Small and Medium Enterprises in Global Perspective

**Employment Generation and WTO**
**Vision 2012**

# Small and Medium Enterprises in Global Perspective

## Employment Generation and WTO Vision 2012

**Dr. C.S Prasad**

New Century Publications
New Delhi, India

NEW CENTURY PUBLICATIONS
4800/24, Bharat Ram Road,
Ansari Road, Daryaganj,
New Delhi-110 002
Tel.: 23247798, 55396605
E-mail: indiatax@del2.vsnl.net.in

Editorial office:
34, Gujranwala Town, Part-2,
Delhi - 110 009
Tel.: 27247805, 27138192
Fax: +91-11-27464774



---

**First Published 2004**
**Reprint: 2023**

ISBN: 81-7708-073-3

Published by New Century Publications and printed at Singhal Print Media, Delhi -110 007

PRINTED IN INDIA

## About the book

Small and Medium Enterprises (SMEs) have emerged as an engine of growth in several developed and developing economies of the world. In India also they have emerged as a vibrant and dynamic component of Indian economy by virtue of their significant contribution to GDP, industrial production and exports. However, the most important contribution of this sector is towards employment generation which is second only to agriculture.

The experience of recent years shows that while employment in agriculture sector has been declining, large industries are also experiencing jobless growth. In such a situation, the main responsibility for job creation rests with unorganised sector including small and medium enterprises and the service sector. Considering its potential and ability, the SMEs sector has been assigned a target of 12 per cent annual growth and additional employment of 4.4 million persons.

However, some of the recent developments emerging out of the challenges of increased competitiveness due to globalisation, liberalization and emergence of WTO, and the constraints relating to credit, infrastructure, technology and skill development, many experts are compelled to think about the capacity of this sector to achieve the given targets. The main objective of this book is to examine the constraints and the required changes which could convert the challenges to opportunities so that the SMEs sector emerges as the saviour of the Indian economy in terms of employment generation. The sector has inherent advantage of flexibility and innovativeness and its major constraint of access to economies of scales could be overcome if the strategy of SMEs development is changed to cluster development and formulation of appropriate policies for the service sector. Besides, the focus has to shift to innovative financing, technology development and improvement of productivity.

This book examines all these issues and attempts to suggest measures which would enhance the competitiveness of SMEs in order to enable this sector to put India on global map.

# Author's Profile

Dr. C.S. Prasad, who has recently retired from the post of Additional Development Commissioner and Economic Adviser in the Office of Development Commissioner (Small Scale Industries), Ministry of Small Scale Industries, Government of India, New Delhi, had been associated with the Small and Medium Enterprises sector for over 25 years. Dr. Prasad had the opportunity to watch the performance of this sector by virtue of his various postings in the Government of India. He had also been instrumental in formulation of policies, programmes and schemes for the promotion and development of this sector and also their implementation. He had been instrumental in the formulation of the Credit Guarantee Scheme and the successful conduct of the Third All India Census of Small Scale Industries in the country. Dr. Prasad had also been member and chairman of various committees constituted for the promotion of Small Enterprises.

Dr. Prasad, an M.A and Ph.D. in Economics, belonged to Indian Economic Service (IES) which he joined in 1969. As a Member of IES, he held important posts in the Planning Commission, and Union Ministries of Industry, Agriculture, Defence, Home Affairs, Finance, and Small Scale Industries. He had been Economic Adviser in the Office of DCSSI from October 1992 to August 1995, and Additional Development Commissioner and Economic Adviser from August 1995 to June 2004.

Dr. Prasad had also been closely associated with teaching and academic world. Apart from his earlier stint as Lecturer of Economics in Bhagalpur University from 1964 to 1967, he worked as Professor and Head of the Department of Economics at Lal Bahadur Shastri National Academy of Administration, Mussorie, from 1981 to 1988. Dr. Prasad has authored a book titled *State Taxation in India* which was published in 1997. Besides, he has contributed over hundred articles, quite a large number of them on the subject of Small and Medium Enterprises.

Dr. Prasad has visited a large number of countries and attended a large number of international conferences on SMEs sector, representing India in those conferences.

# Preface

The Common Minimum Programme (CMP) announced by the United Progressive Alliance (UPA) Government on 27$^{th}$ May 2004 has observed as under:

"In the past few years, the most employment intensive segment of the small scale industry (SSI) has suffered extensively."

The rate of growth in the SSI sector has declined from 11 per cent during 1991-94 to 7 per cent thereafter. Similarly, the flow of credit to SSIs as percentage of Net Bank Credit has also declined from 17 per cent in 1997-98 to less than 11 per cent in September 2003. The Third Census of small scale industries (2001-02) has revealed that the employment intensity of the SSI units has declined from 6.3 persons per unit in 1987-88 to 4.5 persons in 2001-02. Along with these developments, the globalisation and emergence of WTO have also brought the SSI sector face to face with new challenges in the form of increased competition. These trends compel one to think whether the SSI sector can achieve the targets of a 12 per cent annual growth and creation of 4.4 million additional jobs during the 10$^{th}$ Plan period.

No one can deny that Small and Medium Enterprises (SMEs) are the driving force behind economic development all over the world. SMEs are widely credited with generating the highest rates of revenue and employment growth in virtually all economies. The major thrust of all economic policies being pursued in India today is to eliminate poverty, generate adequate employment opportunities and to ensure the utilisation of physical and human resources to the best of their potential. Given the scope of generating tremendous employment opportunities, nurturing entrepreneurial capacities and adding to the National Product, the SMEs continue to be the most important economic proposition for a labour surplus economy as India since it promotes growth with equity. Its rate of employment creation is amongst the fastest and it is able to provide employment not merely by creating a few islands of prosperity, but across the length and the breadth of the country.

The growing importance of this sector is due to its inherent advantage of flexibility and innovativeness. To quote from the report of the Abid Hussain Committee (Expert Committee on Small Enterprises 1997) "There are several reasons why one wishes small scale enterprises (SSEs) to develop. First, they are relatively labour intensive and this has implications for equity. Second, they are flexible. Third, they contribute potentially to decentralisation. Fourth, they promote entrepreneurship. But desiring that SSEs develop is one thing, introducing sector-specific programmes to help them flourish is another. Sector-specific programmes need to be introduced only if market imperfections prevent SSEs from developing."

Since market imperfections exist in credit, capital and labour market, leading to non-optimal size of SSEs, there is need for hand holding and specially tailored policies and programmes for the development of this sector. In India, the SSI sector has acquired a prominent place in the socio-economic development of the country during the last 55 years, particularly since the beginning of planning era. Currently, this sector constitutes 95 per cent of the industrial units and contributes 40 per cent of industrial output and 35 per cent of national exports. According to the latest statistics available from the Third Census of Small Scale Industries (2001-02), there are over 10.5 million SSI units in India which employ approximately 25.0 million people. In other words, the sector has emerged as the storehouse of 10.5 million entrepreneurs in the country.

This achievement has been possible due to the consistent and sustained policy support from the government including policy of reservation, fixation of investment ceiling for the SSI sector, priority lending, fiscal support and marketing support. The economic reforms started in 1991 in India further strengthened the commitments and have provided the opportunity for this sector to grow big. The share of exports from SSI in relation to total national exports increased from 2.1 per cent in 1984-85 to 35 per cent in 1997-98. In absolute terms, the exports have increased from Rs. 11,744 crore to Rs. 44,442 crore in 1997-98 and further to Rs. 86,013 crore in 2002-03.

However, with the removal of Quantitative Restrictions and lowering down of import duties, the sector is now exposed to increased competition both globally and domestically. The hitherto protection of the SSI sector by way of reservations and various preferential supports have been removed to a greater extent. More than 160 items which were reserved for the SSI sector have been de-reserved. Many of the de-reserved items such as readymade garments, leather goods, rice milling are those which have been playing important role in terms of production, employment and exports. Some de-reserved items are those which have vast potential in terms of exports such as toys, auto components, and packaging materials.

When we talk about vision for the SMEs sector, we cannot help remember the greatest visionary Pandit Jawaharlal Nehru, the first Prime Minister of India who carved out a definite role for the Small Scale and Cottage Industries in Five Year Plans, as well as in the Industrial Policy announcements which were made from time to time, particularly in 1948 and 1956. The emphasis on the SSI sector, in view of its important role in employment generation, has continued in all the Five Year Plans. A major policy announcement on this subject was made in August 2000 in the form of a Comprehensive Policy Package with the main objective of enhancing the competitiveness of this sector both domestically and globally. It is, however, a matter of concern that in spite of positive support spelt out in this policy, the rate of growth and the employment generation as per potential have suffered. To tackle this problem, the CMP of the UPA Government has also come out with a road map for the SSI sector when it states that the sector will be freed from Inspector Raj and given full credit, technological and marketing support. The CMP also indicates the need for infrastructural upgradation for major industrial clusters and also spells out the need for promotional package for the SSI sector to be announced soon.

In this context, it is high time that we look into the basic requirements of this sector which can be achieved in the short-term and the medium-term, i.e. by 2012 so that the SMEs sector enables India to become a member of the developed nations by 2020. In order to make the SMEs sector as the *Engine of Growth*, certain changes are required in the strategy of development and also in the policies and programmes.

The first change required to be made is with regard to the definition of the SSIs, to make it in tune with the global practices and also to provide opportunities for technology upgradation. This means efforts should be made to move from SSIs to SMEs, to raise the investment. The second change is needed in adopting cluster approach as a strategy of future SMEs development since it lead to optimal utilisation of resources and also provides access to the economies of scales, both key elements in enhancing global competitiveness. Along with these changes, it is also essential to ensure the provision of critical inputs to this sector in the form of credit, infrastructure, marketing and technology. Competitiveness is linked with productivity which is the function of skill development. Hence adequate investment is required in the field of skill and entrepreneurship development.

The type of changes which are required were spelt out by the Abid Hussain Committee in its Report on Small Enterprises (1997) when it suggested that –

- Protection through reservation is unnecessary particularly in the context of removal of Quantitative Restrictions.
- Support must be for small scale enterprises, not for small scale industries. Support from non-government services must be encouraged, such as through clusters.
- District Industry Centres should be replaced by flexible broad-based District Enterprise Promotion Boards.
- The distinction between Term Lending and Working Capital institutions should be scrapped.
- There should be more stringent provisions for non-payment to SSEs in the Delayed Payments Act.

- There should be Limited Partnership Act to encourage Venture Capital.
- There should be a separate law for the SSEs.

While some action on the above has been taken in the past, it is time now to speed up the implementation of other suggestions.

Need for changes in policies and programmes has also been highlighted by Dr. S.P. Gupta in the Special Group Report on Targeting Ten Million Employment Opportunities Per Year (May 2002). To quote from the report, "But of late, because of the opening up of the economy with deregulation and market orientation including withdrawal of several key subsidies, the unorganised sector in general and specially some of its components are meeting with growing sickness and slowing down of activities. Some other macro economic changes including removal of quantitative restrictions and reductions in tariff have also affected their competitiveness in the recent past leading to some economists putting questions above the very viability of these sectors with new economic surroundings. This Group does not agree with this view, especially because the percentage of sickness in the unorganised sector in terms of outstanding debts is much lower than the organised sector. But at the same time it realised that for the unorganised sector, to be made viable and competitive under the new circumstances, suitable policies and programme have to be recommended so that the sectors become more productive and quality conscious. It will also have to be ensured that the role of level playing field is applied for this sector". Apart from the changes in policies and programmes, it is also essential that the basic requirements of the sector must be met.

Credit forms the life line for any business. Adequate and timely supply of credit at reasonable cost is the most important requirement. Hence, any problem on this count constitutes the most important constraint in the successful running of the business. When inadequacy leads to sickness, high cost of credit makes the sector uncompetitive. The SSI units experience both procedural hassles as well as availability constraints. Though credit comes under the priority sector lending programme of the banks, the flow of credit has been declining in percentage terms. It is generally said that the small entrepreneurs are not so much concerned with the cost of credit as much with the timely, adequate and hassle free availability of credit. There are reports that the small enterprises face problems in accessing credit from banks and financial institutions even after offering manifold collaterals. The response of the banks to the SSIs is not very encouraging. The market inefficiencies occurring due to high transaction costs and perception of high default risk in lending to small business are still considered as major constraints. These aspects have been highlighted by several committees particularly Nayak Committee (1991), Abid Hussain Committee (1997), Kapur Committee (1998) and the S.P. Gupta Study Group (2002). In spite of various measures taken in this regard, the availability of credit remains to be the major problem for the SSIs in the country. It is necessary to create a condition in which banks find themselves inclined to finance SMEs sector. In this context, a cheaper and wide network of credit creating institutions for SMEs needs to be created.

After credit, the second most important issue which needs to be addressed is to improve the marketability of the products in the SMEs sector because this is the most important reason for the low performance of this sector. The chief constraint is the inability to find a target market for the products due to competition at either end of the quality spectrum. The SSI units need to be provided with market related information relating to new avenues for their products, both domestically as well as abroad. These units must be made aware of new production and business practices through trade fairs and workshops and increased use of IT network. The industry forums and associations should undertake publication and dissemination of such information in the form of bulletins and journals. The emphasis should be on standardisation, brand equity building and brand positioning strategy to develop a good market presence for these products. This requires standards and code procedures to be available within easy reach of the SMEs.

The small entrepreneurs seem to be intrigued by the presence of Chinese and other cheap foreign goods in the market which lure their customers. There is, therefore, the need to educate them about the effects of WTO on their business. In this context, it is also essential to provide greater linkages between large and small units. Subcontracting has been emerging as the route to success for the SMEs sector. This can be nurtured through better coordination and cooperation mechanisms between small and large companies. There should be close-knit coordination between large industrial houses and SMEs so as to reap the benefits of the small sectors in the production processes. This can be undertaken by the introduction of common exchange platform of projects and organization of large number of vendor development programmes in different parts of the country. The consortium approach has also been successful in increasing the bargaining power of the SMEs and making them stronger.

Next major area of concern is SMEs low productivity, poor managerial ability, and lower level of skill of the workers engaged there in. The human resource constraints have been affecting both the efficiency and productivity of SMEs sector. A massive programme of skill and entrepreneurship development should form the backbone of SMEs development. There should be training programme from the industry associations to upgrade the skill of the workers and to make them acquainted with the skills, compatible with the new technology. Poor productivity of the labour force, being a major concern, can also be addressed through upgradation of skills. Similarly, the labour laws should be made more flexible and simplified but not at the cost of safety and security of the labour force. Training programmes in marketing have been most demanded, particularly in the areas of market development, dealer networking and training. Investment needs to be made in a big way on skill and entrepreneurship development if the goal of sustainable employment is to be achieved.

Entrepreneurship development has emerged as an effective strategy of economic development and employment generation. It helps in widening the industrial base, innovation and harnessing the latent energy of youths. Hence, the entrepreneurs are the harbingers of change. They must appreciate the need for change in the changing environment and must be capable to manage the affairs in tune with the emerging requirements of the time. The entrepreneurs must be an innovator with the ability to provide **forward and backward linkages.** To be competitive in global environment, the entrepreneurs must be conversant with the modern managerial techniques and practices. He must appreciate as to how a change in economic policy of any country is going to affect his own cost of production and demand of his product. Entrepreneurship is no longer an inborn quality. It comes with training and exposure. Hence, our priority should be to launch a bold programme in all parts of the country through National and State level Entrepreneurship Development Institutes.

As economic reforms have come to stay, similarly there is no alternative to small enterprises so far as their role in providing employment opportunities is concerned. Both have to exist as supplementary and complementary to each other. This is possible through what the Hon'ble Prime Minister Dr. Manmohan Singh calls *Economic Reforms with Human Face*. The aim of reforms should be to remove poverty, increase employment through relief to decentralised sectors. Economic reforms must provide opportunities to the small enterprises so that they are able to provide more and more sustainable employment opportunities, which is the need of the hour. All available studies show that the growth and quality of jobs in the unorganised sector has been very much affected by the absence of timely low cost credit, improved technology, good infrastructure, quality consciousness, modern marketing and synergy with large organised industries.

Technology constraints are no less important factor in the context of globalisation. In spite of emergence of facilities like Tool Rooms, Testing Centres, Process cum Product Development Centres (PPDCs), Small Industries Service Institute (SISI) Workshops, technology continues to be a problem because of big gap between demand and supply. Quite a large number of SSI entrepreneurs, particularly from the tiny units, are either not aware of the ability of technology to translate into new markets and reduce costs or they find it a costly proposition. Most of them feel that technology is essentially an expensive proposition which should be deployed only if everything else stops working or if they are certain about the demand that it would generate. The newly launched Credit Linked Capital Subsidy Scheme needs to be modified by enhancing the incentives as well as coverage. The SSIs in India are, by and large, viewed as units producing poor quality outputs using outdated technology. The growth and development of SSIs in India greatly depends on a change in this perception and the reform processes should include a strategy to catalyse the change. The very fact that SSI sector has been consistently contributing 35 per cent to national exports should be viewed as encouraging factor in its endeavour to adopt the latest technology. The contribution will definitely go up since technology constraints would be easier to handle under SMEs concept. Technology can work wonders in transforming the productivity, quality and competitiveness. It has rightly been said that technological strengths are the key to creating more productive employment in an increasingly competitive market place and to continually upgrade human skills. Technology does not only improve efficiency but it is also important for bringing a cost effective solution to environmental pollution.

Along with the above mentioned changes, there is need to bring about a change in the strategy of development. Clusters have emerged as the focal point of growth and development of SMEs sector in most part of the world. Italian industrial districts have revealed that the argument that SMEs do not have access to economies of scales is no longer true. The cluster approach has worked well and has been appreciated by entrepreneurs in all the regions. Schemes and programmes encouraging the use of clusters must be encouraged. Instead of distributing limited resources to all parts, it is better to put them to those areas which can optimise the return and maximise the growth. It has ultimately to emerge as the new strategy of small enterprise development in the country.

The main issue for consideration is whether the small enterprise sector is capable of achieving the set target of employment generation and economic growth. If we go by the past trend of growth in employment, it can be seen that the economy has always been achieving higher employment than targeted. During the Ninth Plan while the target for additional employment was 2.5 million, actual achievement was 3.2 million. During the first two years of Tenth Plan, the increase in employment has been somewhat lower than the target. In fact, if we go by the employment figure in the SSI sector as revealed by the Third Census of SSI, the actual employment was 25.0 million in 2001-02. The targets of employment will have to be reworked in the light of data from the Third Census of SSIs. The SSI sector has vast potential which has not been tapped so far. Given the right type of support, the sector is capable of providing employment to over 30 million people by the end of Tenth Five Year Plan and about 38 million by the end of Eleventh Plan i.e. 2012.

The main objective of this book is to examine the constraints and potentials of the SMEs sector in this regard. It also tries to examine the required changes in the structure, policies, and programmes so that the sector ultimately emerges as the Engine of Growth by 2012 and enables India to emerge as a developed nation by 2020.

Chapter I *Small Enterprises: Global Experiences* looks into the definition of Small and Medium Enterprises as followed in different countries. In most of the countries while the term SME is in vogue, in India it is called SSI. Similarly, in most of the countries the SME sector is defined in terms of employment or turnover, in India it is defined in terms of investment in plant and machinery. To be in tune with the requirements of globalisation and WTO, there is need to change the definition as per the global practice. The chapter also examines the contribution of SMEs in various economies. It is observed that the sector has emerged as a vibrant and dominant sector of economy in almost all countries.

Chapter 2 *Development of Small Enterprises:Policy Measures in India* traces the growth of policies which have been formulated from time to time since independence to promote this sector. Because of its contribution to employment at low capital cost, the sector has always been assigned an important role through various Industrial Policy Resolutions, Comprehensive Policy Package and during various Five Year Plans. The creation of Small Industries Development Organization (SIDO) as an apex body for the promotion and development of SSI at the central level in 1954 has been crucial in this regard. The SIDO has been a link between policy planners and grass root level small entrepreneurs. Through its specific organizations for technology development, entrepreneurship and skill development and schemes for credit, infrastructure, marketing, quality upgradation, the SIDO has given a positive direction to the growth and development of this sector. While the promotion and development of SSI is primarily the responsibility of State Government, the Central Government through creation of a separate Ministry and organizations like SIDO and NSIC have provided the necessary structure to the body edifice of small enterprises in India.

Chapter 3 and 4 *Small Enterprises and WTO* and *Small Enterprises in India and WTO* respectively, are important in order to understand the implications of globalisation and need to improve the efficiency and competitiveness of this sector. One must understand the implications of various provisions of WTO and how they are going to affect the SMEs sector now and in the distant future. The structure of small enterprises is changing in India. Service sector is gradually becoming more important. The protective measures are now being replaced by facilitating instruments. Subsidies are being phased out. Environmental issues are receiving due attention. Since the future of Indian exports depends on the contribution of small enterprises sector, it is essential that small entrepreneurs are fully sensitised with provisions of WTO, including IPRs.

Chapter 5 *Challenges and Opportunities for Small Enterprises in the Globalised World* goes into the positive and negative aspects of globalisation. While on the one hand it has brought this sector face to face with challenges, it has also brought new opportunities. Challenges exist in the form of increased competition and opportunities exist in the form of lower import duty, access to better technology, better raw material and a wide open market. It is essential to understand them and get the best out of the situation. The ultimate survival of this sector and capability to provide sustainable employment depends on the ability of this sector to convert the challenges into opportunities.

Chapter 6 *Innovative Financing of Small Enterprises* is devoted to tracing out various stages of financing which are linked with the stage of economic development of the economy. It has been observed that debt financing has been taking maximum time and in developing economies crossing this stage is like achieving takeoff. In the context of meeting the critical input of production, this chapter discusses the role of innovative financing particularly equity financing, lease financing, venture capital etc. which must be encouraged as new instruments, apart from strengthening of the traditional instruments of working capital and term loan. The emergence of Micro Credit as a tool of poverty alleviation and employment generation has also been discussed. The Indian economy has witnessed widespread structural reforms in the past 14 years and the reform process is still continuing. The Capital Market, Money Market and Foreign Exchange Market are deregulated to a considerable extent and market forces are allowed to operate in them, as compared to the pre-reforms period. Institutional reforms cover the banking sector also and this sector has also undergone major deregulation with the entry of foreign and other private banks. The Small Industries Development Bank of India (SIDBI) set up exclusively for the SMEs sector will be required to play more proactive role in this regard, particularly in the field of direct financing and Micro Credit.

Chapter 7 *Enhancing Competitiveness: Role of Technology* looks to the basic issue on which the survival and future of small enterprises depend in India, i.e. enhancing competitiveness both internationally and domestically. In this connection, technology upgradation assumes special significance. It is stressed and rightly so that the Indian SSIs should remain competitive in the era of globalisation. Competitiveness is possible only if there is a technology upgradation and adoption of new technologies. There is a need to introduce new tools and equipments for production, changes in manufacturing process, improvement in the quality of products and quality assurance, introduction of new designs and diversification, use of new raw materials and usage of modern management and IT tools.

The situation in technology upgradation is, however, not uniform. While larger SSI units have been going for better and state-of-the-art technology, quite a large number of small SSI units, called tiny units, are not in a position to go for modern technology. In fact, whenever the SSIs feel the need, they are quick to take up technology upgradation and adopt it. However, it is felt that the definitional limit in investment in plant and machinery should be increased if technology is to be upgraded. It should increase from the present limit of Rs. 1 crore to Rs. 5 crore as has already been done in respect of several items belonging to hand tools, knitwear, pharmaceuticals and stationeries. The challenges and opportunities attributable to the SMEs entrust a greater responsibility on the government to sustain their growth in the era of globalisation, the cross border changes have almost the same degree of effects as the domestic changes on a nation's economy. Against this backdrop, the need of the hour is not only to convert the challenges into opportunities but to be a step ahead of the competitors in terms of knowledge and technology.

Chapter 8 *Strategy for Cluster Development in India: The Italian Experience* focuses attention on growing realization on the merit of clusters in small enterprise development which has the advantage of economies of scales. It is now being realised that there is need to adopt this as the future strategy of small enterprise development in India. Cluster development programmes which have transformed the Italian economy through its industrial districts need to be adopted with suitable modifications in India.

This chapter also suggests the approach which needs to be adopted to have the maximum results. In this context, need for a holistic approach has been suggested. Clusters can be utilised as a tool of employment generation if the emphasis is laid on skill development and full capacity utilisation. The historical clusters need not only infrastructural support but also common facilities which individual units cannot afford.

Chapter 9 *Export Potential of Small Enterprises in India* examines the scope of Indian Small Enterprise emerging as a focal point of world trade. How can we raise our share in world trade from 0.7 per cent to 1.0 per cent by 2017? One of the major contributions of small enterprises in India is in terms of their significant contribution to national exports. The future of Indian exports depends very much on the growth of exports from this sector. What are the positive and negative points and what are the product lines having potentials for the future. In the context of increased emphasis on quality and competitiveness and changing trade conditions under WTO agreements, this issue assumes greater significance.

Chapter 10 *Employment Potential of Small Enterprises in India* goes into the details of the performance of this sector with regard to employment generation in the past, the present position and prospects of achieving a higher target of employment by 2012 i.e. by the end of Eleventh Five Year Plan. Employment generation is not only an economic proposition but also a social obligation. It requires co-ordination with various Ministries/ Organizations both at the Central and State Government levels and can be achieved only if a *Mission Mode* approach is adopted for the same. By its very nature, the SMEs sector, which is capable of generating large scale employment opportunities, cannot be left to the mercy of market forces. It requires certain positive support from the government and a hand-holding. Left to itself the SMEs sector cannot compete with the large scale companies since it has no advantage of economies of scale. In addition, the sector suffers on account of resource crunch, capital scarcity and being mostly one man shows, it is unable to employ qualified managers. The large companies do resort to internal measures like reducing the cost of production and increasing the productivity of their existing workers or increasing the employee strength and also reducing raw materials procurement and other costs. These are beyond the means of Small and Medium Enterprises. The large companies have also tried to increase the productivity by deploying generators and increasing shifts. Because of limited resources, SME units cannot afford the above. However, it is also a fact that the SMEs must be enabled to overcome these deficiencies. Among the factors which have contributed the most towards growth are market related forces and IT factors like rise in e-commerce and usage of internet. The task of poverty reduction through employment generation is a National Commitment and all concerned agencies should come together for achieving the goal.

Chapter 11 *Small Enterprises in India: Vision 2012* takes us to the changes which are taking place and also to the changes which must take place in this sector if this sector is to survive amidst challenges posed by globalisation. Among all the changes, the most important change that must take place is with regard to attitude. Role of government in a market led economy is that of a facilitator. However, considering the weakness with which this sector suffers, the role of government in providing a level playing ground will always be true. Much depends on the new generation entrepreneurs many of them are technocrats. They can appreciate the changing requirements of the markets better. SMEs will be under pressure to innovate constantly, not only in changing their products and services but in the way they deliver them. The extent of services depends on their ability to innovate in fast changing environment. They must create knowledge through IT related solutions.

To conclude, the main mantra for the existence and survival of Indian Small Enterprise is that they must become competitive. For this, all the preparations and changes which need to be introduced must be completed by 2012 so that the period between 2012 and 2020 is utilised as period of consolidation. If the task as spelt out above particularly those relating to adoption of the concept of Small and Medium Enterprises, removal of inspector raj, provision of adequate credit including introducing innovative financing, infrastructural developments of clusters, formulation of suitable programmes for skill development, entrepreneurship development and technology development are completed only then the sector can claim to be a part of the developed economies by 2020. The change will come automatically once the people concerned start thinking positively. In this context, I will like to quote from Shri A.P.J. Abdul Kalam and Y.S. Rajan's book *India 2020–A Vision for the New Millennium,* "India is a nation of a billion people. A nation's progress depends upon how its people think. It is thoughts which are transformed into actions. India has to think as a nation of a billion people. Let the young minds blossom – full of thoughts, the thoughts of prosperity.

Small and Medium Enterprises have the potential, there is a vast army of over one billion entrepreneurs in this sector. Many of them are disciplined and dedicated, are technocrats, IT professionals, scientists or those with long experience of working with the government defence and large companies. They have proven records of their managerial ability. They are achievers. We have to harness their capabilities to introduce necessary changes in the structure and efficiency parameters of the SMEs sector. They have to become the harbingers of change for sustainable employment generation and in placing India in the category of developed nations.

**Acknowledgements**

Employment generation is one of the set goals of the UPA Government as spelt out in the Common Minimum Programme. Basic issue is how to achieve it through small enterprises which have the capability as well as potential. The task is not easy since the sector is faced with several constraints, along with the need of proving more productive and competitive since these are the requirements of globalisation and WTO. Employment generation is not only an economic proposition but also a social commitment. The task needs proper coordination and a *Mission Mode*

*Approach*. If there are problems arising out of globalisation and WTO agreements, these need to be properly addressed to so that the challenges are converted into opportunities. How to achieve this has been one of my major concerns and I have been thinking over this issue for quite some time. Whatever I have been thinking on this issue appeared in the form of various articles in various issues of *Laghu Udyog Samachar*, a quarterly journal of the Office of Development Commissioner, Ministry of Small Scale Industries, Government of India.

This book is an updation and compilation of my articles on this subject which appeared in *Laghu Udyog Samachar* and other journals since 1997. My colleagues have been suggesting to me from time to time to write a book on the role of Small Enterprises in Employment Generation in the context of needed changes which are the requirement of a market led economy. However, they were of the view that as employment generation is one of the immediate requirements, this book should suggest a short term or at the most a medium term strategy which could be implemented/ introduced in the near future, at least by the end of the Eleventh Five Year Plan i.e. by 2012. Hence, this book with vision for 2012.

The immediate provocation for bringing out this book came from the two targets which have been set for this sector in the Tenth Five Year Plan. These two targets are an annual rate of growth of 12 per cent and additional employment of 4.4 million from Small Scale Industries and of 10.5 million from the Small Enterprises sector covering both modern and traditional small industries. Dr. S.P. Gupta, Member Planning Commission's Special Group Report on Targeting Ten Million Employment Opportunities Per Year and the Tenth Five Year Plan document which contained the above targets, also spelt out road maps on how to achieve them. For sustainable employment generation, the two documents lay stress on improving productivity and this can be achieved by adequate investment on skill development and a properly tailored HRD policy. I had the opportunity to attend meetings of Employment Group in Planning Commission and had also the occasion to discuss my ideas and strategy on achieving them with my senior colleagues and bosses in the Ministry of SSI and the Office of DC(SSI). In particular, I would like to mention my fruitful discussions on the subject with Shri Ashok Pradhan, Shri S.K. Tuteja (who was also DCSSI), the then Secretaries of SSI, Shri B.S. Minhas, the present Secretary SSI and Shri Suresh Chandra, Additional Secretary and Development Commissioner (SSI) who has not only helped me in conceptualising the strategy but also clarified certain doubts.

I acknowledge with great regards the guidance and support which I received from Dr. S.P. Gupta, Member, Planning Commission, Shri Ashok Pradhan, Shri S.K. Tuteja, Shri B.S. Minhas and Shri Suresh Chandra. I would also thank my colleagues Shri M.P. Singh, Shri Praven Mahto, both Directors in Economic Analysis Division of the Office of DCSSI and Shri Harish Anand, Deputy Director (IFC) for their inputs in various forms. I also acknowledge the help and cooperation of my personal staff, particularly Shri Sethu Raman who assisted me in bringing out my articles which appeared in *Laghu Udyog Samachar*.

I will be failing in my duty if I do not thank my wife Mrs. Usha Shekhar and my children Vineeta, Niharika and Ashutosh who found an author in me and have helped me directly and indirectly.

Finally, thanks are also due to my publisher New Century Publications, New Delhi, for showing patience and extending cooperation to make my work see the light of the day.

Delhi
July 10, 2004

Dr. C.S. Prasad

# Contents

# 1

# Small Enterprises: Global Experiences

Schumacher was right when he said, "Small is beautiful." The experience of Small Enterprises (SE) development during the last two decades all over the world has proved it so. Small and Medium enterprise (SME) have emerged as an engine of growth in the new Millennium. The SME sector has already proved its mettle as a dominant player in most of the developed economies by giving a new dimension to their growth perspectives. It has helped in generation of large scale employment at lower capital cost, balanced regional development, generation of exportable surplus and in the establishment of a more flexible, innovative and competitive structure. Even in developing economies, it is being accepted as key to sustainable economic growth.

Small enterprises exist in the form of factories, workshops, trading and service organisations and range from the most modern and up-to-date enterprise to the simple and traditional units. The operational range varies from independent enterprises to ancillaries, subcontractors and vendors engaged in catering to the needs of the markets, extending from the domestic to the global horizon. These enterprises exist in various forms such as proprietorship, partnership, companies or co-operatives. Mostly these are set up in the private and co-operative sector. Co-operatives are in fact more popular in the service sector or as provider of common facility service. Though the main objectives of SMEs are almost the same, they are defined and viewed differently in different countries. In this chapter an attempt has been made to have the comparative position of definitions of SMEs followed in different countries.

Small and medium-sized enterprises (SMEs) are a key component in economic life, not only because of their number and variety but because of their involvement in every aspect of the economy, their contribution to regional development, the complementary role they play in support of the large sector and on the ground of innovativeness and adaptability. They can be seen as a kind of industrial breeding ground, a source of constant renewal of industry and commerce, and wellspring of competition and dynamism. Small enterprise could be termed as seed of industrial growth. The developmental role of small enterprises has now been well recognised.

Even in those industrialised countries of Europe and America where the large scale industries dominated the scene during sixties and seventies, there has been major turn around since and the SMEs are now on the Centre stage. One of the reasons which have helped the SME sector in occupying predominant role in the economies of advanced countries has been as an income distributor in society. To quote from Dr. P. M. Mathew's book (*Towards a Vibrant Small Enterprise Economy in India*, published by the Institute of Small Enterprises and Development, Cochin, Kerala on 30th April, 2000). "A theoretical articulation of this from a sociological angle has been provided by the eminent German sociologist, Erhard. He says that, the major problem of Germany in the post-World War era, was the sharp polarisation of the industrial society. In order to create a balance in society, a strong middle class is necessary. Viewed from this angle, small businesses have been perceived as an income distributor in society."

The argument advanced in the literature for promotion of small scale enterprises involved both certain desirable characteristics of such enterprises e.g. their labour intensity and related positive distribution effect and their advantages in terms of flexibility and innovativeness, smaller requirement of inventory and their positive contribution towards dispersed development and last but not the least important is the role played in the development of entrepreneurship. Also there is a common belief that under normal market conditions either too few or the wrong combination of resources will be employed by the SMEs as they suffer from certain handicaps and do not have access to the economies of scales leading to units with less than optimal size. This affects their existence sustainability in the long-run.

According to the Abid Hussain Committee on small Enterprises (Expert Committee on Small Enterprises 1999) "the basic imperfection which might lead to a less than optimal size of the small scale industries (SSI) lies in the area of factor markets of both labour and capital .... In most economies and in developing countries in particular capital market imperfections are more basic to the non-optimal size of the SSI than labour market imperfections."

The advantage of flexibility available with small enterprises has been found to more than compensate the disadvantage of the non-availability of the economies of scale. This is clearly emerging from the new theory of economics-cum-organisation which was developed in the 1990s by scholars like Doughlas North. To quote from Dr. Mathew's book, "It points out that economies of scale are important; but in order to achieve it, full ownership of a large enterprise is not necessary. It agrees that privatisation is not the ultimate solution as it leads only to inefficiency; what is needed is managerial restructuring. There is large and growing literature on new competition and flexibilism. The argument is that flexible technologies, management strategies, labour relations, institutions and event culture can lead to much better results than those achieved in rigid set up."

At times a question is raised as to which enterprise (large or small) is more efficient in real terms. It is said that labour used in large enterprise is priced well above the levels it is used in small enterprises while the capital is generally much cheaper for the larger firms. No doubt per unit of labour cost is higher in large units but when compared in relation to output, the real cost for labour is lower in large units. The advantage of small units lies in per unit employment and that becomes a critical factor in a labour surplus economy. This brings out a strong case for adopting support policies which would encourage the development of small enterprises beyond the point which the sector might attain left to free market forces. In order to decide which component of industry needs the support; it is necessary to define the concept and segregate the segments.

## 1.1 Meaning of Small Enterprises in Different Countries

There is no universally accepted definition to an SME. One study has identified more than 50 definitions in 75 countries. Some of these definitions are given in Table 1.1. Frequently, criterion defining an SME in a country may be based on the purpose for which the identification is required. Within the same country, different definitions of SME may be prevalent for different purposes, these could be based on

- turnover or
- persons employed or
- capital invested.

Such variations make inter-country comparisons very difficult, even when data are available.

**Table 1.1: Definition of Small Enterprises in Different Countries of the World**

---

**India**
Tiny units: <2.5 million rupees in plant and machinery
Small Industries: <10 million rupees in plant and machinery, < 50 million rupees (in respect of item like knitwear, hand tools, pharmaceuticals and selected stationary items)
Small scale service and business enterprises, Rs.1 million fixed.
**Criteria:** Assets (other than land building)

**Australia**
Manufacturing: Small enterprises <100 employees
Services: Medium enterprises <20 employees
**Criteria:** Employment

**Belgium**
Annual staff average of 50 employees
Annual turnover.
**Criteria:** Employment, Assets

**Canada**
Manufacturing Units: Independent firms having <200 employees.
**Criteria:** Employment

**France**
10-499 employees
**Criteria:** Employment

**Germany**
<500 employees (enterprises employing fewer than 20 persons are not included in industry statistics)
**Criteria:** Employment

**Greece**
Small enterprises 0-49 employees, Medium enterprises 50-500 employees
**Criteria:** Employment

**Italy**
Small enterprises <200 employees
**Criteria:** Employment

**Japan**
Manufacturing: <300 employees (or <Y 100 million in asset capitalisation)
Wholesale trade (<50 employees or <Y 30 million in capitalisation, Retail Trade and services <50 employees or <Y 10 million in capitalisation.
**Criteria:** Employment. Asset

**Holland**
All private enterprises excluding agriculture and fishery, employing <100 employees. Small enterprises; <10 employees. Medium enterprises 10-100 employees
**Criteria:** Employment

**Portugal**
<500 employees. <Esc 2 400 million in sales (value for 1993) is not controlled (more than 50%) by any company (nor does it hold over 50% of any other company).
**Criteria:** Employment, Sales

**Spain**
Small enterprises <200 employees. Medium enterprises <500 employees.
**Criteria:** Employment

**Sweden**
Autonomous firms with <200 employees.
**Criteria:** Employment

**USA**
Very small enterprises <20 employees, Small enterprise 20-99 employees, Medium enterprise 100-499 employees
**Criteria:** Employment

**China**
Varies with industries, usually <1000 employees.
**Criteria:** Employment

**Korea**
Manufacturing: <300 employees. Services: <20 employees.
**Criteria:** Employment

**Taiwan**
Manufacturing: <NT $ 40 paid-up capital. <total assets of NT$ 120 million Business, transport. Other services. Sales of <NT$ 40 million,

**Criteria:** Paid-up capital assets and sales

**Indonesia**
<100 employees.
**Criteria:** Employment

**Thailand**
Labour intensive sectors: <200 employees. Capital intensive sectors: <100 employees.
**Criteria:** Employment, Capital.

**Malaysia**
Varies <RM 2.5 million and <75 employees.
**Criteria:** Shareholders, funds, employment

**Singapore**
Manufacturing: <S$ 12 million fixed assets. Servicces: <100 employees.
**Criteria:** Fixed assets, Employment

**Vietnam**
No fixed definition, generally <200 employees.
**Criteria:** Employment

**Philippines**
<200 employees. Revenue <P 40 million.
**Criteria:** Assets, Employment.

**Hong Kong**
Small and Medium Enterprises Manufacturing = < 100 Employees Non-Manufacturing < 50 employees
**Criteria:** Employment

**Mexico**
Micro Enterprises = 1-15 Employment, Small Enterprises= 16-100 Sales, Medium Enterprises = 101-250
**Criteria:** Employment, sales

**Pakistan**
According to Punjab Directorate Employment of
Industries PDI) Small Unit = < 10 million rupees,
Medium Units = < 10 million - 100 million rupees
According to Punjab Small Industries Corporation (PSID)
Small Unit < 20 million rupees Medium Units = 20 million rupees
**Criteria:** Assets

## 1.2 Contribution of Small Enterprises in the Economies of Different Countries

SMEs play a significant role in the economies of most countries, industrialised as well as developing (Table 1.2).

A qualitative definition could stipulate that an SME is one in which all relatively important administrative, managerial and technical decisions are taken by one or two owner-entrepreneurs.

Going by the criterion of the number of persons employed and nature of activity undertaken, it is possible notionally to group manufacturing SMEs in three broad categories:

- Cottage or artisan units (i.e. less than 10 employees).
- Organised small-scale units (up to 50 employees).
- Medium sized industries (between 51 and 200 employees).

The economic impact of SMEs can be measured by their contribution to output, employment, income, investment, exports and other economic indicators. Unfortunately, the available statistical data for many countries are not adequate. However, ad-hoc surveys have confirmed following characteristics of the SME sector.

- A large majority of workers are found in small scale enterprises, particularly in household and cottage industries;
- SMEs make an important contribution to total manufacturing output, albeit in general to a lesser extent than their contribution to total manufacturing employment.
- The bulk of small enterprises are located in rural areas, where handicrafts and cottage industries are an important source of employment;

**Table 1.2: Contribution of Small and Medium Enterprises (SMEs) in Various Economic Aggregates in Different Countries of the World**

| Country | Index | Shares |
|---|---|---|
| United States | Less than 100 Employment | 34% employment and 32% Sales (1982) |
| Japan | Small scale Manufacturing | 99% of all establishment<br>72% of employment<br>52% of output<br>13.5% of exports |
| Federal Republic of Germany | Small Scale Industrial Sector | 40% of production<br>35% of all |
| France | Less than 9 employees | 99.9% of all firms |
| Chile | Less than 9 employees | 99% of all firms<br>39% value addition |
| Republic of Korea | Small Industry | 38.4% value addition |
| Brazil | Small-scale sector | 43.6% employment<br>29.6% production share |
| Philippines | Small-scale Manufacturing | 90% of all establishment<br>50% of employment |
| Singapore | SME | About 33% of value addition<br>97% of establishment<br>32% of output<br>16% of exports |
| India | Small Scale Industrial Sector | 40% of production in the industrial sector<br>35% of all exports<br>45% of employment in industrial sector |
| | Small and Village Industries Sector | 50% of production in the industrial sector<br>over 50% of exports<br>over 80% of industrial employment |

Source: *Handbook of FDI by SME - Lessons from Asia,* UNCTAD, Geneva 1998; DCSSI, Government of India, New Delhi.

- Most of the final products of small enterprises cater to the basic needs, such as food, clothing and housing of the majority of the population;
- SMEs use relatively less imported materials and equipment while the large business sector is very much dependent on such imports;
- As industrial restructuring takes place in industrialised countries, developing countries become natural ground for sourcing of parts and components, and SMEs can play and significant role in meeting such demand; and
- SMEs are often the source of new products and innovations.
- Service sector has been growing at much faster rate in recent years than the manufacturing sector as revealed by the Third All-India Census of SSIs 2001-02 conducted by the office of DCSSI, Ministry of SSI, New Delhi.

In India there exists a clear cut definition for small scale industries (SSI). This is defined as a unit which has investment in plant and machinery not exceeding Rs. 100 lakh (Rs. 10 million). There also exists a definition for micro enterprises popularly known as tiny units. A tiny unit is one having investment in plant and machinery not exceeding Rs. 25 lakh (Rs. 2.5 million). Industry related service and business are also included within the purview of SSI sector if their fixed investment is not exceeding Rs. 10 lakh (Rs. 1.0 million). Small Scale Industrial (SSI) sector forms an important constituent of unorganised manufacturing sector in India. By the end of 2002-03, there were 35.14 lakh SSI units whose contribution to production was Rs. 7,63,013 crore and they provided employment to 199.65 lakh persons. Data for exports available for 2002-03 reveal that it stood at Rs. 86,012 crore. The third Census of SSIs has however revealed that the number of small enterprises in India in 2001-02 was 10.5 million and out of these about 1.4 million are registered working units and 9.1 million are unregistered units. Further their contribution to employment stood at 25.0 million i.e. 2.5 crore.

Considered as the modern segment of small enterprise sector, their share in industrial production was about 40 per cent, in industrial employment 45 per cent and in national exports 34 per cent. Small enterprise however, is a wider term and it includes even the village and small industries. Other segments of small enterprises are handlooms, handicrafts, sericulture, coir and khadi and village industries. Contribution of all these segments including modern SSI sector comes to about 50 per cent of industrial production, 55 per cent of exports (particularly by the SSIs and the handicrafts sector) and over 80 per cent of industrial employment.

As against clear cut definition for SSIs, in India, 'Medium Enterprises have not been defined. The categorisation of industries is restricted to large and small categories. When we talk of medium enterprises in India, given the present level of investment limit for the Small Scale Industrial sector, conceptually Medium enterprise could be one having investment over Rs. 1 crore and up to Rs. 10 crore. The S.P. Gupta Group constituted by the Planning Commission (2001) has also recommended Rs. 10 crore limit of investment in plant and machinery for the medium enterprises.

The Indian small sector has evolved with time. The sector produces about 8000 items covering wide range of products inclusive of auto-components, garage equipment, cycle and parts, general engineering and variety of hand tools, light engineering, air conditioning and refrigeration, plastic goods and machinery, leather goods, ready made garments, chemicals and pharmaceutical products, toys, sports goods electrical items, electronic goods, processed food and host of consumer goods and utility products. Traditionally, we have had industries both in the urban as well as in the rural areas. The Third Census has revealed that the number of registered and unregistered small enterprises in India was more than 105 lakh by the end of March 2002.

# 2

# Development of Small Enterprises: Policy Measures in India

The legacy of the present policy framework for development of small scale industrial enterprises (manufacturing, service and trade) in India derives from a conscious attempt to reconstruct and recontextualise pre-colonial and pre-capitalistic mode of production in the fabric of modern manufacturing activities. On the other hand, this approach was a political necessity to rehabilitate millions of distressed rural craftsmen, who could not survive the onslaught of the forces of colonial economic imperialism; on the other hand, such compulsions forced the planners to make an attempt to evolve a development strategy to integrate this segment of the country in the overall ambit of successive Five Year Plans in India.

While the promotion of small scale industries has been one of the major objectives of economic planning in India, the policies and strategies have undergone change from time to time. In this chapter the readers can have an idea of various policies which have been followed since the beginning of planning era in India.

The initial model of industrial planning in India, known as Mahalanobis model (named after its architect, P. Mahalanobis), relied heavily on what is known as the economic philosophy of capital fundamentalism. Its central emphasis was to develop a production base for manufacture of capital goods it needed. The role of small scale sector was envisaged as supplier of consumer goods. It obviously implies that this strategy can be sustainable only if small scale sector can generate enough surplus to sustain and support a programme of heavy industrialisation. This called for a separate component of planning to promote modern small scale industries within the overall gamut of rural, village and small industries.

Contrary to the theory of deploying the surplus labour in large enterprises as propounded by Arthur Lewis and which was followed by many countries during fifties and sixties, India from the very beginning followed a somewhat different approach based on the economic philosophies of Gandhi (Gram Swaraj) and model given by Nehru and Mahalanobis. These enterprises were visualised as an effective link between the government and masses on the one hand and between the rural and urban areas on the other. The result is the wide base that these enterprises have created from the manufacturer of 'pickle, chutneys and papad' to the development of software and service provider in information technology. In fact the task of taking the benefits of bio-technology including food technology and gene-technology now rests with small enterprises. The concept of entrepreneur has also undergone a sea-change. From a traditional artisan managing the manufacture of shoes and chappals or from a father-son entrepreneurship, he has turned into a Management oriented enterprise effectively managing time, resources, knowledge and latest technology has also become an innovator.

The existing framework of policy support were evolved essentially in the environment of 1950s and 1960s and then continued with appropriate changes based on the requirement of the time. The main plank of development strategy of the Small Scale Industries (SSIs) in India is built around a system of institutional support mechanism and structure of incentives. One of the major policy of the Government of

India has been to provide an environment leading to unhindered growth of the small scale industries. It is with this objective that the registration of SSI continues to be voluntary and there is no licensing restriction.

## 2.1 Policy Support

After Independence, the foremost task for the government was to achieve rapid industrialisation of the country within the overall framework of a welfare state. The plan objective of economic growth with social justice was kept in view in the overall strategy of industrial development. Large, medium and small industrial units have been assigned a mutually complementary role with a view to facilitate an integrated and harmonious growth of industrial sector as a whole.

Right from the inception of development programmes, the revival of various stagnant village and cottage industries was given a prominent place in the country's economic agenda. The guiding principles were enshrined in the Directive Principles of State Policy in the Constitution of India, which enjoined upon the state to strive to minimise income inequalities and regional disparities, and promote cottage industries in the rural areas. Because of the historical background and the constitutional mandate, the Government of India, while framing the industrial policy, accorded special status and importance to the "Small Scale Industries."

The industrial policy of the government from 1948 has aimed at a balanced growth between different manufacturing sectors. It recognised the basic dichotomy of large scale and small scale manufacturing units including decentralised industries. The Industrial Policy of 1948, stated that cottage and small scale industries are particularly suited for better utilisation of local resources and achievement of "local-self-sufficiency" in respect of certain types of essential goods.

The policy for the small scale sector was first enunciated in the Industrial Policy Resolution of 1956. The basic framework of overall industrial policy is visible in the following paragraphs of the 1956 Resolution:

"The Government of India would, in this context, stress the role of Cottage and Village and Small scale Industries in the development of the national economy. In relation to some of the problems that need urgent solutions, they offer some distinct advantages. They provide immediate large scale employment; they offer a method of ensuring a more equitable distribution of national income and they facilitate an effective mobilisation of resources of capital and skill which might otherwise remain unutilised. Some of the problems that unplanned urbanisation tends to create will be avoided by the establishment of small centres of industrial production all over the country."

No doubt, in the past 55 years, some adjustments have been made in this policy to meet the changing needs of the overall economy but the basic thrust remains unchanged. The policy framework underwent changes in accordance with the course of industrial development in the country through the Industrial Policy Statements of 1977, 1980, 1990 and 1991 only as a corrective measure. However, a significant policy announcement on small enterprises emerged on 30th August, 2000 which is in vogue till date. The various components of this policy have been outlined subsequently in this chapter. Up to 1970, the thrust was on development of infrastructure which was visible in the form of large number of industrial estates, developed plots and sheds to accommodate the small scale industries in almost all parts of the country with the hope that it will attract small industries and lead to regional development. However, the initial investment could not bring the desired result and as many estates languished in the absence of maintenance and some of them have turned into industrial slums. the hope that the NGOs will automatically take over the maintenance could not materialise. This however, does not negate the role that the industrial estates have played in the development of focal points of development.

Directional strength was imparted to the sector by the Industries (Development and Regulation) Act 1951. Section 11-B provides the power to define small scale industry and Section 29-B provides for the reservation of products for exclusive production in the small scale industrial sector.

After the formulation of First Five Year Plan (1951-56), a Committee was appointed by the Planning Commission with Professor D. G. Karve as its Chairman. The Committee outlined specific measures for protection of the village and small scale industries sector. The important among these measures are:

- Reservation of certain items only for Village and Small Industries;
- Restriction on capacity expansion of large industry and
- Management of supply of raw materials.

Accepting the recommendations of the Committee, the government formulated the common production policy and programme for the balanced development of large scale, small scale and village industries.

The development of small scale sector received a new thrust after the adoption of the Ford Foundation's Perspective Plan in 1953-54. Thereafter consistent efforts in successive industrial policies as well as Five Year Plans for development of small scale industries have been made by raising investment limits, providing incentive, infrastructural facilities and other assistance.

In the Industrial Policy Statement of 1977, more emphasis was laid on reservation of items. It was the policy of the government that "whatever can be produced by small and cottage industries must only be so produced." As a follow-up of policy measure, 324 items were reserved on 26th April, 1978, on the basis of exhaustive analysis and the list was significantly expanded to 504 items as compared to 180 items earlier. The Industries (Development and Regulation) Act, 1951 was amended in 1984 to give statutory backing to the policy of reservation. The Reservation Policy has the objectives to:

- Ensure bulk production of consumer goods in the small scale sector.
- Expand employment opportunities through setting up of small scale industries.

The reservation of economically viable and technically feasible products for exclusive manufacture by small scale industries which began in 1967 with only 47 items, was greatly extended to many more products and now stands at 675 after dereservation of 51 items last year. Non-SSI units can manufacture the reserved items only if they abide by a minimum of stipulated export obligation.

The central government, in the interest of stepping up of exports, has been permitting expansion or creation of new capacities, by industrial undertakings other than the small scale industrial undertakings in respect of items reserved for exclusive manufacture in small scale sector if they undertake an export obligation of a minimum of 50 per cent (reduced from 75 per cent in December, 1997) of the new or additional annual production to be achieved within a maximum period of three years. If units presently manufacturing a reserved item in the small scale sector wish to go beyond the SSI limit, they would have to obtain a licence from the Secretariat for Industrial Approvals. The licence pegs their production capacity at current levels. There is no regulation or restriction on marketing the reserved items by large industries.

The Policy Statement of 1977 also stressed upon the integrated approach for effective promotion of cottage and small industries widely dispersed in rural areas and small towns. The District Industries Centres (DICs) as a nodal agency were set up in 1978 as the focal point for local industrialisation and single window clearances. The Industrial Policy announcement of 1980 recognised the need for growth of the small scale sector, for a rapid and balanced industrialisation of the country. It emphasised the complementary role of the large and small sector so that an integrated growth of the industrial sector could become possible through the process of mutual reinforcement. DICs are continuing even now as nodal point of industrial development within a district but they could not emerge as the Centre for single point clearances/single window clearances. Though they are engaged in registration of SSI units and in implementation of schemes like the Prime Minister's Rojgar Yojana (PMRY) and other employment schemes but there is need to redefine their role to address to the requirements of time in the form of information technology, incubation centres, arrange prompt payments to the SSI units by acting as a 'factor'.

The new concept of "Tiny Enterprises" was introduced in 1977 for the first time. The Bhatt Committee (1971) had recommended a separate category - 'Tiny Sector' to address the problems of the local small entrepreneurs, which utilise local raw material, local skill, local technology and cater to local market. To promote service enterprises, this category was defined in 1980 and its scope was further enlarged to business enterprises also and categorised as Small Scale Service and Business (Industry related) Enterprises (SSSBE) in 1991.

The definition of these enterprises has been changed from fixed investment of Rs. 5 lakh to Rs. 10 lakh in September 2000 consequent upon the announcement of a comprehensive policy package for the small scale industries and tiny units on 30th August, 2000. These enterprises are eligible for benefits as admissible to tiny units. In view of the fact that service sector is having the highest rate of growth and contributes about half of the national income and has also emerged as the major employment provider, the enhancement of investment ceiling is a timely action in right direction. Tiny sector now forms the base of the SSI sector as it accounts for 96 per cent of SSI units in the country. According to the Second All India Census of Registered SSI units (base year 1987-88), this segment accounted for 58.5 per cent of production and 79.4 per cent of employment in the small scale sector. Employment intensity in tiny units was also found very high i.e. 5.9 persons per lakh of fixed capital as against 2.1 persons in other SSI units. As per the Third Census, the share of tiny units is over 98 per cent of total small enterprises in the country.

As a part of the process of economic reforms and opening up of the economy, separate policy measures for promoting and strengthening small, tiny and village Enterprises were announced on 6th August, 1991 for the first time. The salient features of this policy are:

- De-regulation and debureaucratisation;
- Simplification of regulations and procedures;
- Improving the flow of credit;
- Technology upgradation;

- Exports development;
- Promotion of entrepreneurship.

In the context of on-going programmes of economic reforms, restricted list in small scale sector is completely disbanded. There s now total deregulation in the small scale sector so far as the licensing is concerned i.e. "No licensing for SSI units employing less than 50/100 workers with/without power." Specific attempts have been made to liberalise environmental laws wherever possible as applicable to small scale industries. In fact, except for 17 categories of polluting industries other industries have only to file a memorandum of information which shall serve the purpose of consent.

Besides wide ranging measures, the government has decided to allow equity participation by other industrial undertakings in small scale sector. The relevant para in the policy (para 3.2) reads as follows:

"To provide access to the capital market and to encourage modernisation and technological upgradation, it has been decided to allow equity participation by other industrial undertakings in the SSI, not exceeding 24 per cent of the total shareholding. This would also provide a powerful boost to anciliarisation and sub-contracting, leading to expansion of employment opportunities".

Further, to empower the SSI Sector legislatively, an Act was passed by the Parliament in 1993 to provide for and regulate the payment of interest on delayed payments to small scale and ancillary industrial undertakings. The objective of the Act is to ensure prompt payment on goods supplied by small scale and ancillary units. There had, however, been some suggestions to amend some of the provisions of this Act to make it more effective. This was done in 1998 which additionally provided for creation of

Facilitation Councils at States/UT levels.

Considering the important role that the small scale and agro and rural industries play in Indian economy Government created an exclusive new Ministry of Small Scale Industries and Agro and Rural Industries in October, 1999. In order to provide focussed attention on the development of small-scale industries and separately for rural and agro-industries, the Government divided the Ministry into two parts in September 2001. At present there are 2 separate Ministries of Small-Scale Industries and Agro and Rural Industries. In order to provide necessary strength to the growth in the context of the emerging requirements of the New Millennium, the Prime Minister announced a comprehensive policy package for SSI and Tiny Enterprises Sector on the 30$^{th}$ of August, 2000. Policy decisions by the Government have never been unilateral. These have been based on the demands emerging from the representatives of the SSI sector and/or based on the recommendations of the Committees which have been set up by the Government from time to time. In the context it is relevant to mention the committees which have been set up after 1990.

During 55 years the investment ceiling has gone up by 20 times. Though changes in investment ceilings are said to be governed by factor like inflation, however, it is difficult to find the equal correspondence between the two variables.

1. Nayak Committee on SSI credit and related issues set up by the RBI - 1991
2. Abid Hussain Committee by the Government of India - 1995 (Expert Committee on Small Enterprises).
3. S.L. Kapur Committee on SSI Credit by the RBI - 1998.
4. S.P. Gupta Study Group by the Planning Commission - 1999.
5. Group of Ministers under the chairmanship of Sh. L.K.

Advani, Home Minister, Government of India - June-August 2000.

6. Working Group on SSI credit constituted by the Reserve Bank of India in February 2004 under the chairmanship of Shri Ganguly.

The Expert Committee on Small Scale Industries in December 1995, under the Chairmanship of Shri Abid Hussain addressed itself to the need of reforms in the existing policies and design new policies which would facilitate the growth of viable and efficient small scale Industries to make them globally competitive. The expert Committee in its report laid emphasis on the removal of protection, abolishing reservation, enhancement of SSI investment limit and restructuring supportive, specialised and financial institutions. It also emphasised on cluster approach for future strategy of development.

In 1999, the Planning Commission had set up a Study Group Small Enterprise Development under the Chairmanship of Dr. S. P. Gupta, Member, Planning Commission. The Group submitted its interim report in July 2000 and final report in January 2001.

A Group of Ministers on SSI under the chairmanship of Sh. L.K. Advani, Home Minister was constituted by the Prime Minister on the 28th of June, 2000. The group suggested several policy measures for the development of SSI in the country. The announcement of a comprehensive policy package for small scale industries by Shri Atal Behari Vajpayee, the Prime Minister on 30$^{th}$ of August, 2000 has been based upon the recommendations of the Group of Ministers.

## 2.2 Small Enterprises and Economic Efficiency

Questions often asked are to what extent labour and

capital employed in small manufacturing enterprises are efficient and more productive as compared to large enterprises. Empirical studies made on this subject do not present an unanimous view in this regard. According to Little, Mazumdar and Page who studied this subject in greater detail for the World Bank in respect of some selected industries (Small Manufacturing Enterprises: A Comparative Analysis of India and other Economies - A World Bank Publication, 1987).

1. Employment size is a very poor indicator of capital intensity and productivity, and of total factor productivity or technical efficiency for narrowly defined industries; and for policy purpose it is essential to look at narrowly defined industries.
2. There is considerable evidence that many small enterprises with less than 10 workers, are often not the most labour-intensive and their capital productivity and technical efficiency are very rarely the highest and the whole size range of establishment in the industry.
3. When measured by employment size, firms in the medium-size-range of 50-200 workers have the highest capital productivity and total factor productivity, in most industries in all the countries examined.
4. The very small (less than 10 workers) should not be looked to for their efficient employment of factors of production. But at the same time they should not be discriminated against. They are there and they still provide the bulk of employment in the lower-income developing countries.
5. Lending agencies tend to lend toward the upper end of any limit established as the definition of "small". There is no reason to suppose that this is to be regretted.
6. There is no doubt that India has greatly increased direct

employment by protecting traditional processes. However, it is far more doubtful whether the demand for labour has been increased when indirect effects are brought into account.

7. Intermediate technologies and products are not always socially desirable.
8. The, policy of reserving a great many products for the small has serious disadvantages. It tends to segment product markets and reduce the element of competition not only for the protected sector but also for large firms. It tends also to freeze the structure of the industry and inbuilt the organic growth of firms beyond the protected size. It must also inhibit the organic growth of firms beyond the protected size. It must also inhibit exports in that larger firms have economies of scale in foreign markets, as evidenced by the fact that small firms typically export a much lower portion of their production than larger firms. These effects are unquantifiable but may be serious in the long run.

## 2.3 Investment Limits

The small scale sector is currently defined in terms of investment in plant and machinery. However, in the fifties the definition was both employment as well as investment based. In a capital scarce economy, it was felt that the SSI Sector should be defined in terms of investment.

The investment limit for small scale industries has undergone drastic changes since 1950 onwards as a policy follow-up. In 1950, the upper investment limit in fixed assets was fixed at Rs. 5 lakh with an additional condition of less than 50/100 people with or without power. In 1960, the employment criteria was dropped and the small scale industries were defined in terms of the upper ceiling of investment in plant and machinery (original value), alone since 1960.The definition of small scale industries has undergone changes over the years in terms of investment limits (Table 2.1).

**Table 2.1: Changes in Investment Limits for Small Industries**

| Year | Investment Limits | Additional Conditions |
|---|---|---|
| 1950 | Up to Rs. 5 lakh in fixed assets | Less than 50/100 persons with or without power |
| 1960 | Up to Rs. 5 lakh in Plant and Machinery | No condition |
| 1966 | Up to Rs. 7.5 lakh in Plant and Machinery | No condition |
| 1975 | Up to Rs. 10 lakh in Plant and Machinery | No condition |
| 1980 | Up to Rs. 20 lakh in Plant and Machinery | No condition |
| 1985 | Up to Rs. 35 lakh in Plant and Machinery | No condition |
| 1991 | Up to Rs. 60 lakh in Plant and Machinery | No condition |
| 1997 | Up to Rs. 300 lakh in Plant and Machinery | No condition |
| 1999 | Up to Rs. 100 lakh in Plant and Machinery | No condition |

Source: *Engine of Growth–2002-03*, Office of Development Commissioner (SSI), Government of India, New Delhi.

## 2.4 Strategy for Small Enterprise Development

Development strategy for SSI sector has three elements:

- Protective discrimination,
- Integration between large and small industries, and
- Institutional support, assistance and incentives.

**2.4.1 Protective Discrimination:** Policy of protective discrimination seeks to ensure adequate demand for the products of SSIs through statutory restrictions. Reservation of items for exclusive manufacture in SSI sector is statutorily provided for in the Industries (Development and Regulation) Act. The reservation policy has the objectives to (i) ensure bulk of increased production of consumer goods in the small scale sector and (ii) expand employment opportunities through setting up of small scale industries. 675 items currently stand reserved for exclusive manufacture by the SSI sector (2004).

Under this system, any large scale manufacturer, if willing to expand its production of a reserved item after the date of its reservation, can do so only under the export obligation of 50 per cent of the incremental production (in case of knitwear, hand tools, pharmaceuticals and some selected stationary items, the limit has been raised to Rs. 50 million). If any entrepreneur intends to invest more than the stipulated investment ceiling in any of the reserved item, he has to undertake the prescribed export obligation. Reservation of an item is done through a Committee which decides about the techno-economic viability of manufacturing the item within the prescribed investment limit and its employment potential.

Reservation seeks to protect the SSI against possible unfair trade practices by the large-scale units. This policy has got the operational difficulty that item of any description, when reserved, implicitly presumes that there is unique technology available for this item and even if various technologies are available, the items produced are perfect substitutes and cannot be significantly differentiated. The policy of reservation is an open policy. A Committee headed by the Secretary, Ministry of Small Scale Industries of the Government of India, considers various proposals for reservation of new items or dereservation of reserved items.

Apart from product reservation there also exists provisions for marketing reservation, but the later does not enjoy statutory backing. 358 items have been earmarked for purchase to be made by the Government for its own consumption from the small scale sector. In addition, price preference to the extent of up to 15 per cent is also given to SSI products on purchases by the Government Departments. SSI lending comes under the priority sector lending programme of the banks; this is also a form of protection. Statutory provision for reservation of products for exclusive purchase from small business enterprises to the extent of 23 per cent by the Government exists in USA. Product reservation, though to a limited extent, existed even in Korea till 1990.

While one or the other form of protection to small enterprises exists in almost all countries, the term has lost its acceptability in recent years. To quote Abid Hussain Committee Report again, "Efficiency and growth objectives would be seriously jeopardised if SSIs are allowed to grow in a protective environment without exploiting economies of scale or attaining technical efficiency".

In a market driven economy, the protection which brings distortion is not permissible but even WTO conditionalities permit those protective measures including subsidy which are across the board and are not meant for a particular industry or unit. Moreover, it is now being realised that the era of protection is gone and the role of the government should be as facilitator.

**2.4.2 Integration between Large and Small Industries:** The Industrial Policy Resolution of 1956 advocated an effective integration between small and large sectors. Government is promoting ancillarisation through organisation of buyer-seller meets, ancillary development seminars, exhibitions displaying the ability of small industries to fulfil the requirement of large units through sub-contracting. Sub-contracting exchanges located in the major Small Industries. Service Institutes maintain liaison with the public sector enterprises for implementation of ancillary development programmes. The current linkage between large and small scale industries is very weak. It is this strong linkage between the two which could bring phenomenal growth in SSIs in countries like Japan, Korea, Italy etc. Though provisions of equity participation up to 24 per cent in small units by large units and outsiders exist, but experience so far reveals that not many outsiders have been attracted to make investment in SSI units. A group of people feel that this limit is inadequate and could be raised to 49 per cent.

**2.4.3 Institutional Support, Assistance and Incentives:** The support system can be classified into two categories: those administered by the Central Government, and those by the state governments. At the Centre, the Office of the Development Commissioner, SSIs known also as the Small Industries Development Organisation (SIDO), which is an organ of the Ministry of Small Scale Agro and Rural Industries (SSARIs), Government of India is the apex body to formulate the development policy and support system for this sector. Under the office, there are 30 Small Industries Service Institutes (SISIs) and 28 branches of SISIs which undertake techno-economic and managerial consultancies, disseminate trade and market information, undertake surveys, conduct training in various trades/ activities and provide workshop facilities. In addition, there are 4 testing centres, 10 tool rooms/tools design institutes, 6 product-cum-process development centres and central footwear training centres for providing modern technical facilities and training in the areas as their names suggest.

In addition to training provided by the above institutes there are exclusive institutes namely, National Institute for Small Industry Extension and Training (NISIET), Hyderabad; National Institute for Entrepreneurship and Small Business Development (NIESBUD), New Delhi and Indian Institute of Entrepreneurship, Guwahati, which conduct entrepreneurship development programmes at national and international levels. Of particular mention is the Indian Institute of Entrepreneurship at Guwahati which caters to the training requirements of the north-eastern part of the country.

The National Small Industries Corporation (NSIC) created in 1954 along with SIDO, an autonomous body under the Ministry of SSI. It provides machinery under hire-purchase and equipment leasing scheme, marketing support under consortia marketing, procurement of bulk orders, brand franchising, technology assistance, development and training activities etc. It also operates several schemes of export promotion.

In the state governments, the Directorate of industries are the nodal agencies to promote the small scale sector. At the district level, District Industries Centres are envisaged as a single window interacting agency to provide services and support to small entrepreneur under a single roof. They are the implementing arm of the Central and state governments of the various schemes and programmes. Registration of small industries is done at the district industries centres.

Central and state governments have evolved a substantial structure of incentives and facilities for small enterprises. Apart from various facilities and incentives extended by the Central Government which have been mentioned in the foregoing paragraphs, the most important and meaningful support to SSI is that of fiscal support.

## 2.5 Role of State Governments/Union Territories

Promotion and development of SSI is primarily the responsibility of the State Governments. The support and facilities offered by the state governments include land, developed plots and sheds on concessional terms, infrastructural facilities, investment subsidy in selected areas at varying rates, seed capital for setting up new units, financial assistance for preparation of project reports, assistance in purchase and marketing, subsidy for technical know-how, testing of products in approved test houses and modernisation, subsidy in power and generating sets, water at concessional terms, interest subsidy, exemption/deferment on sales tax, stamp duty, etc., Monitoring cells/ committees for rehabilitation of sick units also exist at the state level. The State level inter-institutional committees which exist under the Chairmanship of State Secretary Industries have been playing important role in the rehabilitation of sick SSI units. State Level Bankers Committee (SLBC) also plays an important role in assessing and co-ordinating the credit needs of the state including those for the small enterprises.

## 2.6 Recent Policy Initiatives

The national economy of India has entered into the phase of economic reforms with emphasis on liberalisation, privatisation and globalisation since 1991 and a separate policy exclusively for SSI sector was announced on 6th August 1991 for this purpose.

As a sequel to the new policy initiative, a number of administrative reforms were introduced. Licensing restriction in production in small scale sector has been removed, locational restrictions have been reduced to minimum, industry related services have been brought within the fold of small scale development programmes, registration procedure has been simplified, steps have been taken to transform the enforcement of labour laws for SSIs from a regime of regulation to an era of self-discipline and voluntary compliance, environmental clearance procedures for SSIs have been rationalised and simplification in the administration of the excise tax regime. Major policy decisions have been taken in the field of SSI credit, extending fiscal benefits and removal of anomalies to provide impetus to technology upgradation, entrepreneurship development and in other concerned areas.

**2.6.1 Measures Initiated after 1991:** These include,

1. Ensuing adequate credit (calculated on normative basis) and improving the quality of its delivery. This is based on the Nayak Committee recommendations made in 1992. Presently, for SSI units with turnover of Rs. 5 crore, working capital requirement is computed @ 20 per cent of projected annual turnover.
2. Providing infrastructural support in integrated manner in selected rural and backward areas through Integrated Infrastructure Development Scheme.
3. Enhanced technology support for modernisation and quality upgradation by opening of five new Tool rooms with Danish and German assistance.
4. Financial incentives for SSI units which acquire ISO 9000/14001.
5. Enhancement to entrepreneurship development programme by involving voluntary agencies and strengthening entrepreneurship development institutes.
6. Strengthening special employment generation programmes by way of self-employment through Prime Ministers Rojgar Yojana (PMRY) schemes. This subject

has now been transferred to the Ministry of Agro and Rural Industries.

7. Restructuring the system of collection of SSI data and information on SSI by computerisation of Director of Industries and selected 138 DICs and also computerisation of selected Small Industries Service Institutes.
8. Simplification of export procedures and providing incentives for higher production and maximising export earnings.
9. Amendment of Interest on Delayed Payments Act to tackle the problem of settlement of dues of SSI units by large companies was brought out in 1998.

## 2.7 Policy Support to Meet Credit Needs

Credit forms the most critical input to production and is arranged themselves out of own resources or as loan from relatives, money lenders or institutional sources. While term loan requirements are met by the State Finance Corporations (SFCs), the working capital needs are met by the commercial banks. After the nationalisation of banks, the availability of credit to small entrepreneurs has been increasing continuously. A major landmark of credit policy has been bringing SSI sector under "priority sector lending programme" of nationalised banks. A Single Window Scheme (SWS) for financing of fixed assets and working capital of tiny and SSI units was introduced in May, 1988.

Another major policy initiative, was the setting up of Small Industries Development Bank of India (SIDBI) in 1990 as principal financial institution. SIDBI acts as an apex bank for priority re-financing of small loans to meet the credit requirement through various schemes. Small Industries Development Bank of India has diversified and increased its operations and has come up with new schemes such as factoring services, venture fund and schemes for modernisation and technology upgradation. Today, small entrepreneurs can avail credit facility not only for initial investment and working capital, but also for modernisation and expansion of their enterprises.

To accelerate the need-based credit flow to small scale sector, the Nayak Committee was constituted by the RBI in 1991 which submitted its report in 1992. The RBI accepted the major recommendations and necessary instructions were issued to the banks before the end of December 1994 for ensuring timely and adequate credit to the SSI sector. Among the number of promotional measures, the working capital limit is to be computed on the basis of a minimum of 20 per cent of their projected annual turn over, whose credit limit in individual cases is less than Rs. 5 crore while this has been hailed as the most important recommendation of the Nayak Committee, this has also been criticised by the SSI Associations the most on the ground of its non-adherence by the banks. In his budget speech in 1995-96, the Union Finance Minister had laid down a Seven-Point Action Plan, including, setting up of specialised SSI branches in 85 identified districts, delegation of powers at the branch and regional levels, conducting sample surveys of their performing SSI accounts and simplification of procedural formalities, etc. 417 specialised commercial bank branches for SSI have already been set up by March 2004.

Though several measures have been taken in recent past to improve the flow of credit in pursuance of Nayak Committee recommendations and subsequent guidelines issued by the Reserve Bank of India, a large number of SSI units and their associations have been complaining that the credit being made available to them particularly, the working capital is inadequate, costly and often delayed.

There has been demand for introducing an effective monitoring mechanism. It was precisely with this intention that a seven point SSI credit plan was introduced in 1995-96 budget and also the scope of National Equity Fund Scheme being operated by the Small Industries Development Bank of India (SIDBI) was expanded and a new Scheme of Technology Development and Modernisation Fund with SIDBI was launched that year.

Despite the steps taken by the RBI, the problems continued to persist. Concerned with the continuing problem and non-adherence of the RBI guidelines on credit to SSI sector, the RBI had set up a High Powered Committee under the Chairmanship of Sh. S. L. Kapur, former Secretary (SSI and ARI) to review the working of credit delivery system for SSIs. The Committee submitted its report to RBI on 30th June 1998. The Report contains 126 recommendations. About 60 recommendations have already been accepted and implemented by the RBI and the Government's decision on remaining recommendations is awaited.

Major Policy changes relating to SSI credit were announced in the Budget of 2000-2001 to improve the flow of credit. These are:

1. Collateral security dispensed with, for loans up to Rs. 5 lakh.
2. Composite Loan Scheme limit was first enhanced to Rs. 10 lakh, then to Rs. 25 lakh and further enhanced to Rs. 50 lakh in 2003.
3. Specialised SSI banks branch to be set up in each district and SSI clusters. However, this target has not been achieved primarily because the specialised bank branches have not been found to be performing satisfactorily. Now the specialised bank branches have also been permitted to lend for non-SSI activities to

some extent. What is needed is that all the bank branches in the country should engage in SSI lending and for this they should earmark a nodal officer for small enterprise sector.

4. Technology Development and Modernisation Fund Scheme of SIDBI extended by another 3 years. Further extended by two years in 2003.
5. Credit Guarantee Scheme was announced in August 2000 to provide collateral free loan up to Rs. 25 lakh. For this Credit Guaranteed Fund Trust has been created at Mumbai by its two promoters, namely the Government of Indian and the SIDBI. A fund of Rs. 25 crore is to be created to be shared by GOI and SIDBI in the ratio of 4:1. By the end of March 2004, a fund of about Rs. 700 crore has already been created.
6. National Equity Fund Scheme to cover projects up to Rs. 25 lakh. Subsequently, the scope of the scheme has been extended to all the areas of the country.

The year 2000-2001 has been a landmark in the history of development of SSIs in the country. A large number of credit related announcements have been made by the Prime Minister on 30th August 2000 which have made major improvements over those policies which had been announced in February 2000 by the Finance Minister.

The SIDBI had set up a Technology Development and Modernisation Fund (TDMF) Scheme in April 1995 with a corpus of Rs. 200 crore for direct assistance of small scale industries to encourage existing industrial units in the sector, to modernise their production facilities and adopt improved and updated technology so as to strengthen their export capabilities. Assistance under the scheme is available for meeting the expenditure on purchase of capital equipment, acquisition of technical know-how, upgradation of process technology and products with thrust on quality improvement in packaging and cost of TQM and acquisition of ISO-9000 series certification. The operation of this scheme has been extended by another three years though the announcement under Union Budget 2000-2001 made by the Minister.

## 2.8 Credit-related Developments since 2002

Based on the Kapur Committee recommendations, specialised bank branches for SSI lending have been set up. By March 2004, there were 417 such bank branches in the country. However, studies have revealed that they have not achieved the desired objectives of improving the flow of credit.

By March 2004, it was found that the availability of credit continues to be a major problem with the small enterprises. The credit to small enterprises as percentage of net bank credit has declined from 17.5 per cent in March 1998 to 11 per cent in March 2004. The Standing Advisory Committee of RBI had been constantly reviewing the position and consequently a Working Group was constituted by the RBI in February 2004. To reduce the cost of credit in the SME sector, the Finance Minister announced creation of an SME Fund of Rs. 2,000 crore in January 2004.

Some other credit related developments in recent years are preparation of exclusive credit plans for 60 clusters by the banks. These plans have to be subsequently merged with Annual Credit plans of the States. Another measure is launching of an exclusive programme of Micro Credit to address to the problem of poverty alleviation and creating sustainable employment opportunities. NGOs and Self-help Groups are important players in this scheme which is being operated through SIDBI. The recovery in micro credit has been found to be as high as 98 per cent. Third major development is acknowledgement of the need for creating separate credit rating agencies to apprise the credit worthiness of small enterprises. This will enhance the confidence level of the banks in small loaning who find this segment as risky one due to greater and higher NPAs.

## 2.9 Regional Developments

As a part of the planned industrial growth throughout the country, the Industrial Estates Programme was started in 1952. The main objective of the programme has been to encourage and support the creation, expansion and modernisation of SSIs through provision of factory accommodation, common service facilities and other assistance, etc. The programme also assumed the role of regional development with the requisite facilities and services in semi-urban rural and backward areas.

As per the Second All India Census of Registered SSI units conducted for the year 1987-88, it was found that 42 per cent of SSI units are located in rural areas and 62 per cent of SSI units are located in backward areas. The position shows marginal change as per the result of the Third Census. For promoting industrialisation of backward and rural areas in an effective manner, the government of India, announced in 1988 setting up of Growth Centres and Integrated Infrastructure Development Scheme. Under this scheme, projects up to Rs. 5 crore are financed 40 per cent by way of grant from the Centre and 60 per cent as loan from SIDBI or by the State Governments. No doubt, several measures have been announced by the Government for the dispersed development of SSIs in the country but the available data do not prove the same. Industries have the tendency to grow only in those areas where infrastructure is relatively strong. The result is that the North Eastern states with Eastern States even now lag behind in this respect. Several corrective measures have been taken exclusively for the development of small industries in North Eastern States during the last 7 years i.e. after 1997.

**2.10 Fiscal Measures**

In line with government's policy of encouraging small scale industries, a wide range of concessions and exemptions from payment of excise duty are available to small scale manufacturers to enable them to stand in competition with large scale manufacturers. Under the general small scale excise exemption scheme introduced in 1986, small scale units producing a wide variety of excisable goods are allowed excise duty concessions.

Till 1997-98 any SSI unit, whether registered or unregistered was entitled to full exemption from duty up to the annual turnover of Rs. 30 lakh and concessional duty up to the turnover of Rs. 100 lakh. For the first time in 1997-98 concessional duty at the rates of 3 per cent up to turnover of Rs. 50 lakh and 5 per cent between Rs. 50 lakh to Rs. 100 lakh was prescribed. As a result, the SSIs are not required to maintain complicated records. This benefit is however, limited to total annual turnover of Rs. 300 lakh. In budget 1998-99, clearances up to Rs. 50 lakh were made fully exempted from excise duty. Flat rate of duty is chargeable @ 5 per cent ad valorem on the clearances between Rs. 50-100 lakh. There is also an option to avail MODVAT route. Among all the support/assistance going to SSI sector, excise duty exemption/concession is considered as the most important and effective support to enable the SSI sector to reach a level playing field. As part of the comprehensive policy package announced by the Prime Minister on 30th August, 2000, the excise exemption limit has been substantially enhanced to Rs. 100 lakh. The new enhancement has been made applicable with effect from the 1st September, 2000. Thereafter, various measures have been taken towards rationalisation of duty and providing a delta between the raw material, intermediates and the finished products. It may however, be mentioned that all tariff lines are not included in the SSI General Excise Exemption Scheme. Further, from time to time several new items have been brought out of exemption list and some new items have also been included in the exemption list.

Direct tax benefits in the form of tax holidays, tax relief for new SSI units have also been announced from time to time particularly for the North East and hilly and backward areas.

## 2.11 Technological Support

The SIDO plays a pioneering role in the field of technological development. The Government is providing technical support to SSIs through the following institutions:

1. Tool Rooms: Tool Rooms have been set up with the objective of:

- Assisting SSI units in technological upgradation by providing quality tooling facilities.
- Increasing efficiency of SSI units by providing consultancy and common service facilities in the areas of design and production of tools, jigs and fixtures moulds and dies etc.
- Designing and manufacturing of precision tools such as press tools, moulds and dies for metal castings, jigs and fixtures and special purpose tools.
- Conducting long term training courses in tool and die making, machining and fitting and short term courses on related subjects to personnel working in the industries.

Apart from the existing tool rooms at Calcutta, Ludhiana, Jalandhar, Hyderabad and Mumbai and Training Centres (four), three new Indo-German Tool Rooms have been set up at Indore, Ahmedabad and Aurangabad along with two Indo-Danish Tool Rooms at Bhubaneshwar and Jamshedpur. These tools are equipped with latest machinery and the state of the art technology.

2. Product-cum-Process Development Centres (PPDCs): PPDCs have been set up to look into specific problems of an industry, develop new technologies, render technical support services and manpower development. Besides, strengthening the existing Process-cum-Product Development Centres (four) located at Meerut (Sports goods), Agra (Foundry), Ramnagar (Electronics) and Bombay (Electrical Instrumentation) two new Centres have been set up at Ferozabad (Glass Industry) and Kannauj (Essential Oils).
3. Testing facilities to SSIs, engaged in the production of different products including export worthy products, are provided by the Regional Testing Centres. These Centres provide performance testing, type testing, acceptance testing, calibration services and development of processes for various products. A scheme to provide assistance to industry associations/ voluntary agencies to set up testing centres is also being operated since 1994-95. It has now been decided to involve NGOs in this scheme.
4. Central Footwear Training Centres (CFTCs) extend support to small scale industries by training of manpower in leather and footwear products. CFTCs at Agra and Chennai have undergone modernisation with UNDP assistance. The centres have started training courses in Footwear Technology based on the syllabus

of CFL, London.

5. Integrated Technology Upgradation and Management Programme (UPTECH): A new scheme on Upgradation of Technology (UPTECH) has been operationalised. It covers all the facets of technological improvements such as quality upgradation, energy conservation, pollution control, process modifications, modernisation etc. 10 clusters have been identified in the above scheme which would be taken up during the current Five Year Plan period.
6. Financial incentives have been designed for SSI units which acquire ISO 9000 or similar international quality standards. Under the scheme of promoting ISO 9000 certification, SSI units are given financial support by way of reimbursing 75 per cent of their expenditure to obtain ISO 9000 certification subject to a maximum of Rs. 75,000. Over 4000 SSI units have already availed this scheme by March 2004.

## 2.12 Export Promotion Measures

Small scale units account for about 35 per cent of national exports. This is definitely not a small achievement and proves the capability of Indian SSI products to compete in international markets. In case of items like ready-made garments, leather goods, processed foods, engineering items, the performance has been commendable both in terms of volume and their share within the SSI sector while in some cases like sports goods they accounted for 100 per cent of total exports.

Export promotion from the small scale sector has been accorded a high priority in India's export promotion strategy which includes simplification of procedures, incentives of higher production of exports, an exclusive SSIs Market

Development Fund, simplification of duty draw-back rules etc. Products of SSI exporters are displayed in international exhibitions free of cost.

The Import-Export Policy allows various export/import entitlements to exporting units under the schemes covered by the policy. These schemes primarily relate to advance licensing, imports under EPCG, scheme of 100 per cent EOUs, setting up of units in FIZs/EPZs. The proposals received from SSI units are considered and recommended for granting of various licences/entitlements to the importers to help them to meet their requirements of materials etc. Imports under some of the schemes are allowed without payment of customs duty or at concessional rate of customs duty. The import-export policy provides for double weightage on exports from small scale units for recognition as export/trading houses.

To acquaint exporters of the latest packaging standards, training programmes on packaging for exports are organised by the SIDO through the Office of the Development Commissioner, Small Scale Industries. Trade delegations and sales-cum-study teams are sponsored from the small scale sector under the Market Development Assistance Scheme of the Ministry of SSI. To encourage quality, National Awards for quality products are given by the Ministry of Small Scale Industries, every year.

Export promotion has been one of the objectives behind the policy of product reservation in the SSI sector. Any large scale unit in India or abroad can set up industries even in respect of reserved items provided it agrees to abide by the condition of 50 per cent exports. This stipulation which was earlier 75 per cent of total manufacture has been reduced to 50 per cent with effect from 18th December, 1997. The reduction in export obligation has been considered as an inducement for induction of latest technology in areas having high export potential in the SSI sector.

## 2.13 Entrepreneurship Development

Small and tiny enterprises create dispersal of economy throughout the length and breadth of our country. To utilise the potential of youth of our country by setting up small scale and tiny enterprises, proper guidance is given through Entrepreneurship Development Programme (EDPs). Over the years, these programmes have created confidence in our youth which has led to self-employment and creation of further employment. The SIDO through the network of SISIs have been the pioneer in conducting such EDPs for various target groups. These courses generally have a duration of four to six weeks. Product-oriented courses, such as hosiery, food products, leather products, herbal cosmetics, electronics, etc., have been found to be useful by the trainees.

The strengthening of existing national level training institutes, such as NIESBUD, NISIET have also been undertaken by the Ministry of SSI.

EDPs have attracted the attention of the educated unemployed youth. To meet the demand, the EDIs have set up with government assistance in different states. They are located in Lucknow (UP), Dharwad (Karnataka), Bhopal (MP), Aurangabad (Maharashtra), Bhubaneshwar (Orissa), Madurai (Tamil Nadu), Parwanoo (HP), Cochin (Kerala) etc.

## 2.14 Comprehensive Policy Package for Small Enterprises (August 2000)

Major Announcements by Prime Minister on the occasion of the National Conference held at Vigyan Bhavan,

New Delhi on 30th August, 2000

- To improve the competitiveness of Small Scale Sector the exemption for excise duty limit raised from Rs. 50 lakh to 1 Crore.
- Composite loans limit raised from Rs. 10 lakh to Rs. 25 lakh.
- Industry related service and business enterprises with a maximum investment of Rs. 10 lakh will qualify for priority lending.
- Capital subsidy of 12 per cent for investment in technology in select sectors. An inter-ministerial committee of experts will be set up to define the scope of technology upgradation and sectoral priorities.
- To minimise harassment to Small Scale Sector a Group will be set up to recommend within three months, means of streamlining inspection. This will include repeal of laws and regulations applicable to the sector that have since become redundant.
- A fresh census of Small Scale industries will be conducted covering inter-alia, the incidents of sickness and its causes.
- To encourage total quality management, the scheme of granting Rs. 75,000 to each unit for opting ISO 9000 certification will continue for the next six years i.e. till the end of the 10th Plan.
- To support the Handloom Sector "Deendayal Hath-kargha Protsahan Yojana" has been announced. The scheme has a total financial implication of Rs. 447 crore and will provide comprehensive financial and infra-structural support to weavers.

The Hon'ble Prime Minister also announced that Ministry of SSI and ARI will announce some more measures for Small Scale Sector. The announcements made by the

Ministry on 31. 8. 2000 are as under:

## 2.15 Other Decisions Announced by the Ministry of SSI and ARI

- The investment limit for the tiny sector will continue to be at Rs. 25 lakh.
- The investment limit for the SSI sector will continue to be at Rs. 1 crore.
- The Ministry of SSI will bring out a specific list of hi-tech and export oriented industries which would require the investment limit to be raised up to Rs. 5 crore to admit of suitable technology upgradation and to enable them to maintain their competitive edge.
- In the National Equity Fund Scheme, the project cost limit will be revised from Rs. 25 lakh to Rs. 50 lakh. The soft loan limit will be retained at 25 per cent of the project cost subject to a maximum of Rs. 10 lakh per project. Assistance under the NEF will be provided at a service charge of 5 per cent per annum.
- SIDO will have a Market Development Assistance (MDA) programme, similar to the one obtaining in the Ministry of Commerce. It will be a plan scheme.
- The eligibility limit for coverage under the Credit Guarantee Scheme has been revised to Rs. 25 lakh from the present limit of Rs. 10 lakh.
- Self-certification will be progressively encouraged in lieu of inspections, which should be prescribed under the three following conditions:

1. On receipt of specific complaint
2. Selection of unit for sample check (say 10 per cent of total units); and
3. For audit and safety purposes.

- The Integrated Infrastructure Development (IID) Scheme

will progressively cover all areas in the country with 50 per cent reservation for rural areas.

- Regarding upgrading the industrial estates, which are languishing, SSI Ministry will draw up a detailed scheme for the consideration of the Planning Commission.
- Setting up of incubation centres in sunrise industries will be supported.
- Capacity building in the SSI sector, both for entrepreneurs as well as workers will be given top priority. SSI Ministry and Labour Ministry will work out the strategy jointly.
- The Reserve Bank of India is being requested to appoint a Task Force to go into the question of how to strengthen and popularise factoring services and on how to encourage bills culture, without recourse to the SSI suppliers. The Task Force shall give its report within six months of its constitution.
- The Limited Partnership Act will be drafted quickly and got enacted. Attempt will be made to bring the Bill before the next session of the Parliament.
- A plan scheme for cluster development will be drawn up.
- The Department of Economic Affairs will appoint a Task Force to suggest revitalisation/restructuring of the State Finance Corporations.
- The Nayak Committee's recommendations regarding provision of 20 per cent of the projected turnover as working capital is being commended to the financial institutions and banks.
- RBI is being requested to take up with the banks the question of sub-allocating overall limits to the large borrowers specifically for meeting the payment

obligations in respect of purchases from the SSIs, either on cash basis or on bills basis.

- RBI is being requested to draw up revised guidelines for the rehabilitation of currently sick but potentially viable SSI units. Such guidelines should be detailed, transparent and non-discretionary.
- The funds available under the non-lapsable pool for the North East will be made use of for Industrial Infrastructure Development, setting up of incubation centres, for cluster development and for setting up of IIDs in the North East including Sikkim.
- The TBSE set up by SIDBI will be strengthened so that it functions effectively as a Technology Bank. It will be properly networked with NSIC, SIDO (SENET Programme) and PCTT.
- SIDO, SIDBI and NSIC will jointly prepare a compendium of available technologies for the R&D institutions in India and abroad and circulate among the industry associations for the dissemination of the latest technology related information.
- Commercial banks are being requested to develop schemes to encourage investment in technology upgradation and harmonise the same with SIDBI.
- The Vendor Development Programmes, Buyer-Seller Meets and Exhibitions will take place more often, and in dispersed locations.

### 2.16 Policy Package for Tiny Sector

- 20 per cent of the projected annual turnover of the tiny units would qualify for working capital loan.
- The National Small Industries Corporation will continue to give composite loans up to Rs. 25 lakh to the tiny sector and continue to charge one per cent concessional

interest rate.

- SIDBI will continue to give concessional rate of refinance to the tiny sector which is now at 10.5 per cent as compared to 12 per cent for the SSI sector. This policy will continue.
- Under the Integrated Infrastructure Development (IID) Scheme, 50 per cent of the plots will be earmarked for the tiny sector (as against 40 per cent done earlier).
- Preference will be given to the tiny sector for loans for technology upgradation.
- Under the National Programme for Rural Industrialisation, cluster development is being taken up by KVIC, SIDO, SIDBI and NABARD. The major beneficiaries of cluster development programme will be tiny sector units. The sponsoring organisation for each cluster will provide for design development, capacity building, technology intervention and consortium marketing. A cluster development fund will be created under the Plan.
- Preference will be given to the tiny sector while organising buyer seller meets, vendor development programmes and exhibitions.
- Under the Prime Minister's Rozgar Yojana, which finances setting up of micro enterprises and generates employment for the educated unemployed, the family income eligibility limit of Rs. 24,000 is revised to Rs. 40,000 per annum.
- Under the National Equity Fund Scheme, 30 per cent of the investment will be earmarked for the tiny sector.
- Action has been completed on all components of policy package barring those relating to Limited Partnership Act and Enactment on Factoring Services.

## 2.17 Environment Dimensions

India became a party to the Montreal Protocol in June, 1992 to phase out Ozone Depleting Substances (ODS) by the year 2010. As per India Country Programme, for implementation of Montreal Protocol, Office of the Development Commissioner SSIs has been charged with the responsibility of effecting phase out of ODS in the small scale sector. To co-ordinate this work on behalf of the Ministry of Environment and forests, "Ozone Cell" has been constituted in SIDO. The Cell will represent the small scale sector in the Ministry of Environment and Forest. Basic information exposure, awareness and training mechanisms for small entrepreneurs will be developed by this Cell to facilitate phasing out of ODS in the small scale sector. The SSI sector is now engaged in the energy audit of polluting industries.

## 2.18 Assessment of Policy Framework

From a review of policy support accorded to small enterprises in India it is clear that all the support measures are the product of time and are based on its requirement of the small enterprises in India. The Government of India took a lead role along with the State Governments in the promotion and development of the small enterprises, since no other organisation was forthcoming. The SSI Associations and other organisations either did not exist or were too weak to take a lead role. Some people think that the Government has been over possessive and thus had been over protective; as a result the small enterprises could not have a natural growth. This criticism, however, is not correct. The Government was protective when it has needed and has switched over from its earlier role of protector to facilitator when it realised that the small enterprises are no longer infant. Moreover, such support measures through Government exist in all the countries. All literature on 'Small firms' have established the need for such support to small enterprises to bring them nearer to its optimal size in the economy. In fact, there is strong case to introduce support mechanism to small enterprises to provide them a level playing ground as they do not have access to the economies of scale. This is however, correct that prolonged protection has induced many small enterprises to remain small. In some cases this has affected their competitiveness and has led to their horizontal growth. A sound policy framework is one which induces the enterprises to grow vertically. A small unit must become medium in 10 to 15 years time and should become a large in 20 years time.

The sector must grow because growth means increase in employment, output, exports, growth of entrepreneurship and regional development. Another feature of small enterprises development has been its growth in isolation. The sector could not achieve an organic linkage with the large scale enterprises. In most of the advanced countries where small enterprises have been playing dominant role, there exists a strong bondage between the two sector. Even in the case of ancillaries, there are instances that while the large units (mother unit) grew or modernised themselves, they did not take the small units along.

The policies for small enterprises development pursued since independence could be summed up under four broad phases as under:

**Phase I: 1947 to 1977: Period of Conceptualisation**
**Phase II: 1977 to 1990: Period of Construction**
**Phase III: 1991 to 1999: Period of Consolidation**
**Phase IV: 2000 onwards - Growth Propeller**

The foundation for SSI development was laid during the

1947-1977 phase, particularly during the second Five Year Plan and more specifically through the second Industrial Policy Statement which was announced in 1956. The policy unambiguously chose equity as the guiding principle for small industries development. The Office of the Development Commissioner also known as Small Industries Development Organisation (SIDO) was set up and small scale industries Board was created with a view to give a direction to small industries development. Its role in employment generation, entrepreneurship development and regional development was recognised. Some protective measures were conceptualised during this phase. By this time the public sector had assumed the commanding heights in the Indian economy.

The period 1977-1990 emerged as a high watermark in the evolution of the policy on small industries which got its manifestation through the Industrial Policy Statement of 1977. It aimed at consolidating the gains conceptualised during the first phase through a cover of protection. The policy announced that "whatever can be produced by the small and cottage industries must only be so produced". The policy of reservation conceptualised during the first phase led to construction of a somewhat protective environment The number of reserved items has raised from 180 to 504 and further to 807. Need for special attention to tiny sector was realised during this period. An attempt was made to take the mission of SSI development to the masses through creation of District Industries Centres (DICs) as the focal point of decentralised development. To give impetus to construction phase of the movement, technological institutions in the form of Regional Testing Centres, Field Testing Stations, Workshops, Tool Rooms, etc. were created. Several institutes of entrepreneurs development were also set up. All these helped the sector to achieve a high rate of growth, perhaps the highest rate of growth achieved so far. During the Seventh Plan, the sector achieved an average growth rate of about 13 per cent.

1990-91 was the year of economic crisis in the Indian economy. The Economic reforms introduced thereafter reaffirmed its faith in the market forces. The phase which started in 1991 with Economic Reforms could be termed as a period of consolidation in the face of competition. The phase witnessed challenges emerging out of liberalisation, privatisation and globalisation. It brought the sector face to face with competition. The protection enjoyed so far was drastically reduced through delicensing, reduction in excise and custom duty rates, placement of several items on OGL list and by making credit worthiness as the criteria for credit disbursement. For the first time, a separate policy for SSI development was announced in 1991 whose primary objective was to impart greater vitality and growth to this sector. Focus moved from cheap credit to adequate credit through the implementation of the Nayak Committee recommendations. To provide additional support to employment generation, need for direct intervention was realised which led to the introduction of the Prime Minister's Rojgar Yojana with the target of creating one million additional jobs through micro-enterprises during the last 3 years of the Eighth Five Year Plan. New tool rooms, process-cum-product development centres with latest technological back up were set up to enable the sector to upgrade technology, improve quality and competitiveness. This phase saw the sector emerging successfully in the face of competition as it succeeded in recording a higher rate of growth than large industries and in making a convincing global presence. In fact, this phase led to the realisation of vast potential as a precursor to an era of hope for future.

Phase IV starting from the year 2000 has recognised small scale enterprise as an engine of growth for the new millennium. In the history for policy initiatives, the day 30th August 2000 has emerged as a landmark. Based on the recommendations of the Group of Ministers, the Prime Minister announced a comprehensive policy package for the small scale enterprises with the objective of enabling this sector as the GROWTH SECTOR for the Millennium.

The last 55 years has seen the small enterprise sector emerging as a vibrant and dynamic sector of Indian economy. It has vast potential. The sector, however, has not contributed as per its potential so far due to lack of organic linkages with crucial sectors of economy and due to use of traditional and somewhat obsolete technology. Lot of scope exists for improvement in productivity, efficiency and competitiveness. Many economic parameters are not in its favours. The ratios of economic efficiency indicates enough scope for improvement. Even in export sector where its share is 35 per cent, it cannot be forgotten that SSI exports are less than 10 per cent of SSI production. A large segment of SSI sector which has remained broadly confined to traditional products, traditional technology and traditional market, calls for urgent technology upgradation and modernisation. Some of the major continuing problems which need to be addressed are provisions of adequate credit, adequate infrastructure including power, improvement in marketing opportunities ensuring timely payments on their supplies to large units, and reducing the hassles of complex laws, rules and regulations and thus reducing the rigours of inspector raj.

The problem of unemployment continues without solution. Today when our population has crossed the one thousand million mark, employment in agriculture is declining and large industries are experiencing jobless growth. The only ray of hope is small scale and cottage industries. It is the only sector with potential to achieve enhanced industrial production, accelerated exports and at the same time generate large-scale employment. To achieve the best of results, the guiding principle for small enterprise development should be upgrade technology, improve quality of labour and output and enhance competitiveness.

The sector requires a responsive business environment which means adequate and timely supply of credit, institutional support services, technological and infrastructural support assistance, and last, but not the least a reduced rigour of 'Inspector Raj'. Export promotion requires special attention which should include facilities for hi-tech products, exploration of new markets, product specific packaging and development of common brand names. Creation of marketing and export consortia should be focus in this area. The strategy of growth should lay more emphasis on holistic development of clusters both natural and induced as the economies of scale lie there. If service sector has been emerging very fast both in terms of growth and employment it is necessary to have policy framework to address to the needs of the service sector.

The Indian SSE sector must gear itself to face the challenges and avail the opportunities emerging from the WTO. It must address itself to the requirements of the WTO environment. The need of the hour is to prepare the sector to face the era of change and challenge successfully. There is a need for change in strategy of small enterprise development by evolving variety of linkages between large and small industries, between government and people through non-governmental organisations, between technology and quality and finally between economic cost and social benefits. Small enterprise development should take the shape of mass movement.

# 3

# Small Enterprises and WTO

The world is changing into a global village. The change is visible in multiple forms and from multiple directions. Starting from reforms with emphasis on liberalisation, privatisation and globalisation, the world has witnessed emergence of World Trade Organisation (WTO) which has altered the basic principles of trade, regional groupings, barrier free movements, mergers and acquisitions, foreign direct investments, bilateral and multilateral agreements, etc. which have become the orders of the day. The world is in the grip of technological changes and revolution in the field of information technology.

Service sector has emerged as the most powerful segment of national income in most of the economies including India. Labour standards and environmental situation in our country affect the cost of production and competitiveness of products in other countries. Marketing strategy has changed. There has been a major change in consumers attitudes and preferences. Their pressure for better quality and hygienic products has once again proved that consumer is the king.

Amid so many changes around us, the Indian Small Industries Sector which has been playing very important role in terms of its contribution towards employment, output and exports, has remained relatively oblivious to the these changes. So far, it has survived amid somewhat protected environment which exist in the form of product reservation, market reservation, price preference, priority sector lending, fiscal exemptions/concessions, etc. With the emergence of WTO along with its conditionalities protection may be considered as discriminatory or barrier to trade. Many of the existing support systems in place for protection and promotion of small scale sector will have to compete on their own and to find a place for themselves in domestic as well as international market.

The small enterprises will have to upgrade its technology and modernise, adopt modern marketing, management practices and improve the quality of its products and be efficient and competitive. This will involve complete transformation of this section. It is rightly said that the small enterprises in the new millennium will be entirely different and that the existing small industries are going to become some what redundant in their present structures in the new economic environment. What does WTO mean to the SSI sector in India? It is necessary to examine the implications of the various provisions of the WTO. For this, it is essential to understand the origin, objectives and conditionalities of the WTO. The emergence of WTO is one of the major developments of the last century which will have major influence in deciding the shape of world trade in the present century. This chapter traces the factors leading to the emergence of WTO.

### 3.1 Emergence of WTO

The economic boundaries of nations for all practical purposes have expanded enormously much beyond their geographical limits and the rules of trade are no longer different for domestic zone and international zones. Trading partners are required to follow uniform rules of trade. Moving away from the erstwhile policy of 'Beggar thy Neighbour', the nations are now required to accord 'National Treatment' to the trading partners and follow certain disciplines.

The process of disciplining international trade started with the signing of an Agreement in 1947 in Geneva immediately after the Second World War by 23 non-communist countries. This agreement was called General Agreement on Tariffs and Trade (GATT). Since the idea of having an international trade organisation under UN could not fructify, the GATT was the only agency for promoting non-discriminatory trade among member nations. Though its membership rose to 96 in 1988, GATT remained confined to two basic functions, viz., tariff reduction and removal of non-tariff barriers. GATT took major decisions by having discussions and negotiations through meetings. Between 1947 and 1986, the GATT had seven rounds of meetings. The eighth round began in Uruguay in 1986 and concluded in 1994 which led to the emergence of the World Trade Organisation (WTO).

The World Trade Organisation came into being on 1st January, 1995 as an outcome of the signing of final Act on 15th April, 1994 at Marrakesh. The WTO has emerged as the only institution dealing with the Rules of Trade between the nations. With headquarters in Geneva, Switzerland, it has 148 members at present (March 2004) including India. China joined the WTO in December 2001. 27 countries are trying to have the membership. As the only regulatory body for the world trade, WTO's objective is to ensure freer, more transparent and more predictable trading regime in the world. It is based on a sound legal system and its Agreements are ratified by the Parliaments of the member countries.

The WTO's Agreements cover all the original treaty provisions of the GATT relating to trade in goods and also cover new areas like trade in services, trade related intellectual property issues and trade related investment measures. The basic objective of WTO is to ensure global free trade and reduction of tariff and non-tariff barriers. The ultimate objective of WTO is to expand production and trade and allow the optimal use of world resources. It acknowledges the need of special concern for the less developed countries.

In this context it is worthwhile to have a look to the preamble of the Marrakesh Agreement which clearly visualises the need for securing a better share for the developing countries, "there is need for positive efforts to ensure that developing countries and especially the least developed among them, secure a share in the growth in international trade commensurate with the needs of their economic development." Its procedures are based on the principles of **transparency, predictability and certainty**. WTO has an effective dispute settlement mechanism with built-in cross retaliatory provisions and is poised to become a forum for continuous negotiations. The ministerial conference is the forum for discussion and thus an apex body for decision making. The conference meets every two years. So far, four conferences have been held. The first in Singapore (1996), second in Geneva (1998), third in Seattle (December 1999), fourth at Doha (November 2001) and fifth at Cancun, Mexico (September 2003). In the fifth conference 146 member nations were present.

### 3.2 Activities of WTO

The activities of WTO cover the three areas of **trade in goods, trade in services and trade relating investment**.

**3.2.1 Trade in Goods:** Covered under the General Agreement on Tariffs and Trade, this includes all industrial products and consumer durables. There are large number of Agreements relating to trade in goods. These are as under:

**A. General Agreement on Tariffs and Trade (GATT)**

**B. Other Agreements**

- Agreement on Valuation of Goods;
- Agreement on Pre-shipment Inspection;
- Agreement on Technical Barriers to Trade (TBT);
- Agreement on Sanitary and Phytosanitary Measures (SPS);
- Agreement on Import Licensing Procedure;
- Rules applicable to exports;
- Agreement on Subsidies and Countervailing Measures;
- Agreement on Safeguard Measures;
- Agreement on Anti-Dumping Measures;
- Trade Related Investment Measures (TRIMS);
- Market Access Negotiation;
- Agreement on Textiles and Clothings (ATG);
- Agreement on Agriculture;
- Agreement on Government Procurement and;
- Agreement on State Trading Enterprises;

**3.2.2 Trade in Services:** Covered by the main Agreement, trade in services comes under the General Agreement on Trade and Services (GATS) and includes activities like banking, insurance, consultancy, etc.

**3.2.3 Trade related aspects of Intellectual Property Rights (TRIPS):** This covers patents, copyrights, trademarks, industrial designs, layout designs, trade secrets, etc.

The WTO Agreements can be classified broadly in 3 categories:

1. Those affecting the Quantitative Restrictions (QRs) and tarrification of products e.g., General Agreement on Tariffs and Trade (GATT), Agreement on Agriculture, Agreement on Textiles and Clothings (ATC).

2. Those which deal with Intellectual Property Rights e.g., Agreement on Trade Related Aspects of Intellectual Property Rights (TRIPS), and
3. Those which deal with barriers to trade, standards, investment and subsidies, e.g., Agreement on Technical Barriers to Trade (TBT), Agreement on Application of Sanitary and Phyto-sanitary Measures (SPS), Agreement on Subsidies and Countervailing Measures (ASCM) and Agreement on Trade Related Investment Measures (TRIMs)

### 3.3 Principles of WTO

In order to understand the implications of the Agreement, it is essential to understand the basic principles of WTO. The basic principle on which these Agreements are based is non-discrimination which means:

- **Most Favoured Nation Treatment (MFN):** This means any trade concession offered by one member of WTO to another member must be offered to all other members.
- **National Treatment:** This means imported goods should not be discriminated against the domestic goods meaning thereby that same treatment has to be accorded to both the domestic and the foreign markets.
- **Same Rule for All:** This implies restricting Governments or organisations from 'distorting' normal trade by way of subsidising, dumping, discriminatory licensing policies etc., which can hurt the business within the country or outside the country. This calls for rationalisation of Government's policies to eliminate the distorting effects e.g., WTO visualises exports to be relieved of all indirect taxes as excise duty, sales tax, etc., having a cascading effect on the cost of the product.
- **Freer Trading System:** This means that barriers which

exist should come down and if there are problems, it could be sorted out through negotiations.

- **Predictable Trading System:** This means that the foreign companies, institutions and Governments should be confident that trade barriers including tariff, non-tariff barriers and other measures would not be raised arbitrarily. More and more tariff rates are 'bound' against subsequent increases.
- **More Competitive Trading System:** This is to be achieved by discouraging unfair practices which exist in the guise of export subsidies and dumping of products below cost of production.
- **Special Consideration for the Less Developed Countries:** WTO has given more time for them to adjust, greater flexibility and special privileges exist particularly for the Least Developed Countries (LDCs).

Detailed guidelines exist for administration of Agreements. Government or traders have right to information, Right to present evidence etc.

## 3.4 Main Provisions of Agreements

**3.4.1 General Agreement on Tariffs and Trade:** The entire edifice of GATT is built on five basic rules.

- Protection to domestic industry to be provided through tariffs only.
- Non-tariff barriers like import licensing quotas, other form of restrictions will have to be eliminated.
- Reduction in tariff and other barriers to trade are to be done through negotiations. Tariffs are to be bound against subsequent increases on most of the products.
- Most Favoured Nation Principle - No discrimination among member countries. Exceptions however, exist for regional preferential agreements like EU, NAFTA,

ASEAN, SAPTA, etc., form the MFN rule.

- National Treatment - same treatment to imported products and domestic products.

**A. Phasing out of Quantitative Restrictions:** Since overnight elimination of Quantitative Restrictions (QRs) was not possible, flexibility was granted for eliminating QRs in a specific time frame. Developing countries including India were given more time to adjust. Delayed removal of QRs was allowed to countries having Balance of payments problems to restrict imports. The Agreement requires the developing countries to take price based measures (such as import surcharge) instead of quantitative restrictions (as restrictive import licensing). Quantitative restrictions were abolished by WTO Members in agriculture and in its place tariffs were applied, making the process more transparent. Similarly for textiles, quotas levied by many developed countries on import of textile products from developing countries are to be phased out in a specific time frame by 1st January, 2005 completely.

**B. Subsidies:** While some subsidies are not allowed (called Prohibited Subsidies), there are a few subsidies which are listed as Conditional Permissible (Actionable Subsidies) and there are others which are Permissible (Non-Actionable Subsidies) called Green Subsidies.

**Prohibited Subsidies:** Two categories of subsidies are prohibited by Article 3 of the Agreement on subsidies and Countervailing Measures (SCM). These are subsidies on export performance (Export Subsidy) and subsidies based upon the use of domestic over imported goods (Local Content Subsidy). These subsidies are prohibited because they are designed to affect trade and thus are most likely to have adverse effects on the interests of other members. Export promotion policies like tax exemptions under Section

80 HHC, EPCG, DEPB are being targeted under this category. Precautions will have to be taken in their use. India has some cushion in this regard since its per capita income is less than $ 1000 per annum at present and hence it can give prohibited subsidies but these could be subject to countervailing action by the other member countries. The European Union has imposed anti-subsidy duties against some Indian exports citing the above schemes and some other countries are contemplating similar action.

**Permissible Actionable Subsidies** arc those which are permissible as long as they do not hurt the interests of other Members e.g., a subsidy specific to an enterprise, group of enterprises, industrial sector or designated geographical location, is permissible. They are essentially production subsidies which are not prohibited but are actionable and subject to challenge either through multilateral dispute settlement mechanism or through countervailing action, if they cause adverse effects to the interests of another member.

**Permissible Non-Actionable Subsidies** are those which are granted on the basis of objective criteria that are economic in nature and horizontal in application and do not favour certain enterprises over others and are not specific. There are 3 subsidies in this category:

- Basic Research and pre-competitive development subsidies. This is a major subsidy used by developed countries to the advantage of their domestic agro-industries.
- Assistance to disadvantaged Regions: This is available provided it is not limited to specific enterprise or industries within the region. It should go for regional development of a disadvantaged area/regions.
- Assistance to adopt existing facilities to new environ-

mental requirement. It should be on one time basis and limited to 20 per cent of adaptation cost.

Importing countries cannot levy countervailing measures on Non-Actionable subsidies e.g., subsidies given by the government to small and medium enterprises (SMEs) identified on the basis of their size or number of employment would be non-actionable.

**C. Unfair Practices:** GATT rules deal with two types of unfair practices which distort conditions of competition. These are:

- If the goods benefit from the subsidies and
- If goods are dumped in the foreign market.

The Agreement on Anti-Dumping Practices and Agreement on Subsidies and Countervailing Measures authorise countries to levy compensatory duties on import of products benefiting from 'unfair trade practices'. The criteria and procedures employed by both the Agreements for determining injury are similar.

Provisions under Anti-dumping Duties are based on price behaviour of exporters and not the exporting country as a whole. Dumping exists when export price is less than the normal value and injury or threat to domestic industry and causal link are required to be proved. De-minimise levels consist of 2 per cent for dumping margin, 3 per cent for export volumes of a country and 7 per cent for all dumped imports from all countries. It is required to be proved that the above limits have been crossed in order to take anti-dumping action.

Similarly the instrument of countervailing duties deals with the problem of direct and indirect government subsidies. Action is primarily oriented against the policies and programmes of the Government of the exporting country. Injury or threat of injury to domestic industry and causal link must be proved. De-minimise provided are:

- 1 per cent subsidisation or negligible volumes for developed countries;
- 2 per cent subsidisation and 4 per cent for one developing country and 9 per cent collectively from all developing countries.
- 3 per cent for Annexure VII countries (like India) having per capita income of less than US $ 1000 per annum.

**D. Trade Related Investment Measures (TRIMS):** Governments often impose conditions and restrictions on direct flow of foreign investment in accordance with certain national priorities. Conditions that can affect trade are known as Trade Related Investment Measures. The Agreement prohibits use of five types of TRIMS which are as follows:

- Local Content Requirement (LCRs) involving use of certain kinds of local inputs in production.
- Trade Balancing Requirement limiting use of import content in proportion to exports of investing companies.
- Trade Balancing Requirement placing restrictions on import to an amount or value of the product exported.
- Exchange Restrictions implying restrictions on access to foreign exchange to an amount of foreign exchange earnings attributable to the enterprise.
- Domestic sales requirement requiring a company to sell certain products locally.

TRIMS were to be reviewed before the 1st January, 2000. India notified two TRIMS viz., Local Content Requirement in the production of certain pharmaceuticals and dividend balancing requirement in the case of investment in 22 categories of consumer items.

**E. Tariff Cuts:** Developed countries are required to cut tariff by 40 per cent and developing countries by 30 per cent in five equal stages so as to reach the agreed rate by 1st January 2000.

**F. Binding of Tariffs:** The market access schedules are not simply announcements on tariff alone. These represent commitments not to increase tariffs beyond listed rates. These are called bound rates which serve as a ceiling. Bound rates have been fixed at 40 per cent for finished goods and 25 per cent for intermediates. However, for agriculture goods, the bound rates are 100 per cent for agricultural commodities, 150 per cent for processed food and 300 per cent for edible oils. However, in the Union Budget for 2000-2001, the highest import duty rate was fixed at 35 per cent with 10 per cent additional duty on it, thus the maximum bound rate on manufacturing goods can go up to 38.5 per cent

**G. Agreement on Textiles and Clothing (ATC):** World trade in textiles and clothing has been subject to an array of bilateral agreements over the past three decades termed as the Multi Fibre Agreement (MFA). The arrangement when terminated in 1994 had a Membership of 39 countries (mostly developing or exporting) and had around 90 bilateral restraint Agreements. Textiles and Clothing have now been brought under multilateral discipline replacing the erstwhile MFA. The Agreements prescribe removal of QRs in four phases within ten years ending in January, 2005.

**H. Government Procurement:** In almost all countries Governments and agencies controlled by them are significant buyers of goods and services amounting to the tune of 10 to 15 per cent of the GNP. The rules of GATT specifically exempt products procured by Government from two important rules i.e., MFN and National Treatment Principle, that means that these provisions promote purchasing agencies to buy their requirements from a domestic manufacturer even at higher prices if they so wish. However, there is a plurilateral Agreement on Government procurement, which requires the signatories to accord MFN and National Treatment to Government's purchases as well as on agreed purchases. India is not a party to this Agreement (Plurilateral means some countries whereas 'multilateral' refers to all member countries).

**I. Labour Standards:** Trade and labour standard is a highly sensitive issue. Till date, there is no mention of inclusion of social clause or labour standards in WTO. Some industrialised nations do realise this issue now and are insisting that the subject should be studied by the WTO as a first step towards bringing the matter of core labour standards into the organisation. There is great divide between most of the industrialised nations and developing countries on this subject. The developing countries including India which is one of the most vocal countries on this issue, look at it as a ploy of developed nations to annihilate their comparative advantage of labour cost and argue that ILO is the right forum to discuss the issue and not WTO. This issue is of great concern for unorganised manufacturing sector where sometimes use of child labour is alleged in some activities.

**J. World Trade and Environment under WTO:** The WTO has no specific Agreement dealing with environment but a number of Agreements include provisions dealing with environmental concerns. These are:

- **GATT Agreement Article:** Policies affecting trade in goods for profiting human, animal or plant life or health or measures relating to conservation of exhaustible natural resources which are exempted from normal GATT discipline under certain conditions.
- **Agreement relating to Technical Barriers to Trade**

**and Sanitary and Phyto-sanitary measures** (animal and plant, health and hygiene), recognition of environmental objectives.

- **Agreement on Agriculture:** Environmental programmes are exempt from cuts in subsidies.
- **Subsidies and Countervailing Measures** allow subsidy up to 20 per cent of the firm cost for adopting new environmental laws.
- **Intellectual Properties:** Government can refuse to issue patents that threaten human, animal, plant life or health or cause damage to environmental and policy affecting trade in service for profiting human, animal, plant life are exempt from GATS and certain conditions.

**K. World Trade and Environment Agreement on Technical Barriers to Trade and Sanitary and Phyto-sanitary Measures:** This is of great concern for the small enterprises. Hence, it is essential to understand its provisions. The Agreement on Technical Barriers to Trade (TBT) provides that mandatory standards adopted by Governments to protect health and safety of the people and to protect environment should not be applied as to cause unnecessary obstacles to trade. The Agreement visualises that standards do not create unnecessary barriers, if they are uniform and based on internationally agreed standards. For non-voluntary standards, the code of Good Practices for preparation, adoption and application of standards is an integral part of TBT Agreements.

The Agreement also covers process and production methods standards having special relevance to agro industries, food processing and chemicals. The Agreement on the Application of Sanitary (for human and animal) and Phyto-sanitary (for plants) Measures (SPS) specifies the principles and rules which member countries must use in regulating import of agriculture and food products to protect human, animal or plant life or maintain health. SPS Agreement allows discrimination owing to differences in climate, incidence of pests or disease in different countries. The emphasis is on adoption of international standards.

**L. Safeguard Measures:** These measures exist against sudden surge in imports and is available when such a situation has caused injury or have threatened to cause serious injury to the domestic industry. Safeguard measures can be in the form of tariff increase or Quantitative Restrictions. It also concerns issues like structural adjustment, compensation, retaliation etc. and its imposition requires consultations with WTO as well the exporting country at different levels. Further compensation, retaliation etc. come into play if measures continue beyond 3 years.

**3.4.2 General Agreement on Trade and Services:** Services sector has been growing at a fast rate in recent years. There has been phenomenal movement in technologies of telecommunication and information technology related services. The Agreement on Trade in Services (GATS) applies the basic rule of 'trade in goods' to extend to 'trade in services'. It covers all services (any service under any sector) under GATS. The general obligations to be followed are:

- The extension of MFN principle with some exceptions, for a transition period of ten years.
- Transparency of regulations.
- Require all Governments to publish all laws and regulations and to establish enquiry points for information before January 1, 1997.

**3.4.3 Agreement on Trade Related Aspects of Intellectual Property Rights (TRIPS):** India as a developing country had a 5 year transition period which expired on 31.12.1999. An additional period of 5 years, i.e. up o December 2004 is also available for extending product patent protection to areas of technology not protected so far. The provisions of patent has to be both TRIPS compliant and also safeguard for protection of public interest, national security, bio-diversity, traditional knowledge, etc. Adequate provisions are required with regard to patents, trademarks, designs and geographical limitations. Already a new legislation called 'Geographical Indications of Goods (Registration and Protection) Act, 1999 has been enacted.

Till now geographical indications were not registrable in India but protection by general principles of common law exist which permit the aggrieved person to file an action for passing of protection of their rights. Due to the absence of statutory protection in India, Indian geographical indications may be misused by persons outside India to indicate goods not originating from the locality in India.

Existing laws are required to be amended to bring them in conformity with TRIPS. At present, there are no specific laws on geographical indication and trade secrets though action can be taken under common law.

### 3.5 General Implications of WTO

The general implication of WTO can be summarised as under:

- The impact of WTO and its Agreements is being felt over every economic activity be it agriculture, trading, services or manufacturing.
- World markets are opening up due to lowering of tariffs and protections are getting progressively dismantled.
- Developing countries will have greater opportunities in sectors in which they have cost-based comparative advantages.

- Export markets will become tougher because of competition among developing countries with similar comparative advantage.
- There is a wave of standardisation - hence products from developing countries will face tougher quality standards.
- Every company will required to have cost audit and compare itself with global markets.
- International Trade is increasingly becoming 'knowledge-based'.
- Every aspect of trade has legal backing hence every unit must be in a position to fight legally.

The discipline implicit in the operations of the WTO system has given rise to escalating incidence of instances of anti-dumping, non-tariff barriers and other forms of protectionist measures which a country can devise. There are charges and counter charges made on both sides and the common tenor of the criticism is that it is heavily loaded against developing countries, for example while 80 per cent of the 144 members are developing countries, the balance of power and initiatives in practice favour the developed nations comprising Europe, USA, Japan and Canada accounting for 85 per cent of world trade.

WTO includes trade in services which should be of growing importance to us in India. This sector is important as it is the fastest growing sector in the Indian economy and is mostly concentrated in the small scale sector. SSI sector might be facing tough competition in the area of services.

### 3.6 What Makes WTO so Important?

Among all the international level institutions at present, the World Trade Organisation is not only the most talked about but also the most important institution. While there are some countries which find some of the WTO provisions as non-acceptable or find it difficult to implement, yet there is no dearth of countries who want to become its member at any cost and are willing to pay any price and make appropriate adjustments in their internal policies to be in conformity with the WTO provisions. Answer to the above question could be found in the following facts:

- WTO covers much larger agenda than GATT and it is much more visible organisation than GATT.
- WTO came into existence at a time (1995) when the process of globalisation had already set in (1991) and thus it came at a time when the need for such an organisation was felt most to provide a forum to regulate the conduct of international trade. It is in fact coincidence of timing which has made it so important.
- WTO impinges not only the production for outside market but also domestic market, In fact now there exists only one 'Market' and not the domestic and global market. The twin principles of most Favoured Nation Treatment and National Treatment provide it the unique status.
- It has emerged as the fastest and more rigorous dispute settlement system. Its bindings are automatic and cannot be flouted by any country however, strong or powerful it may be. It provides a rule based system which anybody would like to prevail.
- Though WTO may look all pervasive, yet there are many areas which are exclusively the domain of international policy and the WTO does not interfere in those areas.
- Almost all the nations have realised that days of unilateral or bilateral negotiations are over. It is an age of multilateral trade and negotiations and the WTO exactly stands for the same. In fact there is no life in the realm of international trade outside the WTO particularly

after the joining of China.

- The rules of game of WTO are based on the principle of consensus which has given power even to lone objector. No doubt this also makes the task of decision making difficult and time consuming, it gives a feeling of recognition to even the smallest countries. No member country is ignored here.

The emergence of WTO is the most significant development of the closing years of the last century. Its principles are laudable as it sets a rule of game to be applicable to all members whether belonging to the category of developing or developed.

# 4

# Small Enterprises in India and WTO

## 4.1 WTO and Indian Industry

The process of economic reforms with emphasis on liberalisation and globalisation started in India in June 1991 and the domestic industry has been trying to adjust to the changes since then but within the limits of Indian conditions. The programme has been a phased one. The freedom of phasing may not be available once the WTO conditionalities become operative. The Quantitative Restrictions (QRs) on imports maintained on Balance of Payment (BOP) grounds were notified to WTO in 1997 for 2714 tariff lines (at 8 digit level). Within improvement in BOP, the Committee on BOP Restriction had asked India to phase out plans for retaining these QRs. India had an agreement with its trading partners (except USA) to phase out its QRs in next 6 years i.e. by March 2003. For this bilateral Agreements were signed with the trading partners but USA disputed the need for India to maintain QR as the latter's BOP position had considerably improved. India lost in this legal battle and was asked to remove the QRs by 1.4.2001. The task was accomplished with the removal of QRs on 715 tariff items on 31st March, 2001. Indian is still maintaining QRs on 484 items under Article XX (to protect human, animal and plant life on health and public morals etc.) and XXI (security reasons) of GATT. Only 3 member countries of WTO are maintaining QRs on imports. These are Pakistan, Sri Lanka and Bangladesh.

The mechanism to protect domestic industries exist in the form of raising the import duty on the items considered vulnerable to bound rates. This is up to 25 per cent on raw material and 40 per cent for most of the finished manufactured goods. Through the Union Budget for 2000-2001, India reduced the highest import duty rate from 40 per cent to 35 per cent. This has subsequently been reduced to 25 per cent. The country is faced with another dilemma i.e. it can't raise the duty to bound rates of 35 or 40 per cent because the import duty in most of East-Asian countries is as low as 10 to 15 per cent and India is duty bound to adopt a trade policy which is non-discriminatory. Thus domestic compulsions might be at variance with international regulations.

The WTO Agreements are legally enforceable through the Dispute Settlement Mechanism, thus reducing the flexibility available to national governments to adjust policies to the needs expressed by the industrial associations. Industries will have to pay attention to improve efficiency and competitiveness and rely less on protection through policy changes. Policies will have to be WTO compatible.

The partner countries are under obligation to limit their import duties within the limits of bound rates. Incidentally the applied rates of industrial tariffs in India are already lower than bound rates in several cases. India has bound about 67 per cent of its tariff lines (covering 100 per cent of agricultural lines and about 62 per cent of import of industrial goods). Lines remaining unbound includes those on consumer products and some industrial items.

The biggest challenge before Indian industry is to radically change its mindset. Industry cannot continue to survive behind high tariff barriers or non-tariff barriers like import licensing. It cannot hope to get subsidies from Government indefinitely. Indian industry will have to make themselves in line with the best in the world by raising their level of efficiency and competitiveness to meet competition both in domestic and international markets.

Indian industry now faces competition in the Domestic Market from multiple sources consisting of competition from imported goods coming into the Domestic Market at lower import duties, from goods produced in India for the Domestic Market by the Foreign controlled companies having advantages of brand name and latest technology and also from their inability to raise price in the face of low price prevailing in its competitors countries.

Similarly in the international market, Indian industry will have to face competition from newly industrialised developing countries in its neighbourhood and also to face non-tariff barriers like environmental conditions, health, safety and technical standards from other advanced countries. Indian industries whether large or small will have to pay special attention to (a) quality and (b) observance of environmental health, safety and technical standards. What are the likely effects of WTO on Indian small enterprises? What are the challenges and opportunities? This chapter devotes itself to an in-depth analysis of all these issues.

## 4.2 Non-tariff Barriers: How They Impinge Free Trade?

As against barriers which are quantifiable and whose effect on trade can be assessed, there are certain non-tariff barriers in practice and they might constitute a hindrance to free trade. These are measures like anti-dumping duties, import licensing, subsidies, safeguards, etc. which were identified in Tokyo Round of Negotiations (1973-79). A number of WTO Agreements deal with various technical, bureaucratic or legal issues that could involve hindrance in trade. These are:

- Anti Dumping Action:
- Subsidies and Countervailing Measures

- Textiles permitting Quota Restrictions and trade under Multi-Fibre Agreement: This has been taken over by Agreement on Textiles and Clothing to be fully operated by 2005.
- Technical Regulations and Standards which vary from country to country. Having too many different standards makes life difficult for producers and exporters. If the standards are set arbitrarily, they could be used as an excuse for protectionism and thus standards can become obstacles to trade.
- Import Licensing: This is less widely used these days in the wake of economic reforms. It is essential to note that its provisions should be simple, transparent and predictable. A prescribed procedure has to be followed as any omission might mean violation.
- Customs Valuation: WTO Agreement aims for a fair, uniform and neutral system for the valuation of goods for customs purpose - a system that conforms to commercial realities and which outlaws the use of arbitrary or fictitious customs, values, the knowledge of prescribed rules of valuation, expansion, giving precision to the provision of Customs valuation is a must.
- Pre-shipment Inspection: It is the practice of employing specialised private companies to check shipment details essentially price, quantity and quality of goods ordered overseas. The purpose is to safeguard national financial interests (prevention of capital flight and commercial fraud, customs duty evasion) and to compensate for inadequacies in administrative infrastructure. The WTO Agreement established an independent review procedure administered jointly by organisation representing inspection agencies and those representing exporters.
- Rule of Origin: These are the criteria to define where a

product was made. They are essential part of trade rule because a number of policies discriminate between exporting countries through quotas, preferential tariffs, anti-dumping actions, duty etc. It is also used to compile trade statistics and for 'made in labels'.

- Investment Measures: TRIMS applies only to measures that affect trade in goods. It recognises that certain measures can restrict and distort trade and stipulates that no member shall apply any measure that discriminates against foreigners or foreign products. It also limits the scope of local content requirements.

It is essential to have detailed knowledge of all the possible non-tariff barriers and those which are permitted and also details on how to implement them. Lack of knowledge or improper implementation might be taken as hindrance to trade and could be punishable.

## 4.3 Impact of WTO on India

The impact of WTO on any country depends on its stage of economic development and state of awareness of WTO agreements. WTO should not be viewed as an obstacle or monster but a friend and facilitator since:

- WTO provides Indian exporters predictable tariff and non-tariff regimes in markets abroad.
- Provides Indian exporters 'National Treatment" and "Most Favoured Nation Treatment".
- Has emerged as an efficient and effective means of resolving trade disputes.
- Provides a permanent forum for trade negotiations.
- WTO unlike GATT, has expanded into areas other than industrial goods such agricultural goods, services, intellectual property and trade related investment measures.

WTO unlike GATT, is more intrusive as detailed rules,

such as those on agriculture, subsidies, intellectual property and investment measures impact the industry and economy on the whole, and not just exporters and importers. Sovereign policy option are often restricted due to WTO obligation e.g. infant industry subsidies, local content requirement, reverse engineering. Significant information needs arose due to WTO notification obligations such as those for Technical Barriers to Trade (TBT). Sanitary and Physo-sanitary measures and Agriculture agreements which may not have been necessary otherwise.

### 4.4 Impact of WTO on Indian Small Enterprises

The umbrella of the World Trade Organisation is likely to create some far reaching implications for the small enterprises in India, specifically with regard to their competitive ability and integration with the global markets. The small enterprises here should not be viewed in limited terms as Small Scale Industries (SSI) defined in terms of investment in plant and machinery (currently not exceeding Rs. 10 million) but should cover the entire village and small industries sector including handicrafts, handloom, coir, sericulture, powerloom, khadi and village industries in other words, a large segment of unorganised manufacturing sector. Most of the problems arise due to the unorganised nature of this sector, lack of data and information, use of low technology sometimes obsolete technology and poor infrastructure in the country. WTO will affect all types of small enterprises whether producing for the domestic market or for the international market.

The SSI sector which produces over 7500 items will have to be aware of the patents of products including even of the technological patents, trademarks, industrial designs, etc. 98 per cent of the SSI units are in the nature of tiny/micro enterprises and are weak. Many of them are one man show. This is more so in the case of traditional industries which are generally artisan based, use local skills and resources and sell their products locally. Traditional industries mostly cottage based involve lower level of investment in machinery and provide large part time employment. The tiny units defined as one having investment in plant and machinery not exceeding Rs. 2.5 million also find themselves near traditional industries with one difference of providing mostly full-time employment. Their capital base is poor and do not have access to the economies of scale. Their bargaining power is low and do not have access to information and modern management practices. They constitute most vulnerable segment of the SSI sector.

Hence, they will need to be guided and supported since they are also employment generator for the economy. Balance 2-3 per cent of SSI units are in the category of modern SSIs and have already established global links. But, they are also tiny when compared to Small and Medium Enterprises (SME) sector of developed countries. Thus, they have only relative advantage and not absolute advantage and they also need to be guided on WTO provisions and also on the safeguards available to them. It must also be understood that Indian small enterprises have certain inherent strengths which have helped them raise their share in total exports to over 50 per cent even in the face of tough global competition. The SSIs and Handicrafts taken together account for over 50 per cent of India's exports. The SSI sector possesses the advantage of innovativeness and flexibility. Their inventories are low and have weathered many adverse situations successfully and boldly. Indian SMEs have also advantages of local raw material and cheap labour which could be harnessed to the advantage.

## 4.5 Immediate Impact of WTO on India

To understand immediate impact of WTO on Indian small enterprises it would be necessary to understand the following issues:

- Removal of Quantitative Restrictions leading to lower tariffs on imports and hence enhanced competition.
- Removal of TRIMS
- Reduction of tariffs in general.
- A strengthened Intellectual Property Right regime.
- Use of SPS/TBT measure regulated.
- Use of domestic industry protection measures made predictable.
- Better access to foreign markets because of lower tariffs.

At this stage it is necessary to understand where do the small enterprises fit in the WTO framework? WTO agreements are generally 'size-neutral'. Hence SSIs do not have any special dispensation.

Main exception in the subsidies Agreement (Article 2.1 (b) and footnote 2) whereby subsidies automatically granted on an economic bases such as number of employees or size of enterprise would not be deemed 'specific' and thus not subject to prohibition or be actionable through counter-vailing duties.

At the same time, it is essential to note small enterprises vulnerability in the context of emerging global environment resulting into:

1. Loss of protected environment
2. Greater competition from imports;
3. Reduction in conventional subsidy as these are required to be WTO friendly. Many subsidies (viz, export subsidy) are contestable.
4. Widening knowledge and technology gap as a result of revolutionary change in technology.

5. Quality and standard gap.
6. Inability to match the prescribed hygiene and health standards prescribed under Sanitary and Phyto-sanitary Standards (e.g. food, animal, plant disease, other safety standards).
7. Increased export risk.
8. Difficult environmental regulations and costly prescriptions, and
9. Lack of awareness and information on WTO provisions.

## 4.6 Areas of Concern for the SSIs

The provisions/agreements which are likely to affect Indian SSI sector are:

### 4.6.1 Quantitative Restrictions and SSI Reservation Policy

Article XVII of GATT provides for imposition of Quantitative Restrictions on imports for balance of payments reasons. India has built up a large foreign exchange reserve in relation to imports and is under pressure to remove all QRs at the earliest.

India has already removed QRs by bringing more and more items in the Open General Licence (OGL) category. The anomaly which existed due to the continuance of certain products in the reserved list for Small Industry, while being shifted to the OGL category are also being corrected. Already over 160 important items have been dereserved during the last seven years. Due to India losing its case to USA in the Dispute Settlement Body of WTO, physical controls (mainly licensing) had been removed by 1.4.2001. The QRs have been removed gradually since then as under:

| Year | QRs removed |
|---|---|
| 1996-97 | 488 |
| 1997-98 | 391 |

| Year | QRs removed |
|---|---|
| 1998-99 | 894 |
| 1999-2000 | 714 |
| 2000-2001 | 715 |

It may be worthwhile to note that of the above, the QRs removed in 1999-2000 and proposed to be removed by 1.4.2001 are on account of WTO obligation and that about 500 QRs imposed on the basis of the general exception (Article XX) and the security exception (Article XXI) are not being removed; though provision exists for their autonomous review. Already over 700 reserved items of a total 836 reserved items as existing in 1997 have been placed under OGL. Thus the reservation policy has only a limited relevance that too with domestic large scale units. Goods reserved for SSI sector in India were traditionally protected against competition by QRs, which is not the case now.

Due to the total removal of QRs many of the SSI, especially in the consumer goods sector, might face some difficulty. The area of concern is that as the competition will intensify as more imported products find easy access to the Indian market. Items reserved for the SSIs will not face competition from similar products being imported freely except for a low tariff barrier from all over the world and produced by large scale global manufacturers. An analysis of import trend reveals that so far there has not been any surge in import as the import of non-petroleum oil items fell down by 0.92 per cent in 1996-97, and it increased by 7.73 per cent in 1997-98, by 15.48 per cent in 1998-99 and by 1.36 per cent in 1999-2000. The non-surge in import situation continues even now i.e. 2004 with minor exceptions.

When the domestic market is fully open to competition

from foreign goods, the advantage of low labour cost which our small enterprises claim to enjoy may not work beyond a point. The domestic consumers prefer better quality to low cost products. Low-end products will also face international competition from export-oriented developing countries. Even on the cost level, there may be stiffer competition coming from low cost producers from the neighbouring Least Developed Countries (LDCs), such as Nepal and Bangladesh, Sri Lanka and China which are already offering tough competition. Indian small enterprises may be adversely affected because:

- Pace of technological upgradation is slow. The present credit policy is not in favour of the SSIs as it is alleged that there has been costly credit to SSIs as compared to non-SSI units. The recently announced scheme of credit linked capital subsidy scheme may induce the entrepreneurs to go for technology upgradation.
- Industries suffer due to poor infrastructure e.g., power, communication, water, etc.
- Absence of VAT or inability of the tiny units to avail MODVAT (now changed to CENVAT). The raise in excise exemption limit from Rs. 50 lakh to Rs. 100 lakh effective from 1.9.2000 will help the SSI sector to raise productivity as well as productive efficiency.
- Obsolete laws, rules, regulations and harassment leading to diversion of time to compliance at the cost of production. It is expected that single unified legislation to safeguard the interest of SSI will take the shape of an Act soon.
- Lack of awareness among small scale entrepreneurs about implications of WTO provisions through sensitisation programme a good beginning has been made.
- The data base on unorganised sector is very poor. The

comprehensive policy package announced by the Prime Minister on 30.8.2000 included conduct of Third Census of Small scale units. Census results will definitely improve the database of the SSI sector.

- Most of the units do not work in groups or clusters and as such are not able to have the advantage of common facilities and economies of scale. The recent thrust on cluster development by the Government will help to synergise our energy and effort in a focussed manner.
- Lack of international exposure.
- Most of the NGOs are very weak and thus cannot help the small enterprises to renegotiate tariff or prove dumping of products or conduct investigation work on behalf of SSI units, or have their own legal cell to take up the matters in the courts.

Some other issues which come in the way of efficient functioning of small enterprises in India are inadequate and costly credit, plethora of labour legislations, ineffective associations, lack of standards confirming to international standards.

All these might have serious consequences for the small scale sector. Restriction on the export of raw hides and skins and semi-processed leather, etc. is being objected by the European Commission. With the removal of QRs, these restrictions might also have to be removed. Leather industry is a dominant export industry located in the small scale sector and at the same time generating large scale employment. A cautious and conformable policy is needed.

It may however, be noted that the world is not lost with the removal of QRs for the small enterprises in India. Many WTO consistent weapons are available to meet the abnormal situations, e.g.;

1. Applied tariff can be raised up to bound rates.

2. Anti-dumping duties can be imposed if a product is dumped;
3. Countervailing duties can be imposed if a product is subsidised.
4. Safeguard action can be taken if there is surge in imports.
5. Measures can be taken under Article XX of the GATT to protect human, animal or plant life or health, public morals, exhaustible natural resources.
6. Measures can be taken under Article XXI of GATT for national security.
7. Last but not the least important recourse lies in reimposition of QRs under Article XVIII-B of GATT if Balance of Payment position deteriorates.

While these problems are concurrently being addressed to, the impact of removal of QRs can be mixed. With the lowering of tariffs, there is a great possibility that Indian small enterprises may be subjected to foreign competition by way of cheap imports. At the same time opening of global market may help Indian small enterprises to have access to state of art technology, quality raw material and know-how.

The Sector has to take effective steps towards upgradation of technology. Recently announced measures to improve the availability of credit is expected to provide the needed support. Marketing of SSI products also has to be strengthened through more proactive policies. Perhaps statutory backing to existing price and purchase preference policies might help in this direction.

**4.6.2 Tariff Reduction and Reduced Protection:** Indian SSIs have been provided with some protection because they suffer from certain bottlenecks in use and availability of inputs like credit and technology and have no access to economies of scales. As Quantitative Restrictions have been removed, the protection level by way of tariff also has come down. The SMEs have to note that India is committed to a ceiling tariff bindings of 40 per cent on finished goods and 25 per cent on intermediate goods, machinery and equipments. The process of phased reduction to these bound levels has already started. Tariff levels have been already reduced to a substantial extent over the last couple of years, but the international perception is that India has even now one of the highest tariff levels. Reduced protection is said to have already resulted into reduced competitive strength of SSI units. Tariff protection is bound to be scaled down significantly in the future.

Another challenge for the small enterprises arise from high cost of inefficiency and lack of support facilities such as good infrastructure. This calls for adoption of an efficient management practices and investment on development of infrastructure.

**4.6.3 Anti-dumping Practices:** While the domestic market is going to be fully exposed to external competition, the small enterprises may have to be cautious against possible dumping by their competitors from abroad, which may be difficult to establish in many cases. What is also significant is that the cost of anti dumping investigations may be prohibitive. On the other hand, anti dumping charges by the importing countries may do serious damage to the export prospects as well. The small enterprises would need to understand the challenges posed by the Agreement on Anti-Dumping Measures.

There are certain provisions (Special and Differential Provisions) that are intended to benefit the developing countries, but may act against the SMEs when it comes to trade among the developing countries. Article 5.8 of the Agreement provides that the volume of dumped imports shall normally be considered negligible if dumped import from a particular country is found to be less than 3 per cent of imports of the like products, unless countries which individually account for less than 3 per cent of the import of the like products collectively account for more than 7 per cent of the import.

Small enterprises in India may be unable to defend or take counteractive measures primarily due to their ignorance, weak NGOs, lack of necessary data and problem of accessibility to information. Organisations like the Development Commissioner (SSI) [DCSSI], Development Commissioner (Handicrafts), National Small Industries Corporation, State Small Industries Corporations etc. will have to play pivotal role in this regard. Government assistance for fighting legal battles will also be needed which has recently been provided by the Government. The DCSSI's WTO Cell could be equipped with experts to provide the sector needed support.

**4.6.4 Subsidies and Countervailing Measures:** All major subsidies such as Duty Entitlement Pass Book (DEPB) Scheme, Export Promotion of Capital Goods (EPCG) Scheme, Income Tax Benefits under Section 80 HHC of the Income Tax Act etc., are considered as "actionable" subsidies. These are not prohibited subsidies and, therefore, can be continued by the government. However, the importing country can take action (by way of imposing countervailing duty) if it feels that subsidised imports are causing injury to their domestic industry. Indian industry should learn to be competitive even without the present set of subsidies. This is perhaps the most serious challenge for the small enterprises in India.

Small enterprises should be aware of what is permissible and what is not. Experts hold the view that the subsidies by the Government to small enterprises are non-actionable. WTO presupposes that an enterprise knows the implications of all provisions. In a country where 95 per cent of SSI enterprises are tiny units, this "knowledge" needs to be transmitted. This means that SSI unit in 2005 must be different from what it was in 1999.

**4.6.5 Technical Barriers to Trade and Investment Based SSI Definition:** The SMEs would have to take note of growing Technical Barriers to Trade (TBT) in view of high technical standards, set by the developed countries. These are emerging as major non-tariff barriers to access markets of the developed countries. The arrangement on TBT provides for differential and more favourable treatment to the developing country members. But this is hardly respected by the developed countries. One of the basic problems of our small enterprises is their technological weakness.

Investment based on definition of SSI units has at times been found coming in the way of technology upgradation and/ or setting up of units with minimum technological standards. The SSIs are likely to be deprived of market access not only in the case of technology intensive items but even for many labour intensive items. Most of the countries define their SMEs in terms of employment or turnover and thus when any dispute arises they may not treat an Indian SSI as a small enterprise or the vice-versa The first official definition of SSI was fixed in 1950 both in terms of investment in fixed assets and the strength of workforce in the unit. The criterion underwent a number of modifications over the years.

In the later part of fifties, the change effected was a shift from workforce criterion to an investment criterion. In 1966, the original value of plant and machinery was adopted the sole criterion for defining SSI. Since most of the countries use employment or turnover criterion for defining SMEs, there is need to examine the SSI definition in that light.

**4.6.6 Trade Related Investment Measures:** In the domestic market, again there may be reasons to feel concerned when the Agreement on Trade Related Investment Measures (TRIMS) comes into force which prohibits five types of investment conditions. The government may have to do away with the criteria of local area content and dividend balancing. This may prove to be a big jolt to development of sub-contracting and ancilliarisation and result in the loss of domestic market for the SSIs. Impact may be severely felt in the emerging sectors of Indian industry especially in automobiles, consumer electronics, white goods, electrical machinery, electrical appliances, and high-tech items. When the foreign/joint venture companies would be free from the obligation of indigenisation, there may be little incentive for indigenous sourcing of components.

The small enterprises of India may have real problems if they are not competitive and do not go for a major drive for technology upgradation. Technology upgradation thus emerges as the most urgent requirement of the SSI sector in the context of WTO conditionalities.

**4.6.7 Trade Related Intellectual Property Rights (TRIPS):** Intellectual Property Rights (IPR) are considered as a tool to create wealth through knowledge. Inventions and technical information flow very quickly all over the world and they can easily be copied by others. It is essential that fruits of R & D are adequately protected throughout the world under the harmonised protection system. WTO-TRIPS Agreement recognises that widely varying standards in the protection and enforcement of intellectual property rights and the lack of multilateral framework of principles, rules and disciplines dealing with international trade in counterfeit goods, be streamlined in the form of rules and disciplines.

Second hand imports of automobiles has been allowed with the removal of QRs. Import of second hand vehicles from abroad unless properly regulated might have adverse implications for the domestic automobile industry and also for the small scale vendors and sale-contractors. It is essential to understand the provisions of TRIPS in greater detail because violation may attract severe penalties.

TRIPS Agreement covers seven categories of Intellectual Property:

- Patents
- Industrial Design
- Trade Mark
- Copy Right and related rights
- Geographical Indications
- Layout Design of integrated circuits
- Protection of undisclosed information - Trade Secrets.

**Patent Act 1970 vis-à-vis TRIPS Agreement on IPR**

The following implications emerge which must be understood well along with their implications:

- Patent must be available for process/product
- A patent term is of 20 years.
- Micro organism to be patented.
- Effective Sui Generis System for protection of plant varieties.
- Importation of Products to be accepted as patents.
- Compulsory license to be confined to special circumstances.
- Reversal of the burden of proof in infringement actions relating to process patents (obliging the defendant to

prove that the process is non-infringing).

The adoption of the above provisions would bring Indian Patent Law close to general practice in the industrialised world. An apprehension expressed by some of the SSI Associations about the future of small industries is based on the notion that a number of SSI units are thriving on reverse engineering. Under a tough patent regime reverse engineering will be difficult and any infringement would lead to major penalties. This may affect the SSI unit adversely.

While Agreement on TRIPS may have little direct implication for the SSIs, but for those engaged in high-tech industries such as electronics, pharmaceuticals, machine tools, bio-technology, etc., may face the problem of accessing appropriate technology under the TRIPS regime. It is apprehended that both terms and conditions and the cost of technology may be prohibitive. In the new regime ignorance of law will be no excuse as the burden of proof is on the infringer. While transfer of technology cases may increase, any counterfeit trade may invite deterrent action. Care will have to be exercised in choosing the names of companies or products. Problems may come before those SSEs who use protected designs as in the case of garment industry. Employees, sub-contractors, etc., might have to be restrained from divulging confidential information.

**4.6.8 Trade and Investment:** In the event of multilateral Agreement on investment and its eventual enforcement, the small enterprises may have to struggle for survival in a completely unprotected environment in the domestic market. Agreement on Trade and Investment would have to be conducted under the twin policies of 'National Treatment' and 'Most Favoured Nation Treatment'. In that environment, SMEs of the other Member Countries would need to be given same treatment in India as are given to our small enterprises and the implications may indeed be far reaching at least in the short run in the absence of required preparedness on the part of Indian small enterprises.

**4.6.9 Government Procurement:** In India, the Government is a substantially large buyer as well as a large investor. For the SSIs, the Government is a big support as far as market is concerned. There are reservation policies and also price support mechanism for purchase of products from the small scale sector but as against product reservation, these are non-statutory. If it is felt that the market created by the Government may have to be opened up to foreign competition and the system will have to be made more transparent.

**4.6.10 SAARC Commitments:** In addition to the above, negotiations for deepening and widening trade preferences under the South Asia Preferential Trading Arrangement (SAPTA) are continuing. During two rounds of negotiations of SAPTA held in December, 1995 and November, 1996, tariff concessions have already been exchanged on 2459 tariff lines. India has already lifted quantitative restrictions for SAARC countries w.e.f. 1.8.1998. This involves putting over 2000 products on OGL for SAARC countries. These developments are bound to give stiff competition to SSI sector more so if superficial change in the products or raw material imported from India or MNCs set up units for SSI sensitive items in our neighbouring countries.

**4.6.11 Sustainability of Export Obligation:** By March 2004, 675 items were reserved for exclusive manufacture in the field of small scale sector. Earlier, any non-SSI unit which wants to manufacture a reserved item had to undertake 75 per cent export obligation. It was felt that this is too high a percentage as under this dispensation, an undertaking had to export three times of the quantity of products it sells in the domestic markets. It is difficult for many industrial undertakings to achieve this target. In 1997, the Government of India reduced the export obligation for non SSI units to 50 per cent. There is persistent demand from some large industries to reduce further the export obligation as they find it acting as a psychological barrier to their entry to export oriented reserved area. The S.P. Gupta study Group on Small Enterprises in its report (2001) also recommended further lowering down of export-obligation to 30 per cent.

### 4.7 Prospective Issues

**4.7.1 Trade and Environment:** Any Agreement on this is likely to have major impact not only on the production process but also on packaging of products, which, in turn, would affect price competitiveness. But the major question is whether the small enterprises are technologically and financially capable of meeting such challenges? Some enterprises are reported to have already been closed due to environmental reasons. Stricter enforcement in future will create more problems resulting into closure of the units affecting the employment opportunities.

**4.7.2 Social Clause and Core Labour Standards:** Trade and labour standards is a highly sensitive issue. Developing countries like India view it as a ploy of developed nations to annihilate their comparative advantage of lower labour costs. It is also a fact that for a large number of products core labour standards are not adhered to by tiny enterprises who produce mainly for the local markets. The developing countries have, however, objected to linking of these issues to economic matters. Though these issues may not be matters of immediate concern, it is to our advantage if we take cognisance of these issues right now and prepare ourselves accordingly.

To sum up, the small enterprises are required to watch the following issues carefully:

- The impact of removal of QRs on import of SSI sensitive items needs to be regularly watched. The Ministry of Small Scale Industries and other concerned ministries should constantly watch the data on imports of sensitive small industries items where QRs have been removed and also study the impact of QR removal on domestic industries in terms of number of units, production demand and employment.
- Due to TRIMS agreement it may not be possible to follow local content policy after 1.1.2000.
- Adverse impact on small enterprises sector may become more pronounced once the effect of the end of the transition periods in WTO agreements (e.g. TRIMS, TRIPS and Tariff bindings) is felt after 1. 1. 2000 and more particularly after 2005.

Following measures could be taken by for countering the effect:

- Import duties can be hiked to the bound levels for the affected tariff lines. Where there are no bindings, Government is free to hike duties to any necessary levels.
- Macro-economic reviews to assess the impact on small enterprise sector to identify the difficulties that they may face on account of reduction of tariff and NBTs.
- Ensuring adequate flow of finance for running the units and incentives to encourage technology upgradation.
- Although protection to domestic industries are available through anti dumping, countervailing and safeguard action, capacity of small enterprises to take recourse to

these measures needs to be enhanced.

### 4.8 WTO as an Opportunity for Small Enterprises

Small enterprises sector should not view WTO as challenge but an opportunity since

- Lower overheads and higher operational flexibilities in small enterprises may benefit them, at least in niche products, certain environmentally friendly products and low-tech products. For this, identification analysis is required by the Government and NGOs.
- Increasing use of outsourcing, job work, ancillary development by large enterprises/MNCs could sustain SMEs despite trade liberalisation.
- Increasing use of E-commerce could reduce the competitive disadvantages of small enterprises.
- Identification of export thrust small industries items is required and specific measures are required to ensure sustained growth in export performance of those items.
- Small enterprise sector should recognise the role played by service sector in its development and exclusive policy measures are needed to promote industry related services. This sector through its forward and backward linkages can boost the growth of small enterprises in the country.

### 4.9 Task Ahead for Small Enterprises

Indian Small scale Sector (called modern segment) currently accounts for 35 per cent of national export. If traditional industries like handloom, handicrafts, sericulture, etc. are also added, this share will exceed 50 per cent. Though this share looks impressive within the country, when compared with global trade, the picture is rather dismal. India's total international trade constitutes just 0.7 per cent of the world trade. Government plans to increase the share to 1 per cent by the year 2005. The target is challenging since, even within the SSI sector, exports account for only 10 per cent of total production. This share in itself is too low, but at the same time, there exists vast potential that the SSI sector possesses.

With a little improvement in efficiency and competitiveness backed by a bold programme of technology upgradation and facility of information technology can lead to substantial jump in SSI exports. However, for the SSI entrepreneurs, it may not be possible to have full knowledge of WTO conditionalities and also abide by them. They need support from all sources consisting of Government, NGOs, financial institutions, etc. in the form of improved institutional framework. There is need for harmony and bridging the gaps.

### 4.10 Can Small Enterprises fulfil WTO Requirements?

The ability of Small enterprises to benefit from the improved institutional framework will depend on:

1. Their knowledge of the trade rules; rights that are conferred and obligations that they impose.
2. Their knowledge of the new opportunities for trade.
3. That country will be at advantage where a vigilant lobby exists in the form of non-governmental organisations which continuously studies as to what is happening in different parts of the world.
4. The promptitude of the enterprises in beginning their varied problems to the notice of the government so that the same could be raised at appropriate levels.

### 4.11 What Needs to be Done?

- Indian SSEs are at present incapable of visualising the

things in their right perspective because they are technologically, financially, and organisationally very weak as compared to global SMEs. They need to be equipped in these areas. The comprehensive policy package announced by the government in August 2000 has in fact tried to address to many of such requirements of the SSI sector.

- Selected dereservation of certain export oriented items as recommended by S.P. Gupta Study Group could also be considered along with sensitive enhancement of investment ceiling.
- Small industries to reposition themselves in certain strategic sectors where India has proven comparative advantages. It would be necessary to pay more attention to clusters as our future strategy of development.
- Evolve a bold marketing strategy for key SSI products and promote their brand image because even a good quality product needs to be marketed properly.
- A strong SSI desk on WTO will have to be created with a strong legal backup in the concerned Government Departments and Industry Associations.
- Develop India as the Sourcing Point and as a Sub-contracting base. Support to schemes/measures which enhance linkages between large and small units.
- Technological upgradation at par with the best, to achieve low cost of production, better quality and economies of scale.
- Focused attention on key products.
- A Change in the role of government from protection to promotion by assuming the role of facilitator.
- Diversification of SSI export items.
- Building up a strong data base of products, process and cost of production in India and abroad.

- More advocacy required so that small enterprises' role is heard on all forums in India and outside.
- Preparing inventory of technical standards.
- Expanding the role of Information Technology and making full use of Website. E-mailing to be adopted.

Government is fully aware of the likely implication of WTO agreements on SSI sector and has already taken various measures which consist of:

- Sensitisation workshops in various parts of the country. 31 workshops on WTO sensitisation, 16 on IPRs, 14 on Anti-dumping have been completed by March 2004.
- A WTO cell has been set up in the Office of Development Commissioner (SSI) and the cell will be strengthened further.
- A Comprehensive Policy Package has been announced by the Government on 30 and 31 August 2000 to enhance productive efficiency and the competitiveness of the SSI sector through improved supply of credit, better marketing facilities, improved infrastructure and incentive for technology upgradation. The limit of loan without collaterals has been raised to Rs. 25 lakh under launched Credit Guarantee Scheme and a scheme of Credit Linked Capital Subsidy of 12 per cent has been announced for technology upgradation of SSIs.

The small industries sector, however, is required to be alert and watchful and is required to give feedback on Non-Tariff Barriers (NBTs) faced by them in export markets particularly relating to TBT and SPS agreements. Finally, the small enterprise sector needs to put more thrust on quality so that the products can compete with foreign goods both in domestic and foreign markets. Local people generally prefer domestically produced quality goods as service is readily available. There is no escape from competition and the small enterprise sector must face it and also remember that the argument that India is a developing economy is not at all relevant at the world forum. We are all equal there. Similarly, there is nothing like small enterprises or large enterprise but we are just enterprises competing with each other for survival.

# 5

# Challenges and Opportunities for Small Enterprises in the Globalised World

India started its process of integration with the global economy in July 1991. The Government has pursued far-reaching economic and structural reforms in all sectors of economic policy. The thrust of these measures has so far been to integrate the Indian economy with the global economy and enable them to be competitive. The liberalisation policy has posed certain challenges as well as opportunities to the small scale sector. The challenges are in the form of increased competition arising out of reduced protection due to removal of restrictions on imports and lowering of tariffs. Opportunities have come in the form of access to better technology, availability of a variety of raw materials and components, impetus to quality, efficiency and opportunity to restructure and to diversify. Challenges and opportunities due to globalisation come together. While we must be ready to face challenges, one should also be in readiness to get the least out of opportunities. This chapter is devoted to the study of challenges and opportunities and the readiness of the Indian small enterprises to convert the challenges into opportunities.

A redeeming feature of the growth pattern of the SSI sector in the last decade is that it has generally recorded higher growth rates as compared to the overall industry or manufacturing sector. This leads us to a positive conclusion. The liberalisation process has not changed the historical trend of the SSI sector maintaining a higher rate of growth over the overall industrial sector. The downswing in the rate of growth of SSI sector (8 per cent against 11 per cent in 1996-97) during the last two years as against the targeted growth is attributed mainly to the general recession in the industry and economy. The industrial growth has picked up in the year 2000. However, as there is delay of about six months in the availability of SSI data, the corresponding impact of the recent industrial growth on SSI sector is not yet known. It would be safe to say that the small scale sector has not been at the receiving end of the economic reforms process.

Liberalisation has exposed Indian SSIs to unequal competition with its counterparts in the industrially advanced countries. The challenge cannot be effectively met unless domestic economic policy focuses on removal of constraints which limit the competitive strength of India industry and of the economy as a whole. The emerge of multilateral trade regime, WTO conditionalities have added urgency to the task of enhancing competitiveness. It is essential to remove the constraints which limit the competitive strength of Indian industry. It is not only the question of India coping with the WTO regime but for greater issue of how Indian can leverage the benefits of large access to global market.

A major problem faced by the Indian SSE sector is the challenge of globalisation resulting into increased competition both internally and internationally. The fast changes brought out by global trade and new marketing strategy over the past few years has necessitated bringing about structural changes affecting the micro, small and medium enterprises throughout the world. The developing countries need to evolve new policies to suit the requirements of several changes in the field of industry, and trade, besides entrepreneurs adjusting to the new environment. The distinction between domestic and international market is getting blurred. The day is not far off when there will be only one market throughout the world. The market condition will be based on non-discrimination and same criterion for domestic and global market.

The process of globalisation has come to exist over the last few years due to rapid technological advances, speedy and short cycle of products, mergers, splits and decline in the fortune of some of the established companies, productivity sluggishness and rise of service economy. The demographic changes occurring due to movement of more talented and skilled people to prosperous countries and resulting race/ethnic conflicts are also to be taken note of. Further, due to the audio-visual impact by electronic media, expectations of people in all countries have risen beyond the capabilities of meeting them. Masses are demanding better quality products at affordable prices and on the industrial side, new concepts of bench marking, chain marketing and better corporate governance have emerged.

While techniques have developed to control and manage manufacturing process involving materials, machines and equipment, it is yet to change the behaviour of work force and their mindset. The present day work situation has changed from that of managing physical inputs like raw materials to development of knowledge inputs and human skills. With the fast spread of computer technology, workers and management would soon adjust to the new situation.

All of our East Asian neighbours have emerged as exporting nations of the world. Regional groupings are the order of the day. The future trade strategy would not be based on bilateral trade, negotiations with a country but with the group of countries. India has been witnessing rapid spread of computer based information technology, which is revolutionising both manufacturing and services sectors. In service sector, the new concept of Bench Marking is making a trend towards uniformity and making others to imitate or follow the most successful among them.

Mr. W. W. Rostow, an American Development economist, referring to the take-off stage in a Nation's growth process, stressed that at least one major sector with high growth rate and socio-political framework is needed to support the growth of any country. We have witnessed Rostow's theory coming true in the case of South East Asian economies with their thrust on export sector in the fields of automobiles, electronics etc. In India, one should not be surprised, if the lead industry is information technology which has already established its root in the small scale sector. India being an English speaking country with IT skilled manpower is an advantageous position.

Coming to the challenges ahead, it is now certain that industry and trade will be increasingly exposed to demands of market forces at home and abroad. Banking and financial needs met by institutions need a new framework that can balance the requirements of industry and trade with that of safety, stability and operational efficiency. Transitory period is to be prudently managed, as the future is unforeseen and untested.

The impact of developmental projects on the environment is now recognised and the traditional cost benefit analysis is to be extended and modified to factor in the long run socio-economic consequences of ecological impact of the project. The pricing of resource inputs should reflect the cost of depletion and degradation and design a socio-economic rehabilitation compensation scheme for the community.

Competition calls for reduced cost of production which

is dependent on cost of credit and improved quality which is dependent on technology upgradation. Thus there is close link between the technology and the cost of credit. Availability of necessary technology and information on them are no less important factors.

The removal of quantitative restrictions may affect the SSI sector provided import surge is witnessed in those items. With the removal of Quantitative Restrictions all reserved items have become freely importable. The SSI sector will have to be safeguarded, if there are adverse effects of the removal of quantitative restrictions on them. There are certain measures which could be taken in this regard. These are

- keeping import duty at maximum permissible bound rate
- imposition of countervailing duty
- imposition of safeguard measures
- imposition of anti-dumping duties and
- reimposition of quantitative restrictions as last resort.

The Indian SSI sector faces major disadvantage in terms of high transaction cost in relation to global standards.

Firstly, the interest rates in India are way above the rates prevalent elsewhere.

Secondly, the cost of credit is higher for SSI sector as compared to large industrial units.

Thirdly, inadequate infrastructure, particularly power, also compel the SSIs to either produce less than the capacity or to go for costly power using generator sets. Even otherwise, electricity available to industrial sector is costly.

Fourthly, there is no exit policy for labourers or enterprises. Labour laws need reform which facilitate redeployment of workers and for generation of new employment opportunities in SSI sector. The impact of one time settlement scheme announced by the RBI on 27th July

2000 could be known only after March 2001.

As competition from within the country and outside increases, this sector, nurtured hitherto in a protective framework, needs to be enabled to take on the challenges posed to it by the process of on- going globalisation. It calls for proper harnessing of the strengths it has built up over the last five decades and imbibing newer capabilities to meet emerging requirements of liberalisation, globalisation and institutions like WTO. Domestic policies need to focus on removing constraints so that transaction cost of SSIs reduces to international standards.

## 5.1 What Needs to be Done?

The opening up of the world economy in he process of globalisation and the vanishing geographical boundaries and the rapid and extensive use of information technology have thrown up challenges for the small producers and manufacturers who have to not only survive competition but also to create a place for themselves in the global commodity chain, which the new global manufacturing methods have come to characterise with emergence of WTO involving removal of quantitative restrictions and adoption of a non-protectionist and transparent system of trade.

It has emerged that the Indian small enterprises are required to be more efficient and more competitive. This implies technological upgradation on continuous basis to keep pace with rapidly changing technological scenario in the world. Technology, however, is only one of the inputs. There are some other requirements which must be addressed to properly. Following areas deserve attention:

1. Adequate and timely supply of credit.
2. Technology upgradation and Modernisation
3. Creation of Information Technology Infrastructure.

4. Adopting cluster as future strategy of development.
5. Procedural Reforms.
6. WTO sensitisation, and
7. Improving quality and competitiveness.

## 5.2 Credit Facilities

Inadequate and delayed supply of credit continues to be the main problem faced by the small and medium enterprises. The problem is more acute in the case of micro-enterprises. Small enterprises lack access to capital market. Investors are unwilling to invest in unquoted companies. Small businesses are perceived to be more risky in many developing countries as a result the cost of credit to small enterprises is high. It is not possible to have credit rating of SSI units because of the cost involved and also establishing the project viability in relation to a large scale units. Assessing of risk and monitoring of small business involve higher cost. In the case of newly emerging hi-tech areas or newly emerging technologies returns are uncertain.

An alternative source of finance is necessary in the form of Venture Capital Funds. Type of intervention in this regard also varies from country to country. Korea and Finland governments have actively participated in establishments of Venture Capital Funds. This has supported high technology business, with focus on science parks and thus has provided networking. Such business in Korea has generated good number of jobs.

In order to improve the flow of credit in India certain measures have been taken in recent past. In India, SSI credit comes under the priority sector lending programme of the banks. The main problem faced in this regard is inadequate and delayed supply of credit. Nayak Committee (1992) which examined this issue found that SSI units are getting not more than 8.1 per cent of their annual turnover by way of working capital advances from the banks against the normative requirements of 20 per cent. The SSI units also face problems with regard to cost of credit and in meeting the collateral requirements of the banks. In most of the developed countries including USA, Japan, Korea, Germany etc. there exists credit guarantee fund to take care of the problem of perceived high risk in small business finance.

Some measures taken by the government to improve the flow of the credit including those included in the comprehensive policy package announced on 30-31 August, 2000 are as under:

- RBI has issued instruction for providing minimum 20 per cent of the annual turnover (calculated on normative basis) by way of working capital loan by the public sector commercial banks up to Rs. 5 crore. This needs to be monitored properly at all the levels.
- Setting up of 391 specialised SSI bank branches is a good beginning. Such branches should be set up in all the districts and clusters. The focus of these branches should be on micro credit and tiny sector lending.
- A scheme of Credit Guarantee to provide loans up to Rs. 10 lakh (since raised to Rs. 25 lakh on 30.8.2000) without collateral has already been launched from 1st September 2000. This scheme is expected to be operational soon. The present size of the fund is Rs. 125 crores for one year. A long term credit guarantee fund with substantial fund to take care of the vast credit needs of small enterprises particularly tiny sector needs to be created.
- The Union Budget 2000-2001 announced extending the limit of loans without collaterals to SSI sector from Rs. 1 lakh to Rs. 5 lakh. This is a welcome move and it is

essential to monitor its implementation properly.

- Budget 2000-2001 also announced raising the limit of single window composite loan (working capital + fixed capital) from Rs. 5 lakh to Rs. 10 lakh. The limit of composite loan was further enhanced to Rs. 25 lakh by the Prime Minister on 30.8.2000. This is expected to boost the tiny sector.
- The scope of National Equity Fund scheme which provides equity to SSI units at 1 per cent service charge has been extended to all areas including metropolitan areas with effect from 15th March, 2000. The scheme, however, is not very popular with the banks. The reason for the same need to be studied and hindrances coming in the way of effective implementation needs to be removed. Under the comprehensive policy package the cost of project has been enhanced to Rs. 50 lakh to be available at 5 per cent service charge.
- SIDBI has started Venture Capital Fund for financing software development. It is also setting incubation park in collaboration with IIT, Kanpur. More and more innovative finance particularly in sunrise activities could be started. Government will encourage setting up of more incubation centres.
- Export-Import (EXIM) Bank of India provides export finance for export of machinery, manufactured goods, consultancy and technology services on deferred payment terms. EXIM bank finance is also available at export production stages. It also provides certain other services e.g. search for overseas partners, identification of technology supplies, negotiating an alliance and consummating a joint venture. It is essential to remove procedural hurdles coming in the way of exporters in timely execution of orders.

- Cost of credit needs to be reduced since the same is very low in other countries. This will help to achieve cost competitiveness.

## 5.3 Technology Upgradation

Technology upgradation is key to survival in present day world of globalisation and liberalisation. During the recent decades, the world has moved from the State of 'static' technologies to the 'rapidly changing' technologies. While on the one hand the developed countries have implanted technologies in the developing world threatening to widen the gap between the world's rich and poor regions, these very technologies can also be used to work as a link between modern and traditional technologies, between large and small units and between the urban and the rural areas. For developing countries, however, appropriate technology which may fit in the local conditions has important role to play.

To upgrade technology, the government has set up Tool Rooms (10) Regional Testing Centres (4) Production-cum-Process development Centres (6) and workshops in the Small Industries Service Institute (58) which are located in various parts of the country. Small Industries Development Bank of India has been running a scheme of financial assistance under Technology Upgradation and Modernisation Fund. Scheme which has been in operation since 1995. The 2000-2001 Union Budget proposes to extend the operation of this scheme by another 3 years. Adequate financial provision need be made by the SIDBI for this scheme.

Asia and Pacific Centre for Transfer of Technology (APCTT) pays special attention to the development of technology in the SME sector. APCTT provide, SME oriented technology transfer services in the following areas:

- Information on technology opportunities and new technological development;
- Search for and matching of prospective technology transfer partners;
- Support service (market studies, feasibility studies, assistance in contract negotiation);
- Finance syndication and marketing assistance for technology transfer projects APCTT is having 270 technology transfer negotiations every month and over 60 technology agreements every year.

Department of Science & Technology is operating a fund for Technology Development and Application since 1996 through the Technology Development Board. The fund provides financial assistance in the form of equity or soft loan to individual concern including SMEs for development and commercialisation of indigenous technology or for adapting imported technology to under domestic applications. Small enterprises could utilise this fund for the development of technology and its testing before commercial application. The announcement of a credit linked capital subsidy scheme for technology upgradation of SSI sector on 30.8.2000 is expected to provide the needed impetus and incentive for technology upgradation. This is the need of the hour.

## 5.4 Information Technology Infrastructure

In this fast changing economic environment, access to latest information on market, demand supply, technology etc. is key to survival and success. Creating infrastructure for information network is costly proposition requiring Government intervention. In many developed and newly industrialised economies, Governments have created infrastructure where information on business-to-business co-operation can be exchanged. Several governments have created such exchanges. In order to improve the data base for the SSI sector, particularly dissemination of data from field level to Office of Development Commissioner (SSI) 138 Districts Industries Centres and 25 State Directorates of Industries have been computerised. Under the programme of Small Enterprises Network (SENET) 14 Small Industries Service Institutes have already been computerised and other important SISIs are being computerised. The Office of the Development Commissioner (SSI) at New Delhi has also been computerised and a website has been created. The purpose is to improve the accessibility of all relevant information to all concerned.

In India, the government has also been financing setting up of sub-contracting exchanges by providing assistance to NGOs. European Union operates Euro-partenariates to encourages SMEs, to meet one another through partnership across border. The Third Census announced as part of the comprehensive policy package on 30.8.2000 will help update the data base which could profitably be accessed through the Web site.

## 5.5 WTO Sensitisation

The present WTO regime requiring opening up of domestic market, lowering of tariffs, removal of quantitative restrictions and national treatment of imported goods means that SMEs will have to face tougher competition in domestic and foreign markets. Their goods have to meet tougher quality and environmental standards. In view of their insufficient capitalisation, lack of access to capital, know-how and information and low skill level of workers, SME's need assistance by way of policy support and measures from government and other organisation. Information on cost, quality, sanitation, environment, labour standards, patents, tariff rates etc. prevailing in India and in other member countries of WTO is the first and foremost requirement.

One must know what constitutes anti-dumping and what are the safeguards available by way of countervailing duty. It is essential to know the details of all agreements and their implications on the SSI sector. SSI sector enjoys certain subsidies and some protection. Hence it is essential to know which are actionable and non-actionable subsidies. One of the important and urgent requirements emerging from WTO is the phasing out of quantitative restrictions which may affect the SSI reserved sector. SMEs in India will have to build up competitiveness in order to compete successfully after quantitative restrictions are removed. They would need to update technology frequently as this is key to remaining competitive against cheap imports.

To create awareness on WTO agreement, the government has launched a programme of sensitisation of SSI units on WTO provisions. Apart from sensitisation a suitable structure has been created to guide the SSI units on all WTO related matters.

## 5.6 Cluster Approach

An expert committee set up under the Chairmanship of Dr. Abid Hussain (1997) for suggesting measures to improve the Indian small scale sector has recommended a cluster based development approach, which would enable technical support services at the industrial clusters. This approach has maximum demonstrative effect and upgradation of even one individual unit technology has its impact on the whole cluster down the lines and other do not feel shy in adopting new technologies as they have already been commercially proven. This also reduces cost on providing common. To co-ordinate the programme of cluster development, last year (1999-2000) the Government announced a National Programme of Rural Industrialisation for this purpose. Under this programme 100 clusters are proposed to be developed by various agencies in a year. Cluster development should form part of the long run strategy of small enterprises development as it has the advantage of the economies of scales. The Italian experience on industrial districts and cluster development need to be considered.

## 5.7 Procedural Reforms

Plethora of laws, rules and regulations have been found as a major hurdle in the smooth development of small enterprises in India. It is said that there are more than 60 laws covering various areas like labour laws, factory act, fiscal acts, municipal acts, environmental acts and associated inspectors who visit the small enterprises and thus lead to great deal of harassment, delay, obstruction to work and increase in cost of production due to occasional payments. Several returns are required to be filed by the small enterprises which hamper the work since SSI units are mostly one man shows.

Streamlining rules and regulations, bringing harmony in their implementation and reducing the hassles is the urgent necessity. Some states like Andhra Pradesh and Gujarat have taken lead in this area. The Union Finance Ministry has already taken a lead in simplifying fiscal rules and procedures. Similar streamlining should take in the area of labour laws, locational rules and environmental regulations. The Ministry of Small Scale Industries and Agro and Rural Industries has already entrusted a study to the Administrative Staff College of India. The report is expected in early

2001.

## 5.8 Improving Quality and Competitiveness

Selling of SSI Products either in domestic market or in the external market is essentially the function of cost competitiveness and quality. These in turn are the function of technology in use and the readiness of the SSI units to take the advantage without losing time. SSI products are competitive in their own right because of low overheads. The government, however, pays special attention to technology upgradation. Apart from strengthening the existing institutions like Small Industries Service Institution, Regional Testing Centres, Product-cum-process Development Centres, etc. for Government lays emphasis on providing adequate and timely credit at low cost for technology upgradation. It is in this context that a scheme of credit linked capital subsidy for technology upgradation has been announced. Production of quality goods is encouraged through National Quality Awards and incentives for ISO 9000 certification. Government has decided to extent the operation of this scheme to the Tenth Five Year Plan.

Already over 500 SSI units have acquired such certificates in order to provide exposure to SSI products in International market the Government takes part in international exhibitions where SSI products are displayed. Packaging plays important role in export promotion which has become product specific and assumed new areas of sophistication. For this, the Government arranges regular training programmes on packaging. Government also encourages the participation of SSI entrepreneurs in international exhibitions. For this the Ministry of Commerce provides financial assistance under their scheme of Market Development Assistance. In order to pay focused attention on SSI sector, it has been decided to create a similar fund with the DCSSI, at the Central Government level.

Improving of Management is a key factor in improving competitiveness. It has been observed that small business have comparatively low awareness of the benefits of enhancing the quality of management. It is essentially a function of entrepreneurial culture and can be improved through specialised training, technical assistance and general consultancy services coming from professional institutions; Mentors or Master Craftsmen or experienced managers can also provide critical knowledge on running a business.

### 5.9 Recommended Strategy

Most of the developing countries lack capital and infrastructure as a result they are not able to take the advantages which have emerged in the field of productions and marketing. Many of them have surplus manpower but due to absence of skill they can not be put to productive users. There is reluctance on the part of foreign capital and technology to come to these countries due to poor infra-structure including power shortage, inadequate communication net work etc. Plethora of rules and regulation and laws have also made the task of setting up and running an enterprise successfully a difficult job. But all the problems have solutions and no task is impossible to achieve. The developing countries like India have vast opportunities, vast potential and a very large size market. Thus demand and supply coexist. What is required to provide an environment in which the two forces are allowed to have free play. Government's role is gradually changing from protector to provider of infrastructure and facilitator. It is in global interest to strengthen the SSI sector.

Recent developments in the international economy and

the developed world's heightened interest in India shows that opportunity is knocking at our door and our goal should be to seize the opportunity. Global market is not new for Indian SSI sector. The fact that over 50 per cent of exports emerge from small enterprises (modern and traditional industries) shows that they have ability to compete. What is needed is to diversify the export basket by adding new products, covering new areas and making them cost competitive and in tune with the changing design, changing quality and consumers preference. It is possible to achieve all these since the SSI sector has distinct advantage of flexibility, innovativeness and lower inventory. This gives them advantage over the large units despite their inaccessibility to the economies of scales.

International co-operation among small and medium enterprises is very important for the development of small enterprises. SMEs in India or elsewhere are no longer local and have gone global. SMEs have large and diversified presence as well as strong backward and forward linkages to large industry but more efforts are needed to synergise the two sectors. Of late, Indian SSIs in knowledge based industries specially bio-technology and information technology are proving very successful. Indian SMEs can also offer technology to other countries in the areas of textiles, garments footwear, toys basic metal and simple electronics. Exports of Indian SSIs are in fact moving from being resource based to technology based. We must avail the opportunities which have come to us in big way.

The Comprehensive Policy Package for the SSI sector announced by Shri Atal Behari Vajpayee, the Prime Minister of India in Vigyan Bhawan at the National Conference on Small Scale Industries on the 30th August, 2000 and those announced on the 31st August, 2000 by the Government which contains measures relating to credit, infrastructure, marketing and technology are expected to enable the SSI sector to face the challenges of the new millennium with greater confidence. There are however, three advices: the small units must not accept the concessions from the government as the crutch for life and that the units must try to grow vertically and not horizontally and must face the challenge of the market.

Providing international competitiveness to the SSI sector has emerged as the most important task for policy markets. The task must be viewed in totality. Preparedness is required in all fields whether it is credit, technology, marketing, infrastructure or entrepreneurship development. We have to be up to date and of possible ahead of time. For this, it is essential that we also address to the task of promoting research and development innovation and incubation. Specific plan for addressing to the requirements of sunrise, hi-tech and IT related industries, sectoral venture capital and state-of-the art infrastructure in the required areas. The SSI sector will also have to bring about a change in its mind-set for meeting the challenges effectively.

# 6

# Innovative Financing of Small Enterprises

Role of finance has been viewed as a critical element in the development of Small and Medium Enterprises. Traditionally the banks have been playing a key role in the financial system of pooling the liquidity risk of depositors and investing a large portion of their funds in productive projects. Financing the SMEs by meeting the Term Loan (Long term needs) and Working Capital (short term needs) requirements has been one of the important functions of the banks. In the context of developing countries, the banks have better information to assess the risk factor of an investment than the small firm itself. This is because they are continually lending to small firms over extended periods of time and have acquired sufficient insight to be able to make sensible and sound judgement over lending decisions. Banks have more information on small units survival prospects and they evaluate a project whether large or small in terms of its viability and credit worthiness. Larger firms are in better position to avail the services of credit rating agencies than small firms because of cost involved. Typically smaller enterprises face higher transaction costs than larger enterprises in obtaining credit. As a result, inadequate delayed and costly supply of credit have emerged as major constraints in the growth and development of SMEs in India. What are the reasons for this state of affairs? This issue needs to be probed in greater detail.

Apart from the inability to have the report of credit rating agencies and difficulty in proving the viability of the projects, poor management and accounting practices have hampered the ability of small enterprises to raise finance.

Information asymmetries associated with lending to small scale borrowers involving lot of paper work have restricted the flow of finance to small enterprises. However, these problems are not uncommon in the development process. A study of availability, pattern and type of instruments and institutions engaged in SME financing reveal a definite pattern. The behavioural pattern are broken into different stages and apply according to the level of development experienced by any economy. In this context it would be relevant to go into various stages of SME Financing to have an idea of the pattern of financing and visualise the scope of innovative financing of SMEs, which is the subject matter of this chapter.

## 6.1 Stages of Financing of Small Enterprises

An analysis of the pattern and source of credit to the small and medium enterprises sector reveals that there is a definite path of credit availability which comes into operation. Depending on the level of the economic development of the country, the pattern of financing can be classified into five stages; incidentally coinciding with Rostow's Five Stages of economic growth. These are:

**6.1.1 Self Financing:** SMEs may be established with funds provided by the founders and their relatives or friends. This is noticed in the initial stages of economic development since by this time institutional sources are not developed or they are in initial stages of development. Self financing, however, has been found to be playing important role even in the later stages of economic development. In many developed economies also, it has been found that a major finance for SMEs has come from own sources. Self financing has several advantages including that it saves from the hassles of complying with the terms and conditions of the financial institutions. Studies have also revealed that people are more judicious in utilising their own money. There is, however, also evidence to the contrary.

**6.1.2 Debt Financing:** When SMEs expand or undertake major changes, they need to obtain funds for investment from external sources. SMEs are likely to get debt finance first for various reasons. Equity investment in SMEs is regarded as too risky due to the presence of information asymmetries. The owners are often reluctant to lose control by introducing external equity. Reliance of SMEs on debt finance at this stage is almost universal phenomenon because debt markets have traditionally been more developed in almost all countries. In Asia and also elsewhere, credit institutions are traditionally the primary sources of SME growth. Among such institutions, commercial banks play an important role. Duration of debt financing has been found to be rather long and it depends on the time taken by the developing economies in attaining the Take Off Stage of economic development. A shift from traditional way of Term Loan and Working Capital Financing is witnessed after the completion of this stage.

**6.1.3 Leasing Finance:** The stage of innovative financing now starts. A beginning is made with lease financing. In many economies, non banking financial institutions often serve as an important vehicle for SME financing. A typical example is leasing companies. Through leasing contracts, leasing companies accommodate financial needs of SMEs for real estates or certain movable properties. In some countries e.g. US and Japan, finance companies specialising in SME credit are also quite active. Established in some cases by commercial banks as subsidiaries, financing companies extend smaller loans usually by obtaining wholesale loans from banks or by issuing securities.

**6.1.4 Equity Financing:** Traditionally, SMEs have seldom had direct access to capital markets for equity financing. However, recent advancements in technology coupled with financial market globalisation is rapidly changing the scene. Following the remarkable success of NASDAQ in the US, a number of stock exchanges targeted at SMEs have been set up in recent years in Europe and Asia. Such exchanges are beneficial to SMEs by providing them with opportunities for tapping capital markets for their financing and also for fostering the venture capital industry by providing increased exit possibilities. One of the functions of the SME exchanges is to provide standardised information on the listed companies, particularly through their listing requirements. Investments in SMEs which may lack sufficient performance records is considered risky. In fact, many listed SMEs do not survive for long. Active participation of investors is key for the development of capital market. This stage of SME financing has been noticed only in the advanced countries.

**6.1.5 Venture Capital Financing:** While credit is usually a primary financial resources for SMEs to operate and invest, equity capital is also an indispensable element in SME financing. Equity capital is important in particular, in start up phases and rapid growth period. In most cases, SMEs obtain equity capital from the founders and their relatives and friends. However, in some advanced countries like UK and the US, the venture capital industry has developed as an important source of equity capital for SMEs. Venture capital industry is generally comprised of individual "business angels" and venture capital funds/ companies, institutional investors including commercial banks and insurance companies provide funds for the industry through such funds/companies. Venture capitalists provide equity investment for prospective SMEs in expectation of high return later by selling the equity to a third party or in the market when the enterprises grow successfully. A number of successful cases of initial public offerings and acquisitions transactions for high tech SMEs in recent years have created a momentum for the development of the industry in many advanced countries. This however, may be added, that development of venture capital financing may not be the last stage of SME financing. There may be many more developments in store for future.

**6.1.6 Traditional Financing:** Credit institutions are traditionally the primary source of SME growth. Among such institutions, commercial banks play an important role. They examine commercial viability of the business, assess credit risks, administer loan contracts and monitor developments. In advanced countries, credit to SMEs has become an important business for commercial banks as larger enterprises tend to tap capital markets and even external sources for their financing. In some countries credit unions also undertake similar functions but they generally operate locally and on a smaller scale. Next to commercial banks, non bank financial institutions have emerged as important vehicle for SME financing (such as State Financial Corporations, National Small Industries Corporation, Small Industries Development Bank of India). However, a major segment of NBFIs, exist in the form of leasing companies where through leasing contracts, leasing companies accommodate financial needs of SMEs for real estate or certain movable properties.

Banking system has emerged as the most important source of financing. It has played an important role in SMEs financing so far and will continue in future as well.

Traditional financing consists of

- Term loan for capital goods, buildings etc.
- Working capital loans in the form of cash credit, bill discounting, cheque discounting etc.

Typically these loans are available against security of assets outside the factory and within the factory such as land, buildings, plant and machinery, inventories (raw materials, work in progress and finished goods). A typical security is demanded for collaterals in the form of properties etc. owned by the promoters or family members of promoters and personal guarantees from third party with proper financial standing.

**Limitations of Traditional Methods of Financing:** Capacity of SMEs to raise finance depends on

- The ability of the promoters to provide primary (stock/receivables) and collateral security. SMEs find difficulty in meeting these requirements.
- Their own investment in business, shortage of own capital because of low income this inhibits the flow of adequate credit.
- Performance of the unit (on monthly basis) which decides the drawing power of working capital. It is not possible for the SMEs in developing economies to for credit rating because it is either not available or very costly.
- Margins on the debtors and inventory applied to calculate drawing power of the banks.
- Working capital cycle in operation and efficiency shown in working capital management. With increasing competition, falling margins and increase in credit to be offered to customers leading to a higher working capital cycle, this issue has gained prominence. Most of the entrepreneurs find it difficult to manage funds properly

because of short term and long term pressures.

- Lack of transparency in the operations of SME compels financial institutions to look upon them with suspicion.
- Emergence of more rising ventures where success is not yet fully proven such IT, Bio-Technology etc. More and more knowledge based industries are fast emerging. Existing banking system finds it difficult to assess the risk.
- Success of any enterprise depends on the ability to market and existence of market; selling also depends on quality and cost. Marketing has emerged as very uncertain phenomenon as 3-tier market structure (niche, domestic and international market) has given way to the emergence of only one market, i.e. competitive market. With the opening of the economy, globalisation, emergence of WTO, the competition on SMEs have increased tremendously. Limited access to information has been providing a major hurdle in extending the area and scope of marketing in developing economies.

Some of the general complaints, the lending institutions have with SMEs are:-

- They fail to estimate their requirements properly.
- Project estimates based on intuition rather than hard realities
- Failure to manage funds properly.
- In many cases not able to reach sales targets.
- Reluctance on their part to give clear stock statement.
- Utilising short-term finance for long term requirements.
- Diverting funds for personal use.

## 6.2 Initiatives in India

The Government of India being fully aware of the problems being faced by SSI units in obtaining institutional credit, has taken a large number of measures for ensuring adequate and timely supply of credit. These consist of

1. Bringing SSI lending under Priority Sector Lending Programme of Banks. Normally 15 to 16% of Net Bank Credit flow to SSI sector. However, this has been showing a declining trend since 1998.
2. Creating a separate refinancing and developmental bank for the SSI sector in 1990-91 called Small Industries Development Bank of India (SIDBI)
3. Setting up specialised and dedicated bank branches for SSI financing. Currently about 417 bank branches are working in the country.
4. Though term loans are generally financed through State Financial Corporations, however, considering their weak financial position and growing needs of the SSI sector it has allowed the banks to go for composite loaning up to Rs. 5 million.
5. Based on the Nayak Committee recommendation, the Central Bank of the country i.e. the Reserve Bank of India has issued directives that 20% annual turnover up to of Rs. 50 million should be met by the banks by way of working capital advances.
6. To assist the entrepreneurs in meeting equity requirement National Equity Fund Scheme has been working which meets the credit needs of units having project cost up to Rs. 5 million.
7. Government of India launched a Credit Guarantee Scheme in August 2000 to meet credit needs up to Rs. 2.5 million without collaterals, for this a credit Guarantee Fund Trust has been set up at Mumbai. Government proposes to create a fund of Rs. 25000 million of which 80% will be met by the Government of India and 20% by the SIDBI. Steps have also been taken

to set up a Mutual Credit Guarantee Scheme on the pattern of Italy where Associations are directly involved as intermediary.

### 6.3 Status of Credit Flow

The Status of credit flow to SSI sector from public sector banks during the past 6 years is given in Table 6.1.

The quantum of advances from public sector banks to SSIs has increased over the years in absolute terms from Rs. 38,109 crore in 1998 to Rs. 52,988 crore in 2003. However, the share of SSI in the net bank credit has declined from 17.5 per cent as the end of March 1998 to 11.1 per cent as the end of March 2003. As at the end of September 2003, this percentage stood at 11.0%. It is evident that the flow of credit to SSI sector in relation to the net bank credit, in percentage terms has been coming down continuously in the recent years. The continuing decline in SSI lending as percentage of net bank credit since 2000 is a matter of great concern as adequate credit flow is vital for achieving 12% growth rate for SSI sector as envisaged in the $10^{th}$ Plan.

60% of SSI credit is reserved for tiny units (for units having investment in plant and machinery less than Rs. 25 lakh). There has been a decline in credit flow to tiny sector as a percentage of SSI advances from 54.3 per cent in March 2002 to 50.8 per cent in March 2003. However, this has somewhat improved as at the end of September 2003 (53.6%).

### 6.4 Adequate Credit and Employment Generation

For achieving the target of 4.4 million additional employment in the SSI sector and the required rate of growth of 12 per cent per annum in the tenth Five Year Plan, it is a pre-requisite that the sector gets timely and adequate supply of credit.

**Table 6.1: Credit Flow to SSI Sector from Public Sector Banks**

(Rs. crore)

| | As at the end of March | | | | | | As at the end of September 2003 |
|---|---|---|---|---|---|---|---|
| | **1998** | **1999** | **2000** | **2001** | **2002** | **2003** | |
| Net Bank Credit | 218219 | 246203 | 292943 | 340887 | 396954 | 477899 | 479554 |
| Credit to SSI | 38109 | 42674 | 45788 | 48445 | 49743 | 52988 | 52828 |
| Percentage to Net Bank Credit | 17.5% | 17.3% | 15.6% | 14.2% | 12.5% | 11.1% | 11.0% |
| Number of SSI Accounts (in lakhs) | 29.64 | 26.24 | 22.72 | 22.80 | 22.23 | 16.95 | 16.66 |

At present, the small scale industries provide employment to 2.50 crore people as per the Third Census. If we can take into account the total employment provided by the Village and Small Enterprises Sector (VSE), it is more than 6 crore. The Tenth Plan has fixed a target of over 1 crore of additional employment in the VSE sector. If the employment in agriculture is declining and the large scale sector is experiencing jobless growth, one of the important ways to achieve the target of 50 million additional jobs in the Tenth Plan is to help the small scale industries and service sector. Unless the role of the SSI sector in employment generation is appreciated by the banking sector, the above target cannot be achieved.

The Working Group on Small Scale Industries (SSI) for Tenth Plan projected the long-term credit requirements of Rs. 63,357 crore during the Plan period. The requirement of working capital funds from institutional and bank sources has been estimated to be Rs. 1,22,942 crore in the terminal year of the Tenth Plan i.e. F.Y. 2007. According to RBI, advances to the SSI sector up to March 2003 have been Rs. 52,988 crore from public sector banks. Further, Rs. 1,000 crore have been provided to SSI sector by others sources other than public sector banks. Thus, the total credit flow to SSI sector comes to Rs. 64,000 crore up to March 2003.

The Third Census of SSI has revealed a highly disturbing trend on SSI financing that not more than 15 to 20 per cent of SSI units are approaching banks and institutional sources for finance. It is because most of the SSI units feel harassed while approaching the banks. It is agreed that at no point of time all the SSI entrepreneurs would be approaching the banks for loan, at least a good number will feel encouraged if there is proper and friendly atmosphere at the bank branches. With the continuance of credit flow to SSI sector at this pace, there would evidently be a substantial shortfall in meeting the projected credit requirements.

Though SSI lending comes under priority sector lending of banks, there is no sub-target unlike agriculture. As advised by the RBI, the banks have fixed self-target for growth in advances to SSI sector based on the previous year's achievement and overall trends in growth of net bank credit. In order to ensure maintaining a reasonable level of credit, it is essential that the banks fix a target of at least 15 per cent growth over previous year's achievement.

For improving the performance and competitiveness, the SSI sector needs enhanced credit support for inducing modern/latest technology. The banks need to develop more schemes to encourage investment by SSI units in technology upgradation. The flow of credit under various schemes launched for credit support to the SSI sector viz., National Equity Fund (NEF), Credit Guarantee Fund Scheme for Small Industries, Credit Linked Capital Subsidy Scheme for technology Upgradation (CLCSS), etc., have to be enhanced by speeding up their implementation.

There are limitations in SIDBI expanding its direct lending to SSIs owing to its small branch network and SFCs meeting the long-term credit requirements of SSIs in view of a weak financial position of a majority of the SFCs. The SSI units are therefore, largely dependent on the commercial banks for their credit requirements. The banks should encourage availing of working capital and term loan through a single window system to meet both the working capital and term loan requirements of SSIs and composite loan limit should be further raised from Rs. 50 lakh to Rs. 2 crore. This will help in increasing the flow of credit to the SSI sector. Nayak Committee norms for computing working capital on the basis of 20% of the annual projected turnover should be strictly followed.

## 6.5 Problems in Raising Finance by SMEs

Coinciding with its critical role in the life cycle of an economic enterprise, raising of adequate financial resources for meeting diverse requirements poses the foremost hurdle for entrepreneurs. Some of the major problems associated with raising of institutional credit in developing economies are:

1. Inadequacy of credit resulting into sickness of the unit form the very beginning. This aspect has already been dealt alone.
2. Delay in availability of credit leading to cost overruns. Often there is a gap in the term lending by SFCs and release of working capital by banks.
3. The procedural hassles arising from exhaustive and complicated forms and avoidable harassment at the hands of the officials forcing the entrepreneurs to opt for other convenient sources of finance such as traditional money lenders even though at a higher cost.
4. Inability to make available the collaterals and third party guarantees. At times, the amount of required collaterals is as high as two or three times the amount of loan requested.
5. The composite loans through single window are available only for smaller amounts. In India currently it is available up to Rs. 5 million (Rs. 50 lakh).
6. The system of joint appraisal (by supplier of term loan and that of working capital) is often found either lacking, uncoordinated and often working against the interests of entrepreneurs.
7. The indifference on the part of financial institutions to promote loans of smaller amounts due to higher amount

of risk, plethora of paper work and resultant higher administrative cost.

8. Higher rate of sickness among SSI units leads to large NPAs of the Banks, which reflects poorly on their performance.
9. The SSI units find it difficult to their establish credit worthiness. Apart from the fewer number of rating agencies for smaller loans it has been found that the fees charged by the existing credit rating agencies is very costly. This further compounds the problems of the small enterprises.
10. The higher cost of credit in India in comparison to other countries particularly the developed ones, results in the escalation of the cost of production and making the products uncompetitive. The cost of credit to the SSI sector, at present is around 14% p.a. as against 8-9 per cent or less for the large-scale sector. The cost differential makes the SSI sector uncompetitive. The Finance Minister in the Union Budget 2003-04 announced that the rate of interest for SSIs would be in the band of 2 % below/above the PLR of banks. The Finance Minister also made an announcement on 9th January, 2004 regarding the creation of an SME Fund of Rs. 10,000 crore by SIDBI for making available credit to small and medium enterprises at 200 basis points below PLR.
11. The other institutional source of funding such as capital market, foreign investment etc. which are available to large units also do not offer much solace to SSI units. Because of their lower size they cannot have access to the capital market.
12. The weak financial base of SSIs eventually prompts the entrepreneurs to raise the required funds through loans

rather than bringing in capital. As a result, the smaller the size of the unit, smaller the deployment of capital.

13. The SSIs are not in a position to maintain proper books of account, partly because of lack of required knowledge and partly on account of inability to hire the services of professionals for the purpose.
14. - The delay in release of payments by the larger units to small scale units disturbs the whole financial cycle and compels the banks to avoid giving further advances to the SSI units. Factoring, services, which could have eased the problem, to a great extent have not become popular in India so far.
15. There is lack of appreciation of financial data and relevant information as required by the banks and financial institutions.
16. One of the more serious credit related problem is lack of awareness among the bank officials/branches. Although a large number of schemes/programmes are being implemented for the SSI sector, the bank officials at branch level express ignorance regarding these schemes /programmes. It is not uncommon to find bank branches expressing lack of awareness about the existence of Credit Guarantee Scheme even though their banks are members of Credit Guarantee Fund Trust. There is also lack of awareness amongst the banks about RBI guidelines. There are complaints about the non-observance of RBI guidelines. Particular mention may be made of RBI guidelines on collateral free loans up to Rs. 5 lakh and up to Rs. 25 lakh in deserving cases. Guidelines on sickness and rehabilitation, time frame for disposal of loan application are not adhered to.
17. There is lack of awareness amongst the SSI entrepreneurs about the various schemes/facilities being

offered by the banks as several banks are not displaying the existing facilities/schemes in their branches. It may, however, be mentioned that some banks like SBI, PNB, Indian Bank, Canara Bank have already announced SSI charters and quite a good number of banks have also started displaying on SSI facilities and incentives on their websites, but quite a large number of banks are yet to take such initiatives. In spite of Government announcement on collateral free loans almost all banks still ask for collaterals up to Rs. 5 lakh. There is lack of seriousness regarding actual implementation of declarations, facilities and incentives for SSIs and guidelines issued by the RBI to facilitate SSI credit from time to time. Announcement of concessions, schemes at the higher level and their non-observance or ignorance about their existence at the field level brings the government and the institutions concerned into disrepute and creates a poor image thereof in general.

18. Due to lack of knowledge and expertise, the SSI units submit faulty and half baked project reports. There is no nodal officer in most of the bank branches to guide the SSI entrepreneurs.
19. The prescribed concessional rates of interest do not motivate the financial institutions intrinsically to invest in SSI units.
20. Most of the SSI units are run either as proprietary concerns or partnership firms as against company forum of business and thus lack accountability. This basic feature discourages the financial institutions to make available small amounts of loans.

### 6.6 Credit to Small Enterprises by Banks

The banks at times have a disinclination to entertain

certain proposals of SSIs due to (i) adverse risk perception; (ii) lack of credit rating facilities; (iii) fear of incurring NPAs attracting punitive action because of high NPAs in SSI sector which is about 20 % at present and (iv) high transaction cost in processing large number of loan applications as against the single large industry proposal.

Banks feel that for genuine default in SSI payments, there should not be vigilance enquiry as it acts as a deterrent in attending to SSI cases for sanction of loans. Banks often complain that they do not get good and viable projects proposals from the SSI sector. The statistics, however, show that over 1 lakh new SSI units get registered with State Directorate of Industries every year. Even considering that only 10 per cent of them are good proposals, at least 10,000 new accounts should get added every year. Besides this, a much larger number of unregistered units come into existence every year. They also have significant credit needs with large number of bankable proposals. As against all this, it is found that the number of SSI accounts have declined continuously from 29.64 lakh units in 1998 to 16.66 lakh in September 2003.

One of the major problems SMEs must overcome in the search for financing is their relative lack of credibility. This is especially true for start-ups and young businesses which tend to have short credit records and little or inadequate collateral, which are often indispensable in obtaining loans from credit institutions. This gap can be closed by third party guarantees. Such guarantees may be provided by related parties such as associated companies or entrepreneurs themselves and their relatives and friends, but in many countries, there exist well developed guarantee schemes to help SMEs obtain financing.

Credit guarantee schemes can be established in a number

of ways. Such schemes may be created on a local, regional or national level or in a multi layer structure. These schemes may be organised as mutuals, co-operatives or corporations founded by professional or entrepreneurial organisations and sometimes banks or their associations. In most cases, credit guaranty schemes are directly or indirectly supported by local and / or central governments. In some countries, public guarantee schemes for SME loans have been established. In Italy the experience of involving Associations in guarantee process under its Mutual Credit Guarantee Scheme has been found to be more successful and popular.

Experience in advanced market countries shows that well functioning credit guarantee schemes are effective in facilitating the provision of commercial credit to SMEs. However, it is also often pointed out that such schemes induce moral hazard borrowers may be less concerned on their efficiency and lenders may be less prudent in their risk assessment. These schemes need to be designed and operated carefully, sufficiently accommodating to ensure the availability of financing to SMEs but not so generous as to result in significant moral hazard problems.

## 6.7 Role of the Government

In order to promote the growth and development of SME sector, Governments often encourage the participation of SME financing by credit institutions. The governments support can be in the form of interest rate subsidies, credit linked capital subsidy, credit guarantee, credit enhancement facilities, tax incentives etc. Further some governments have established within their arms one or more public credit institutions to facilitate SME financing (as SIDBI in India). Specialised credit institutions can largely be divided into two groups those that are effectively founded by governments and the one established and operated by private sector initiatives though possibly getting public support in some ways. In Asia and many other parts of the world, it is not uncommon to find government related credit institutions that specially target SME financing. They may either be credit institutions that actually extend loans to SMEs or guarantee organisations that facilitate the provision of commercial loans to SMEs. They are established by governments as a means to support the development of the SME sector.

In the context of fast changing world, the needs of credit or finance for the small enterprises are also changing from traditional term loan and working capital to innovative venture capital and risk capital. Change in bank's role from developmental and promotional financing to purely commercial financing can also be seen. People generally, ask if the large enterprise do not need bank finance – is it not the high time that banks adopt a friendly attitude in favour of small enterprises. It is felt that excess liquidity with the banks and the lack of demand from large enterprises will bring the doom for the banking sector. Housing loan, car finance, education loan etc. which have become popular in recent years will not provide sustainability to banking operations in the long run. Hence, for their survival it is high time that banks see the small enterprises as their friends and not so otherwise. Further, it is certain that there will be changes in the type and purpose of credit, hence it is also high time that the institutions and the small enterprises both prepare themselves for innovative means of financing.

## 6.8 Instruments of Innovative Financing

**6.8.1 Bill Discounting:** For the SMEs who are vendor to large financially strong organisations, MNCs etc. with a reputation of timely payments can obtain cheap finance under bill discounting at reasonable rates say lower than Prime Lending Rates. This rate depends on the strength of buyer and volumes of supplies by the vendor. Such finances are available for short term period of 90 to 120 days. This system does not involve demand of security or collaterals. The system of bill discounting is becoming popular in India as SIDBI, foreign banks. Private banks etc. are offering such facilities. Any SME who is supplier to any MNC or corporate body of strength and which accept bills of exchange are eligible for this facility. The rate of interest is normally low for SSIs since they qualify for priority sector obligation of the lenders.

SIDBI has been operating Bills Rediscounting Scheme to help manufacturers in the SSI sector to maximise their sales by offering deferred payment credit facilities to prospective purchasers-users. Facilities under this scheme are also extended to cover purchase of machinery by SSIs. Under the scheme, bills of exchange/promissory notes, arising out of sale/purchase of machinery by industrial concerns in the SSI sector are discounted. Short term BRs facility is also provided against inland supply bills of SSIs to enable SSI units to sell on credit and to encourage bill culture in the country.

**6.8.2 Lease Financing:** Although the business of renting equipment and other items has been in existence for time immemorial, the modern concept of equipment leasing has been around only some 50-55 years. Since its modest inception in the United States in 1950s, it has grown to be a US$ 500 billion industry on a world-wide basis. Approximately one third of the developed and developing countries of the world have some form of cognisable leasing activity. There is however, a major difference between traditional and modern leasing system. This is the emergence of third party financial element in modern system. Whereas a traditional rental business maintained an inventory from which lessees rented equipment for short periods of time, modern financial lessors only buy equipment as requested by their lessees, specifically for lease to those lessees, which necessitates a much longer term. The lessee may or may not have an option to purchase the equipment at the end of the lease term. The present form of three party leasing is new, and quite different from traditional two party rental system.

Most of the leasing economies exist in Asia, prominent among them are Japan, Korea, Peoples' Republic of China, Hong Kong, and Taiwan, Indonesia, India, Pakistan, Malaysia, Singapore, Thailand, the Philippines and even Sri Lanka which has had a significant and sophisticated leasing industry for some time. The combined leasing volume in these countries account for almost 20% of the world's total leasing activity. However, a number of Asian countries have yet to develop leasing sector.

What makes the leasing so popular? According to Mr. Steven Gilyeart, President of the International Leasing Resource the modern leasing system has the following advantages:-

- Allows for better cash management of working capital since it does not involve down payment, fixed payment, presentation of lines etc.
- Provides a hedge against technological obsolescence. The equipment can be returned to leaser at the end of lease.
- Provides a fixed payment, based upon a fixed rate of interest rather than the variable one frequently found with loans. Interest rate risk is upon lessor and not lessee.

- It is a flexible form of financing as it has more entrepreneurial culture than banking and regulations are far less than banking, system normally impose upon the borrowers.
- Provides a hedge against inflation as lease payments are usually fixed over lease term.
- Allows better utilisation of tax benefits by both lessor and lessee and is helpful more to start up enterprise. Tax benefits to enable the lessor to lower the rate on the lease and thereby to reduce the overall cost of equipment.
- Conserves credit lines and expands and diversifies credit sources. It may provide off-balance sheet financing. While a loan is always on the balance sheet, lessees are often off the balance sheet – showing instead as a current expenses on the income statement. Thus it helps to improve various ratios used by credit and financial analysts to assess the financial health of the business.
- The lessor may provide non financial services not readily available from other credit sources, such as equipment service and maintenance.
- The lessee may be able to take advantage of the economies of scale of the lessor's purchasing power.
- It may better accommodate capital budgets than alternative financing.
- It also requires payment for only the value of the property's use when the value of ownership is not needed.
- Leasing is considered attractive to lessors because of extra service, extra return as it is both a financial and equipment business. Lessor provides additional service by taking back the equipment. It has scope for self-differentiation through customer related value added. Lessor can design lease keeping into account the status

of leasee

- Leasing can contribute to economic development of developing economies. Since it allows more business, particularly SMEs access to financing and through increase the domestic capital base. As a financial product leasing needs its own funding which tends to further mobilise domestic capital. It also provides competition to traditional banks by being more pragmatic and situation based financier. Leasing also encourages financial product innovation because leasing companies in their expanding purchases of more and more equipment are very capital consumptive as well. It helps to develop secondary markets.

**6.8.3 Factoring Services:** One of the major problems faced by SME is in developing economies in delayed payments on supplies made by them to other units including Public Sector Undertakings and Large Scale Industries. Factoring services is a time honoured tool for speeding cash flow for SMEs. It has origins in USA in 19$^{th}$ Century, but has spread rapidly in last 30 years the world over, including Asia. In India a modest beginning was made in 1991, but it has very limited penetration so far.

Factoring in financial parlance means purchase of receivables. The basic principle of factoring is same as bill discounting. The only difference is that in this case there will be no bill of exchange.. Finance is made available on the basis of invoice. This eliminates the need for drawing up a bill of exchange and its stamping. Factoring service involves a contract concluded between one party (the supplier- client) and another party (factor), pursuant to which the supplier will assign to the factor, receivables (debts) arising from contracts of selling of goods made between the supplier and its customers. This facilitates finance for the client (loans and advance payments) and helps in maintenance of accounts (Ledgering) relating to receivables. Factoring helps in the collection of receivables, and provides protection against default in payment by debtors.

The factoring are of two types: one covering the domestic sales and the other for exports. Domestic factoring is obtaining finance against local receivables. It is discounting of sales invoices without the Bills of Exchange. There are three parties involved in the domestic factoring. These are

- The client or seller of the good;
- The customer or debtor who is the buyer of the goods, and
- The 'Factor' who is the financial intermediary providing factoring services.

As against domestic factoring, international factoring is a product which is applicable to exporters. An exporter can expect up to 90% of finance and 100% risk protection. The Factoring Company will set up limits for each importer of the exporter and buy exports made within this limit. This facility is available for a tenure of up to 180 days, financing is in foreign exchange. Otherwise the principles of export factoring are the same as domestic factoring.

The Factor performs at lease two of the following services:

- Financing for the seller by way of advance payments.
- Maintenance of Accounts relating to the accounts receivables.
- Collection of Accounts Receivables, and
- Credit protection against default in payment by the buyer.

The tasks performed by the Factors cover finance,

collection of dues ledgering, protection against bad debts etc. These are explained below:

**Finance:** Factor extends advance against debts assigned (referred as prepayment). These could either be transaction based finance or drawing power based upon eligible debts. Normally margin is retained (may vary from between 10-40%) usually 20% to take care of possible rejections. Advance to suppliers are subject to customer wise exposure limits which are fixed and reviewed based on payment pattern and other relevant facts. These advances are usually adjusted against payments from customers.

**Collection:** Collection of dues is arranged through personal contracts, reminders, telephone messages etc. They maintain close liaison with the client/ customers to resolve disputes of quantity, quality, discounts etc. After collection of the dues on maturity, funds are remitted to the client. Factors also review debtors to ensure collectability of debts and submits the necessary returns to the client

**Ledgering:** In factoring services, the entire responsibility of sales ledge administration of the client gets transferred to the factor. This ensures the following:

- The invoices raised represent genuine trade transactions
- Sales ledger of the client is maintained in a scientific and up to date manner, based on last invoice raised and cash received.

**Protection against Bad Debts:** Assuming credit risk responsibility is done by assignment without recourse basis. Debt purchase limits are approved for each customer based on credit evaluation. While prepayments are released after applying the proper margin, the retention money is released after the expiry of the agreed period beyond the due date.

**Advantages of Factoring**: Factoring enables ready cash against credit sales and there is no need to wait for the customary credit period. It is a flexible short term financing option- actual drawing totally in the hands of the client. In the process it provides better liquidity at more competitive terms for customers, and this leads to improved sales, and ultimately greater profits.

Factoring services are however, more expensive as compared with banks on funding as a stand-alone basis. Invoices have to be assigned by the client to the factor, which involves the customer who may not be willing to have his debts factored. All invoices have to be routed through the factors although the factor may not finance all invoices. This may push up the service charges of the client, without

**Advent of Factoring in India**: RBI set up a Study Group in 1988 under the Chairmanship of Sri C.S. Kalyanasundarm former Managing Director, State Bank of India, principally to consider the scope of factoring in various forms in the country. The committee after studying the scenario in India and other countries submitted a comprehensive report in 1989. The Committee found that, as the Indian law at present does not deal comprehensively with various aspects involved in factoring business, promotion of a special legislation as also a few modifications in the existing laws were recommended. The committee estimated potential demand for factoring services at about Rs. 4000 crore of outstanding debts ( of which SSI would account for about 75%.)

SBI and Canara Bank set up factoring subsidiaries in 1991. SIDBI participated 20% in their equity. SIDBI has been providing lines of credit to both these factoring companies on concessional terms against SSI debts factored by them. Banks allowed to undertake factoring departmentally as well. But there was lack of response.

There is need for a separate legislation on factoring

services in India. Currently factoring services have to operate within the existing legislation on contracts, sale of goods, transfer of property etc. These enactments do not comprehensively deal with various aspects involved in factoring business and are found not adequate to provide requisite protection to a factor. The existing law does not require the assignee (factor) to give notice to the debtor that it has taken assignment of the debt. However, in order to prevent the debtor from paying the debt to the client or to a subsequent assignee, and also to enable the factor to claim the payment of debt in his own right, giving notice of assignment becomes necessary. The existing law does not require the assignee (factor) to give notice to the debtor that it has taken assignment of the debt. However, in order to prevent the debtor from paying the debt to the client or to a subsequent assignee, and also to enable the factor to claim the payment of the debt in his own right, giving notice of assignment becomes necessary. There are, however, certain problems coming in the way of enactment of an effective legislation on factoring. Important among them is the payment of stamp duty and registration of assignment.

**6.8.4 Equity Financing:** The most essential requirement of equity financing is the existence of a well developed capital market along with a sound SMEs with brands. One of the major problems faced by developing economies in financing SMEs is inadequacy of capital markets to bridge the credit gaps of SMEs, capital markets take a long time to develop and deepen and do not necessarily work in ways predicted. Often the lack of financial instruments and the number of participants restrict the capacity for financial deepening. In low income countries many family based indigenous enterprises are reluctant to change their corporate status. The development of capital markets helps in introducing efficient and effective mechanisms of regulation and supervision to avoid malpractices. If these are not in place then markets will fail to assess the intermediate risks appropriately, so that new capital does not emerge. As a consequence bank finance is likely to remain the main source of finance for SMEs.

Traditionally SMEs have seldom had direct access to capital markets for equity financing. However, recent advancements in technology coupled with financial market globalisation is rapidly changing the scene. Following the remarkable success of NASDAQ in the US, a number of a stock exchanges targeted at SMEs have been set up in recent years, not only in Europe but also in Asia. Such exchanges are beneficial to SMEs by providing them with opportunities for tapping capital markets for their financing and also by fostering the venture capital industry by providing increased "exit" possibilities.

One of the functions of the SME exchanges (or special SME boards on established exchanges) is to provide standardised information on the listed companies, particularly through their listing requirements. Listing at an exchange should therefore be contributory to closing the information gap between SMEs and investors and thereby should help promote equity investments into SMEs. However, investment in SMEs which may lack sufficient performance records, is essentially risky. In fact may listed SMEs do not survive for long. It should be noted that loose listing requirements to allow SMEs to be listed will inevitably weaken the information providing function of the exchange.

Active participation of investors is key for the development of capital markets Among them, professional, institutional investors are important, particularly for risky markets, such as for SME stocks. Globalising activity of institutional investors of advanced economies is contributory to the capital markets for SMEs in Asia. Moreover, an increasing number of Asian economies have now taken efforts to develop domestic institutional investors such as insurance companies, pension funds or mutual funds.

**6.8.5 Venture Capital:** Venture capital financing is one of the forms of equity financing. While credit is usually a primary financial resource for SMEs to operate and invest, equity capital is also an indispensable element in SME financing. Equity capital is important, in particular, in start up phases and rapid growth periods. In most cases, SMEs obtain equity capital from the founders and their relatives and friends. However, in some advanced market countries like the UK and the US, the venture capital industry has developed as an important source of equity capital for SMEs. Venture Capital Funds bridge the gaps in institutional financing mechanism of the SME sector in respect of units, which due to inherent characteristics of their projects in terms of proposed product/ technology involved may not qualify for assistance through the conventional route of term financing. Normally if serves those ventures which have latent innovative potential in industries like Information Technology (IT), Bio Technology, Food Products (processing to enhance self life and new foods qualifying in terms of emerging requirements of health and hygiene), electronics, new chemicals, drugs and pharmaceuticals etc.

The venture capital industry is generally comprised of individual "business angels" and venture capital funds/ companies. Institutional investors including commercial banks and insurance companies provide funds for the industry through such funds/ companies. Venture capitalists provide equity investments for prospective SMEs in the expectation for high return later by selling the equity to a third party or in the market when the enterprises grow successfully. The financing could be in the form of a package of assistance comprising anyone or mix of instruments such as equity, conditional and normal term loan. A number of successful cases of initial public offerings and acquisition transactions for high tech SMEs in recent years have created a momentum for the development of the industry in many advanced countries.

Governments have taken various steps to promote venture capital investments for SMEs. These measures include not only the promotion of supporting infrastructure, such as exchanges specialised for SME stocks and favourable tax environment, but also the establishment of government supported venture capital funds, though it is not evident yet the extent to which such funds can be successful.

In India Small Industries Development Bank of India (SIDBI) launched Venture Capital Scheme in October 1992, and created a separate VC fund with an initial corpus of Rs. 100 million. The corpus of the fund has continuously been enhanced since then and by now the scheme has been extended to cover 27 SSI units covering a wide range of funds by contributing to the corpus of various national and state level VC funds for extending VC assistance to SSI units. The strategy has been to create a 3 tier venture capital structure of software/ IT industry viz. the regional, national and international level so as to effectively integrate and enhance the opportunities for the SMEs. In India SIDBI and the funds promoted by it are primarily the institutions extending VC assistance to small scale units, while other funds presently focus on larger investment of over Rs. 5.0 million. The efforts are afoot to extend the venture capital activities to other parts of the country.

Based upon the recommendation of Task Force on IT constituted by the Government of India to formulate the draft national policy on informatics, SIDBI has set up the National Venture Fund for Software and Information Technology Industry with a committed fund corpus of Rs. 1000 million with fund contributions of 50% from SIDBI, 30% from Ministry of Communication and Information Technology GOI, and remaining 20% coming from the Industrial Development Bank of India. SIDBI has also promoted two subsidiaries of this National Venture Fund. In order to extend the functions across the national border SIDBI proposes to set up overseas Dollar Denominated Venture Capital Fund in collaboration with Intech Venture Group. In spite of all these VC financing in India is still in nascent stage and there is also shortage of trained manpower in this sector. In India most of the VC funds are IT focused and returns to VC funds are linked with performance of IT funds. This sector is experiencing a downsizing after September 2001 incidence.

The Union Budget (2002 – 03) announced the setting up of Micro Venture Capital Fund for small innovations by building national register of outstanding knowledge and grass root innovations.

**Problems in VC financing**

- Venture capitalists prefer organised units as they find SME financing comparatively risky because they require early stage funding. The expected returns from these investments may not be comparable to those of other VC funds/ private equity investors.
- Providing venture capital to SMEs has its own inherent problems like limited exit opportunities, high transaction costs etc. Non availability of proper exit route has proved to be a major bottleneck in providing VC support

to the SSI units, as it does not offer scope to harvest the investment at appropriate times.

- Failures of project supported under the VC route are significantly larger than through conventional lending and therefore require highly trained and motivated managers.
- Lack of professionalism which is a common feature with developing economies is likely to affect the performance of the funds.

Venture capital is ideal for knowledge and technology based industries. The IT sector, software industry and related business such as E commerce, networking, multi-media, data communication and value added communication services is a growing sector and SME units venturing into these areas need to be assisted. However, player enterprises will have to move up to the value chain from providing low end finance and accounting or customer interaction services to e learning, engineering design, GIS services. SMEs with strong managerial teams and excellent execution capability trying to obtain VC funds should not only be provided with fund support but assistance like information and market access, technological net working and hand holding to manage business more effectively and achieve rapid growth in the internationally competitive environment.

**6.8.6 Incubation Services:** Incubator financing is extension of venture capital financing. An incubator provides a some sort of shelter and a nurturing environment that allows a promising entrepreneur with knowledge of the industry but having no knowledge of running an enterprise to survive and grow. A young start up unit requires some nurturing to help them through the most vulnerable period of their existence. The concept of incubation it is presumed took birth in the laboratories of large universities that had professors and students with promising new technology and business ideas. A physical workspace and equipment were provided to cash in on this intellectual capital in exchange for part ownership of the new company thus formed. This is the traditional "university incubator" concept.

During the economic boom of the eighties and nineties, capital was abundantly available in advanced and newly industrialised economies and a person with an idea was hugely in demand. He was allured by the venture capitalists to provide him with all facilities that would lead to the birth of a great company. The success stories of start up companies making it big at NASDAQ and important stock exchanges accelerated the process of incubation. The demand far exceeded the supply and as is expected under such circumstances and inexperienced entrepreneurs flocked to incubators with hopes of access to facilities and funds.

The main objective of the incubator is to produce successful businesses that are financially viable and free standing when they leave, typically in a couple of years. According to a impact of incubator investment study made in 1997 it was found that 87 per cent of incubator graduates remain in business. This is a healthy trend and an incubator can now aspire to have a positive impact on its communities economy by maximising the success of emerging companies.

When a university/premier institute of higher education offers these services, they are doubly valuable. Apart from the infrastructural on-site management that is built in the system, there is access to top quality mentors, research data and library facilities and the privilege of working in an inspiring learning oriented ambience. Here, the goal is to motivate students to take up entrepreneurship, as it is one of the tools to create jobs, revitalise neighbourhoods, comercialise critical new technologies and strengthen local and national economies. India with large number of young graduates with requisite knowledge offers very good scope for development of incubator services.

All infrastructural facilities are given to the incubates who can then focus on creating a sustainable long term business. Mentoring by professors and a team of experts is available to them. In advanced countries, there is no dearth of companies who meet the hardware and other requirements of in incubators such as air conditioning etc. However, the problem developing economies is lack of infrastructure and supporting environment.

Every incubator must make an arrangement so that talented consultants provide low cost or free services in exchange for opportunities to expand their own businesses. All incubators need to look at themselves as accelerators and gather the expertise around them to speed up their clients successful entry into market. The renowned Institutes of Technologies in India and developing economies posses ideal infrastructure for development of incubator services. SIDBI has started an incubation centre at IIT Kanpur. However, incubator financing has not yet gathered momentum in India so far. Large number of technically qualified graduates available in India, the development of incubator sources is the need of the hour.

**6.8.7 Other Instruments:** Besides the above, there exist a few other instruments to enhance the capital base of the SME sector. These are

- Introducing provisions for limited liability partners, if possible having an exclusive act on this.
- Enhancing the limit of equity investment by outsiders in SMEs. In India currently this limit is 24% which could be enhanced.

- Encouraging vendoring for large companies etc.

### 6.9 Micro Credit

Micro credit has emerged as a powerful tool for empowering poor people for alleviating their poverty and thus bringing improvements in their living standards. Micro credit programmes envisage extending small loans to poor entrepreneurs for undertaking economic ventures which have potential to make a dent on poverty. Micro credit programme in neighbouring countries Bangladesh has become a phenomenal success and is considered worth introduction in countries having large segment of population living below poverty line. Though it is not one of the innovative instruments of financing but as an instrument of removal of poverty and generation of large-scale employment opportunity it has become popular in South Asian countries and also in our neighbouring countries including Bangladesh and Nepal. The future of small enterprises and their linking with global market depends on the extent of utilisation of micro credit as an instrument of change.

Small doses of loans work wonders in changing the life pattern of masses. Self-employment makes them masters of their own destiny. Microfinance is successful because the recovery rate is as high as 98 per cent while repayments are weekly and its operation is simple through NGOs and Self-Help Groups who make financial services available at the doorstep and undertake regular and dedicated monitoring. The examples set by Grameen Bank of Bangladesh as dedicated bank and the role played by BRAC and ASA or the role of Palikarma Sahayak Foundation (autonomous body) as leading NGOs are examples worth study and replication with suitable changes. Cost of credit is higher than average but that is not an issue since the cycle of operation decides repaying capacity.

As a principle of financing, Microfinance is not a new concept and it has been in existence since 1970 but it is definitely not a conventional banking concept. Microfinance is simply applying the principles of markets and capitalism to the poorest of the poor. It is a simple mechanism of helping even those who do not have any formal skill. The experience of Bangladesh has proved how the group behaviour built on past and peer pressure can make the poor people credit worthy. The system works in two ways i.e., advancing of loans and generating savings and both are pursued as independent activities. The additional family income generated by micro credit may be small, but it often makes the difference between survival and destination. There is also evidence that micro credit can help the poor families to break out of the poverty cycle through accumulation of assets and improvement of human capital.

The mission of micro credit has been guided by four core themes:

- reaching the poorest,
- reaching and empowering women,
- building financially self-sufficient institutions, and
- ensuring a positive measurable impact on lives of the clients and their families.

In India, there are over 26 crore people living below the poverty line and their micro credit needs have been assessed at Rs. 50,000 crore. The existing programmes of Micro credit being operated by NABARD, SIDBI, various ministries of Government of India, various State Governments and some leading Associations and NGOs make a total of not exceeding Rs. 5000 crore and thus there is still a vast gap of Rs. 45,000 crore between the demand and supply of micro credit.

The last three decades have seen massive expansion of formal credit network in India. However, there is a perceptible gap in financing genuine credit needs of the poor segments of the society specially in remote and rural areas. Though directed credit programmes and efforts of formal and informal institutions in making financial services easily accessible to the poor have borne some fruit, however, much more remains to be done for those who cannot approach formal banking channels for meeting their financial requirements. Some dedicated Non-government organisations such as SEWA in Gujarat under the illustrious leadership of Mrs. Ila Bhatt and some others in West Bengal, Andhra Pradesh and Karnakata have been operating Micro Credit Programmes with amazing success rates. Such efforts are however limited to certain pockets and have not become a mass movement.

Recognising the need for such kind of programme, the SIDBI as pat of its promotional and developmental role, formulated Micro Credit Schemes (MCS) in 1994 with the objective to provide financial support to well managed NGOs for on-lending to rural poor (individuals/groups) with focus on women, for assisting them in setting up micro enterprises. Since introduction of SIDBI Micro Credit Scheme in February 1994, cumulative assistance of the order of Rs. 200 crore of equity support for meeting capacity building, managerial costs, etc. has been channelised through 170 NGOs. In view of the encouraging response to the Scheme, the SIDBI set up a Foundation on Micro Credit in the year 1998-99 with a Corpus of Rs. 100 crore. The Foundation has the following distinctive features.

- Multi-channel credit dispensation routes through apex-NGOs, Self-help Group Federations, specialised Co-operatives, etc.

- Focus on encouraging micro finance for product innovations.
- Enhanced flow of assistance to the micro finance sector.
- Reorientation in the Security/collateral requirement.
- Simplification in procedures for availing assistance.
- Rating of MFIs/NGOs.

The renewed approach places considerable emphasis on (Micro-Finance Institutions) MFIs as long term partners. These MFIs, which may include NGOs and community-based organisations (CBOs), are selected on the basis of their credibility, track record, professional expertise, management practices, organisational capabilities, growth potential etc. The assistance to their MFIs is based on capacity assessment rating, business planning and resource forecast exercise, appraisals, field visits, etc.

The SIDBI Foundation provides a customised package of assistance to these MFIs consisting of a mix of loan, equity and need-based assistance for capacity building. It endeavours to promote and develop these agencies into strong financial intermediaries which would act as major players in the micro credit segments, especially for reaching out to smaller NGOs and MFIs, and for building their capabilities through management support inputs, training in credit delivery and usage. Besides, the programme also aims at promoting best practices and introduction of innovative features that would contribute to financial viability of micro credit programmes which would, in turn, ensure appropriate financial services to the poor.

In order to make a mass movement some changes needed are

- To make the regional Rural Bank as an agent of Micro Credit's delivery through Self Help Groups.
- To make investment on capacity building development

of infrastructure in rural areas and empowering and assisting NGOs.

- To create a national level institution to plan, supervise and guide the operations of micro credit.

## 6.10 Measures to Modernise Credit System

Adequate and timely credit at reasonable cost is the most important requirement of the SMEs in any part of the world. Creation of large scale employment at low capital cost is the speciality of the SME sector. However in view of the increased competitiveness in the fast changing global environment, it is not possible for any economy at this present juncture to wait for the normal stages of SME financing to follow. There is no time to wait. Hence environment has to be created for the implementation of innovative instruments irrespective of the stages of economic development. While the normal economic development will take care of many hurdles in its wake, special efforts are needed to create a conducive environment by having:

- Focussed Programmes and Policies for the SME sector.
- Concerted and co-ordinated efforts on the part of all concerned Government Departments at the Centre and State level and also on the part of other concerned agencies and associations.
- An effective monitoring mechanism aimed at removal of bottlenecks.
- Creation of credit rating facilities.
- Promotion of SME Brands.
- Development of appropriate capital market.

Small enterprises pay higher premiums for bank finance either due to lack of credit rating (credit worthiness) or where collateral problems in arranging or imperfect mechanism to evaluate risks. It is generally agreed that borrowers net worth measured by current assets and potential future earnings is positively correlated with economic development, while premiums attached to finance are negatively correlated to an enterprise's net worth. As a consequence the problems of financing SMEs ought to decrease overtime with economic development.

# 7

# Enhancing Competitiveness: Role of Technology

The opening up of the world economy in the process of globalisation and the vanishing geographical boundaries with rapid and extensive use of information technology have thrown up challenges for the small producers and manufacturers who have to not only survive competition but also to create a place for themselves in the global commodity chain, which the new global manufacturing methods have come to increasingly characterise. This implies technological upgradation on a continuous basis to keep pace with the rapidly changing technological scenario in the world. And this is true of the entire spectrum of small scale sector across the board. Technological upgradation is an essential ingredient of survival in the WTO environment. There is a pouring awareness that technology provides the cutting edge of success in the world striving to improve the quality of life through better product and services while protecting environment. Productivity is the function of technology in use. Are small enterprises ready to upgrade the level of technology in use? What are the constraints? What needs to be done to prepare a better ground for improvement of technology? This chapter examines the above issues.

## 7.1 Factors Affecting Technology Upgradation

The present day world is witnessing, on the one hand, a rapid introduction of new technology based industries (hi-tech) by a new breed of technocrat entrepreneurs, on the other hand, the recent trend towards liberalisation of industrial policy, opening up of the economy to global competition, more towards privatisation, dereservation of products (161 products since 1997) of small scale sector are a few indicators which clearly demonstrate that the Indian SSI policy environment to a more open and competitive culture and all awareness in this regard are open for consideration. What comes in the way of technology upgradation need to be considered. Many feel the mind set of large number of enterprises is not in favour of technology upgradation partly because of lack of knowledge skill and awareness and partly because of the financial constraints.

Some feel that it is also due to the existence of a ready market for all types of inferior goods by large segment of low income urban market. In fact, it is only the larger among the SSI units who have exposure to outside markets or who find their products in direct competition with large units in the domestic market, who think seriously about technology upgradation. Apart from psychological barriers, the lack of awareness and adequate information on the availability of the technology is also a major hurdle in this regard. Technology has direct impact not only on the productivity but also on the quality of life due to wage differential.

Though, even today, a productivity adjusted wage-labour differential of as much as eight times is found and a major chunk of the Indian small scale seems to have thrived on such differentials, the fact cannot be denied that the Indian small scale map is now dotted with the most modern units which cater to the really technologically high end of the market. While the need for technology upgradation in general cannot be denied, the facilities created by the Government over the last fifty years or so have ensured that even the most traditional units have some kind of technological innovation and upgradation. The issues are whether the SSI units are mentally, financially and physically (labour skill) ready for technology upgradation.

This is a daunting task before any National Government and the Government institutions by themselves have limited reach to cater to the requirements of more than 105 lakh small units in India. The Non-Governmental Organisations, including the industry associations, have to gradually take over the role of information providers on technology and also as the managers of change who hold the hands of the industry though the process of technology identification, its negotiation and implementation.

## 7.2 Present Scenario

Under the present circumstances, the facility for technology acquisition and skill upgradation can be looked at through two distinct sets of mechanisms, which are (a) the institutions created to meet the day to day technical requirements and skill upgradation of the industry; and (b) the institutions which take up application oriented research on behalf of the industry and who do not necessarily cater to the related skills development.

In other words, we may term the first category of mechanism as the industry service and related institutions while the other would fall in the category of R and D institutions. The first category need not necessarily involve spending money on technology, for the improved technology would largely result through improved process or better methods of production. The second set of mechanism would require a third set of institutions which would make finance available for upscaling of technology involved through the application oriented research institutions.

## 7.3 Industry Service and Related Institutions

The Small Industries Development Organisation (SIDO)

which was established in India in 1954, has played a pioneer role in the field of technological upgradation and skill development. It started the mission of entrepreneurship development, skills upgradation, technology upgradation and dissemination of technology and market related information amongst the small industry through a net work of Small Industries Service Institutes (SISIs), spread all over the country. These institutes acted as the friend, philosopher and guide for both new and existing entrepreneurs, teach them about the new technology and manufacturing practices, train them at workshops and also provide common facility services. It is through these institutions that the industries associations are encouraged to start training their members in the relevant fields of activity, be it technology or process or management. Now through the use of information technology, most of these institutions are helping the small scale in gathering information and also in marketing themselves.

Gradually the SIDO added Product and Process Development Centres (PPDCs) for specific commodity groups such as fragrances, glass, leather, sports goods, electrical goods, electronics etc., not only to carry out research in products and process development but also to impart training. Product specific training institutions were also set up. All these centres were subsequently complimented by setting up Tool Rooms for common facility and training as well as Testing Centres to complete the requirements of the industry.

The Product and Process Development Centres (PPDCs) have been extremely useful in as much as they have developed products and processes and handed them down to the industry at very nominal charges. They have direct interface with the industry associations which makes the job of dissemination of information in their areas of activity quite easy. The PPDCs are mainly the R & D centres.

The Tool Rooms have made the modernisation of the industries easy for they do not have to spend a big amount of money in setting up CNC machines or CAD-CAM stations. The Testing Centres have also helped improve quality indirectly.

At the level of the States, the concerned Directorates of Industries help small units through District Industries Centres. The Directorates work in close collaboration with Central organisations/ institutions meant for the purpose.

## 7.4 Action-oriented Research

The action oriented research is carried out through the laboratories under the Council for Scientific and Industrial Research, Indian Council for Agricultural Research and the Indian Council for Medical Research. All the laboratories affiliated to them carry out not only a lot of original research but also take up demand based research. These institutions generally provide "proof-of-concept", which must be upscaled and their techno-economic parameters established.

For the purposes of converting a pilot level technology to a full scale commercially viable technology, either there should be professional organisations which take up these activities and then market the technology on commercial basis or an industrial unit must invest its money in these activities, carry on pre-commercial trials and then launch the product commercially. For this purpose, there are various schemes in operation under different departments of the Government. These are mainly -

- Home Grown Technology of the Department of Science and Technology, under which the technologies available with laboratories are matched with the interests of industries willing to venture into development, design and commercialisation efforts. The scheme normally encourages the participation of NGOs in the programme and seems to be gradually picking up.

- Programme Aimed at Technological Self-Reliance (PATSER) operated by the Department of Scientific and Industrial Research, basically aims at promoting and supporting industry in developing indigenous technology and also absorbing the imported technologies. A partial financial support is provided to joint R & D and design and engineering projects undertaken by industry, R & D organisations and academic institutions.
- The National Research Development Corporation (NRDC) markets the technologies developed by various CSIR Laboratories. It also helps in technology identification, negotiations and patenting etc.

While the above illustrative list does not differentiate between the industrial units of various sizes, specific institutions have been set up to cater to the needs of small scale industries. The examples of such institutions are a number of technical consultancy organisations set up by the Industrial Development Bank of India and the Technology Bureau of Small Enterprises set up by the Small Industries Development Bank of India for providing information to the small units on latest technological developments world-wide and for assisting them in transfer of technology and providing finance syndication for the purpose.

## 7.5 Cluster Approach

An expert committee (1997) set up under the chairmanship of Dr. Abid Hussain, for suggesting measures to improve the Indian small scale sector had recommended a cluster-based developmental approach, which would enable technical support services at the industrial clusters. This approach has maximum demonstrative effect and upgradation of even one individual unit technologically has its impact on the whole cluster down the line and other do not feel shy in adopting new technologies as they have already been commercially proven. The Product-cum-Process Development Centres have been basically aimed at such an approach and have proved to be quite useful.

To quote one example, the Fragrance and Flavour Development Centre (FFDC) located in the cluster for fragrances and flavours at Kannauj has developed and commercialised at least 10 processes of essential oil and raisin extraction and 8 different fragrances. It has also developed a process to recover raisinoids out of sandalwood waste. This last process is particularly remarkable, for the waste which could not be sold even at Rs. 3000/- per ton is today yielding a return of Rs. 15,000/- per ton. Thanks to the work done by this Centre in the field of technology, India today ranks first in the world in so far as products of Mint is concerned, leaving China far behind. Similarly, the PPDC for Sports Goods at Meerut has for the first time designed and developed machinery for making cricket balls, enabling the smallest of the units to manufacture world class cricket balls.

The demonstrative effect of such efforts have been quite remarkable, encouraging even new entrepreneurs to enter the activity of production of various items.

## 7.6 UPTECH

Keeping this in view the SIDO started a specific technology upgradation scheme called UPTECH in select industrial clusters. The notable clusters in which this programme has been undertaken are the foundry and forging cluster at Ludhiana, the Tile industry cluster along the west coast of India, particularly Kerala, the Pharmaceutical cluster in the state of Andhra Pradesh, the Auto-component cluster in Pune, Indore and Chennai, etc. Programmes were also undertaken to exploit the bio-pharmacological, herbicidal and pesticidal properties of the neem tree.

Under the scheme, a team of experts works in select cluster for a long period of time during which they study the processes and help improve them in different units. They also identify the technology which is a distinct improvement over the existing technology. Such identified technology requiring changes or replacement in plant and machinery is demonstrated in the premises of a volunteering unit on the advice of the concerned industry association. The participating unit or the association also shares 50% of the cost of such improvement or replacement of plant and machinery, the rest being met by way of the Government grant.

Spectacular success has been observed in the clusters where this scheme has been in implementation. It has been found that the industry does not lack courage if motivated properly by the team of experts and once it has faith in the expert team, it is willing to risk its money, material and resources. The role of the industry associations in this process has also been positive.

All this underscores the fact that with the right kind of motivation, even if the level of grant is not fully borne by the Government, industry will react to positive change with the help of these associations. Hence empowering the associations is a absolute must.

## 7.7 Lessons Learnt

The industry service institutions have done their job well so far but they would be required to expand their activities.

They will have to not only increase their area of coverage but also always be on a look out for newer technologies and techniques of production and inform the industry about it in time. In the process, they have to continuously upgrade themselves. it is a well recognised fact that increasing the activities of these institutions will require additional resource allocation by the Government which would also imply additional increasing recurring costs. With increasing demand on Government resources from various quarters, it is worthwhile to examine the possibility of making one time expenditure on such facilities, which may be looked after by the industry associations or other NGOs formed for this purpose.

In so far as the action oriented research, its commercial viability and tie up between the academia, the laboratories and the industry is concerned, the relationship apparently seems fairly straightforward. In reality, however, this relationship is non-linear. The approach for each category of institutions varies with their priorities lying in different places. Research is carried out without any a-priori identification of technology needs and hence is a waste.

The other shortcoming of action oriented research has been found to be lack of resources for upscaling and commercialising the technology. The costs for the industry have been found to be prohibitive, for these are also fraught with the risk of ultimately failing and not becoming commercially viable. The risk taking ability definitely increases manifold if it can be taken up as a joint activity by an industry association or an NGO comprising of the members from the industry.

Having recognised the importance of a close linkage between the academia and R & D institutions and the industry, the Department of Science and Technology had started a scheme of establishing Science and Technology Entrepreneurship Parks (STEPS). These parks also aim at promoting entrepreneurship among science and technology experts and to provide R & D support to small units through interaction with research institutions. The twelve STEPS established so far succeeded in promoting nearly 400 enterprises and helped development and commercialisation of more than 200 products and processes. Unfortunately, since no emphasis seems to have been placed on addressing the needs of the industry as a group, their growth slowed down considerably.

On the other hand, while the skill upgradation process thrived in the hands of the industry associations, helped by the service institutes, they did not mature fast enough to take up technology upgradation activities as a collective body. The SIDO has helped the industry associations in setting up their own testing centres. These are to work as self-sustaining bodies. But the fear of the unknown has arrested their growth. The scenario, however, will hopefully change in the future.

Technological upgradation is a function of demand. But it can also be done through demonstration of appropriate technology which is evident from the success of PPDCs. The industry associations at the cluster level can be a very effective tool to encourage the industry at large to adopt modernisation.

The NGOs and industry associations do not seem to be mentally prepared to take up technology upgradation on a large scale. Most of the industry typically favours an established technology which can be bought off the shelf within the limited financial resources available. The sector is also willing to go for process improvement which need not entail a substantial expenditure and the approach of the collectivity, which is the association, is not much different from its individual constituents. The scenario, however, may change given the forces of globalisation.

For skills development, the NGOs have been adequately strengthened in India. Such strengths have normally come through training of entrepreneurs and workers in Government sponsored programmes. Hence, it is not necessarily the Government grant which has enabled them in acquiring these capabilities but basically a small amount of money and an opportunity to perform, which spurred them into activity and become strong.

The realisation for the need for technology upgradation is likely to create substantial demand from the small industries, which may encourage NGOs and associations to take up this job. A demand-driven project is more likely to succeed than a supply-driven operation. Under such circumstances, a one time grant for setting up the requisite mechanism would be sufficient, for which a national fund may be set up.

Interactive technology transfer and upgradation is predicated by the fact that there is national resource base where the technology databank is a valuable and it can be sourced properly for use by the industry. If such national level databases are available in various countries, they can be publicised internationally using the World Wide Web. In that eventuality, technology transfer need not be circumscribed by the need for physical movement of individuals from one country to another, merely looking for availability of technology. World Assembly of Small Enterprises (WASME) should be aiming at such a situation wherein there is free flow of information using internet between technology producers and technology seekers, without the hindrance of geographical boundaries.

## 7.8 Subsidy Scheme for Technology Upgradation

The policy package announced by the Government on 30th August 2000 included a scheme for technology upgradation of SSI aimed at enhancing the productive efficiency and competitiveness of the SSI sector. The scheme is called the "Credit Linked Capital Subsidy Scheme for Technology Upgradation of the Small Scale Industries". The scheme to be implemented from October 2000, will provide 12 per cent back ended capital subsidy on projects of technology upgradation by the SSI units in the specified products/sub-sector such as leather, leather products including footwear and garments, food processing, information technology (hardware), drugs and pharmaceuticals, auto-parts and components, toys, glass and ceramics, tyres, handtools, bicycle parts, foundries etc. The list of eligible subsectors has been raised to 30 from 14.

The scheme covers existing as well as new units registered with the State Directorate of Industries. The scheme will be implemented through SIDBI. The scheme offers an opportunity to the small enterprises to modernise and realise the level of productivity and efficiency.

## 7.9 Technology Upgradation under WTO Environment

In the rapidly changing scenario today, technology is the key for industrial growth. The experience of developed economies of USA, Europe and Japan has conclusively proved that the technology plays a vital role with the objective of bringing about rapid economic and social developments. It is technology alone that adds to the national output level, increases GDP and per capita income and raises the standards of living of people and ultimately the nation's stature in international community. The contribution of technology to GDP in the USA is estimated to be of the order of 10 per cent. The SSEs continue to have obstacles for upgrading the technology and modernising their industries. A vast majority of the units continue to use obsolete production processes and outdated technologies. This underlies the fact that our country can grow faster if technology is resorted to by our small industries and small enterprises.

The technology scenario which has been analysed in the earlier paragraphs indicate the opportunities for SSIs to upgrade their technology to remain competitive. The necessity for technology upgradation becomes more pronounced in view of the implementation of WTO regime.

In the WTO regime, domestic markets will be subjected to increased threats because of lowering of tariffs leading to freer entry of foreign goods and because of foreign companies establishing manufacturing bases locally. The developing countries will have greater opportunities in the sectors where they have cost based competitive advantages e.g. textiles, agriculture etc. It can be noted that the Government of India's Textile Modernisation Fund will help the SSIs in this sector to upgrade their technology. As the world markets get opened up under the WTO regime, SSIs need to upgrade their technology to avail this opportunity to increase their share. The vulnerability of SSEs in the WTO regime could be summarised as follows:

- Loss of protected environment;
- Greater competition from imports;
- Reduction in conventional subsidy, many subsidies are contestable;
- Technology gap;
- Quality and standards gap, and
- Environmental regulations.

This underscores the importance of technology upgradation by SSEs and hence urgent steps are required to facilitate them to adopt new and emerging technologies to remain competitive in the world market. It is high time that some change in investment ceiling of SSIs is also considered so that they get an opportunity to upgrade technology. Already a beginning has been made by raising the investment the ceiling to Rs. 5 crore in plant and machinery in some selected sectors.

# 8

# Strategy for Cluster Development in India: The Italian Experience

Italy is called the Japan of Europe. The most striking feature of modern Italy is its astonishing economic success in the past four to five decades. Even though Italy at the end of World War II (1945) had earned the dubious distinction of being the "sickman of Europe" and was one of the poorest countries in the West, a remarkable turn around was brought about by 1970s. During the 25 year period from 1945 to 1970 Italy's GNP increased by 568 per cent and the per capita income increased by 46.4 per cent. By the end of the 1980s, Italy's economy had registered the fastest growth rate among all the countries in Europe. According to a survey by "The Economist" (in its issue dated 26.5.90), "Italy is now the fifth-biggest economy in the world. Its people are richer than the British. It is by no means fanciful to imagine Italy in due time overtaking West Germany and Scandinavian countries in living standards."

After all the Italian scenario in the late 1940s, i.e. before the advent of the economic boom was bleak and characterised by:

- very few internal resources;
- less than a quarter of the land suitable for farming;
- suffered more from war than any other country;
- widespread destitution;
- high rates of illiteracy and infant mortality;
- 50 per cent of population employed in agriculture and
- High level of inflation.

What happened in Italy was that a peasant based

society/economy, got transformed into urban/industrial economy which in some respects is now perhaps next only to Japan. The level of 50 per cent of its population engaged in agriculture has declined to less than 20 per cent. Italy's industrial production shot up by 20 per cent in the 1950s and 1960s. The inflation rate was brought down from 20 per cent in the late 1940s to 5 per cent by the end of 1970s.

How did this Italian miracle (il Sourpuss) come about?

Economists are in general agreement that the chief factors which have contributed to Italy's post-war economic prosperity are

1. Low and stable labour cost which have resulted in Italian goods being highly competitive in the world market.
2. Profits were high and reinvested; creating employment and accumulation of capital stock.
3. Entry of the Italy into the European Economic Community (EEC) resulted in exposure to European competition in the domestic market. So Italian manufacturers and industries had to modernise and innovate. Consequent to their entry into the EEC, trade barriers were removed, free market competition ensured and consequently Italian producers/industries stepped in to exploit a wider market and goods were exported in large quantities.
4. Energy and imagination of entrepreneurs.
5. Government's ability/courage to break with strong protectionism and take plunge into free trade and open competition.
6. The impressive performance of small and medium sized companies in bringing about Italy's economic growth.

The Italian industrial scene is characterised by a few very large family business giants (viz. Agnellis of Fiat, De Benedettis of Olivetti, Zanussi etc.) and a large number of small enterprises. It is worthwhile mentioning here that 80 per cent of Italy's industries employ fewer than 100 workers.

In the 1980s, Italy witnessed the ascendancy of the private sector. The large firms undertook drastic reforms and attracted a large infusion of foreign capital and became stronger than ever. Small and medium enterprises grew more numerous and highly productive. The private sector in Italy has become more independent from the government and has thus become more dynamic. The strong performance of the private sector in Italy is partly due to the remarkable strength of its export sector. This in turn has been facilitated by the following exceptional ability of Italian business:

- To serve changing consumer demands.
- To produce attractive goods of reasonable prices; and
- To shift into new markets and alternative products.

The government only very rarely helps exporters. Similarly, it never hinders them, even when sensitive matters are involved. For example, even during the height of the cold war, Italian business was busy exporting to Eastern Europe and China.

Another important development in the Italian economy has been the strategic shift from manufacturing traditional items like food products, textiles etc. into new lines of products like clothing (fashion wear, leisure garments etc.), electronics, household appliances, furniture, machine tools, robots, agricultural machinery, jewellery and precision metals and leather products (like shoes, bags etc.).

The rise of the small scale sector in the Italian economy is major contributory factor to its spectacular growth. Set up originally to escape trade union regulations, standard minimum wage requirements and social benefits, small scale enterprises now form the mainstay of the Italian economy. Small enterprises employing less than 15 workers were until recently outside the purview of government regulations regarding the payment of minimum wages, workers' right to form unions, etc. These small scale units, which constitute a new layer of the Italian economy, operate at great cost efficiency and are characterised by high productivity.

Italy is a country of private thrift and public profligacy and Italians have little faith in the State's ability to provide public services successfully. Italians save about 22 per cent of their disposable incomes, one of the highest proportions in the world.

The Government of Italy runs what is proportionately one of the biggest budget deficits in the world some 11 per cent of GDP. In Italy, tax evasion is a way of life. In 1984, one study reckoned that 45 per cent of Italy's total value added tax went uncollected. As per the Italian Government's statistical office estimate for 1987, the size of the 'economia sommersa', the submerged economy, added to 18 per cent of GDP. The then Finance Minister, Mr. Rino Formica, reckons that a quarter of income tax and a third of VAT still go uncollected.

Another socio-cultural aspect of the Italian way of life is the fact that the family is the enduring unit of Italian society. It explains the pattern of business. From the Agnellis down, Italians like to keep control of their affairs within the family. They are therefore reluctant to put their companies on the stock market and risk losing control. Partly because of this, the stock market is paper thin; only 200 or so companies are listed on the Milan Stock Exchange and just 4 groups (Fiat-Agnelli, IRI, Mantedison-Ferruzzi and Assicurazioni Generali) account for two-thirds of total capitalisation. IRI apart, the others like many smaller companies remain in family control despite a public listing. One advantage is the lack of dividend payments that have to be paid to the shareholders and the resulting larger volume of profit which can be reinvested in the firm itself.

Some economists argue that one of the costs of Italy's preference for small family-controlled businesses is that foreigners have been kept out, denying Italy foreign know-how and access to markets. Another criticism is about Italian industry's excessive dependence on low-tech products. Textiles, clothes and shoes accounted for 18 per cent of exports in 1990. However, despite competition from such countries as Taiwan, Brazil and Hong Kong where labour costs are cheaper, Italy still maintains its market share in the world market; thanks to its superiority in design and quality.

Italy's middle-sized and small-sized firms are extremely successful, especially in doing business in the Third World and Eastern Europe. Firms tend to be small in Italy not just because the family wants control; owners have also wanted to keep the work force below 15 in order to escape job-protection laws (though the Government since May 1990 has ended this exemption for small firms) and perhaps also to avoid taxation. Such entrepreneurs are highly nimble; they can meet orders almost instantly, carry out short production runs and quickly tailor products to current fashions or market conditions.

Northern Italy is now flooded with small companies. Sometimes they cluster together - makers of silk in Como, cloth in Prato, ceramic tiles in Sassuolo, shoes in Verona and so on - in order to pool resources for certain purposes like marketing. They are highly automated, often with Italian machine-tools, invest heavily and frequently from their cash flows and borrow very modestly. Often too they sub-contract. Benetton, with shops all over the world, employs fewer than 2,000 workers and puts out four-fifths of its business to a network of small firms.

So Italy's economic boom has been brought about by its

small firm sector with its characteristic clusters. Italy's firms are grouped in self-reinforcing clusters and within that clustering lies the secret of industrial advantage. These are clusters of hundreds of firms in the same geographic location. Two small regions, Valenza Political and Arezzo for example, account for a $2 billion surplus in precious metal jewellery and nearly half of total world jewellery exports. It is the same story with ceramic tiles in Sassuola, furniture in Brionza, knitwear in Carpi and Modena, packaging machinery in Bologna and so on. These are all world class industries but built around hundreds, sometimes thousands of small firms competing with each other but located within the boundaries of the same community.

The resulting intense competition is one reason for their success, giving the impetus for continual upgrading of production processes and the final product. But the very size of the combined turnover of the firms allows industry to gain a local critical mass, creating the very pool of skilled labour and techniques that the state system fails to do. And that critical mass creates a virtuous circle of skills, product, new ideas, specialised support networks, research and development, export success, knowledge of markets and so on.

Italy's highly developed system of local and regional government reinforces this geographic concentration. For instance regional governments license firms to trade on local industrial estates thus adding to the cluster - a ceramic firm for Sassuolo, a knitwear firm for Carpi etc. Local technical colleges are briefed to teach a curriculum that will meet with the needs of local industry. The Central Government has little to do with the Italian industrial success - this is largely a private affair supported by associations of entrepreneurs, organised around families and enabled and encouraged by the network of old city states, dukedoms and principalities upon which the modern Italian state sits.

The significant characteristics of Italian industry are (a) the predominance of small firms, which are mostly family affairs; (b) high productivity growth; (c) constant and continuous upgradation of technology and innovation in design and production techniques; (d) uncanny ability to keep ahead of the market and its adaptability and flexibility to changing demand and (e) ability to cut cost through fragmentation of production.

## 8.1 Growth of Small Enterprises: The Italian Experience

In the field of economic growth one of the greatest surprises of recent years is the astonishing economic success of Italy. The story of recent decades has been the miracle of industry particularly small enterprises. Until 1970, parts of Italy were like India drawing their main income from agriculture. The country had approximately the same form of mixed economy with large and to some extent inefficient public enterprises. Like India, it had and still has, the problem of regional disparities (between rich North and poor South). In fact a deep probe into the nature and structure of two economies would reveal several other similarities in the two countries. Some of these could be summed up as:

1. Late industrialisation;
2. High concentration of industries in some areas;
3. Very high rates of growth (around 9 to 10 per cent) in recent years;
4. Family domination of big business (Fiat in Italy; Tata and Birla, Modi groups in India);
5. Existence of very strong sub-governments at local levels e.g. Collectors at district level in India, and Prefects at provincial level in Italy;

6. Autonomy in implementation of programmes listed by states in India and by regions in Italy;
7. Famous for production of specialised items in the traditional sector e.g. carpets, textiles, sericulture, handicrafts items in India, shoes, clothing, glass items, furniture, etc. in Italy.

In order to consider the possibility of development of small enterprise in India on the Italian model, it is necessary to understand the basic features of the growth of small enterprises in Italy. Some of the salient features of the Italian model of growth of small enterprise in the North, particularly in the 3rd Italy (comprising Veneto, Emilia Romagna and Tuscany regions), are discussed in the following paragraphs:

**8.1.1 Industrial Districts and Regional Specialisation of Products:** One of the salient features of the growth of small enterprises in Northern Italy is the development of specialised products on a cluster basis. The specialisation has been so intense that some of the regions have become world leaders e.g. silk from Como, clothes from prato, ceramics in sassuolo, shoes in Verona, glass in Venice, engineering items in Padova, Bologna, etc. The remarkable performance of these districts in international markets has played a crucial role in Italy's emergence during the 1980s as the world's largest exporter of clothing and textiles, the second largest exporter of footwear (after Taiwan) and the third largest exporter of machine tools (after West Germany and Japan). Some advantages of industrial districts are:

- They allow the units to have economies of scale;
- Sub-contracting becomes easier;
- Development of specialised infrastructure is possible and
- Manufacturing becomes easier.

**8.1.2 Fragmentation of Production and High Degree**

**of Inter-firm Co-operation:** Most of the small units are specialised in a single phase of production and the firm responsible for marketing the final product is engaged only in assembly and planning. Sometimes the production is sub-contracted by a designer and marketing company with little capacity of its own. This inter-firm co-operation in these districts is also associated with a distinctive style of technological innovation in which firms specialising in complementary activity collaborate in developing novel solutions to common problems. This method of fragmentation also helps in reducing costs.

**8.1.3 Strong Emphasis on Design and Quality:** This is achieved through constant research undertaken by the small units at their own level, keeping in mind market preferences not only at the present time but also in the future.

**8.1.4 Use of Advanced Technology:** Most of the firms use advanced technology even if they are only engaged in one phase of production. Such firms are highly flexible and no less efficient than those employed by large companies. Key examples are the widespread use of CNC machines tools in metal working shops, micro processing controlled sensors in ceramic kilns, computer aided design, robots etc. Industrial districts and fragmented production help small firms to develop capacity to develop new products, devise new machines, increase production and productivity, cut costs, develop new design and go for strict quality control.

**8.1.5 Family Business and Self-finance:** Another striking feature is that most of the units have been set up at a place engaging in different phases of production of the product by members of the same family. The family is the basic unit of Italian society. Italians like to keep control of their affairs within the family. They are reluctant to put their company on the stock market or to obtain large bank finance and risk losing control. In several cases it has been found that the unit starts working with very low capital and then goes on reinvesting the same and multiplying the units in the name of different members of the family.

**8.1.6 Role of Banks:** Although many entrepreneurs prefer to keep away from bank finance and use only family income to start the business, there are banks, particularly one separately created for artisans, which provide both working and fixed capital and also provide machinery and equipment at a lower rate of interest. Recently banks have started new functions such as leasing or export assistance, factoring services and financing venture capital requirements.

**8.1.7 From Blue Collar Jobs to Entrepreneurship:** A distinctive feature of small enterprise in Italy is that they are set up mostly by persons who have earlier work experience and had worked in another small unit. They bring with them technical skills, know-how and knowledge of products and market. This has helped the units to be managed efficiently.

**8.1.8 Role of Consortia and Associations:** One of the major factors which has contributed to the rapid development of these enterprises is the role of consortia and associations. Consortia are formed by the clubbing together of 20 or 25 firms to obtain common benefits often in a single aspect of business. It could be procurement of raw materials or the arrangement of finance or marketing. This is done with the purpose of generating economies of scale. This saves both time and energy for individual units.

A major role is played by associations of small entrepreneurs set up at regional level such as CNA (Confederasione Nazionale Dell' Artigianato) and Confin-dustria.

The CNA handles the general accounting of "artisan shops" and small units by preparing their pay roll and helping employees to file tax returns. Apart from personalised services, they provide many general services such as:

- development of industrial parks in association with local authorities and arranging sites for manufacturing;
- organisation of technical and management courses;
- representation of member firms at trade fair and exhibitions and providing market information;
- assistance in forming co-operatives and consortia;
- assistance with computers for all applications, providing technical and consultancy services;
- negotiation of labour contracts with trade unions;
- identifying financial resources;
- data bank and
- a forum for political lobbying.

Confindustria serve 20-25 units and confine themselves to one or two activities.

**8.1.9 Role of Government:** Instead of providing direct assistance to the units in the form of subsidy, cheap finance, machinery, sheds, product reservation, the government's role in Italy is largely one of non-intervention. They provide the basic infrastructure through Regional and Provincial governments. The developmental activities of regional and local governments include assistance in business expansion and setting up new enterprises to generate employment, technology transfers services, information, export market grants and low cost loans for introducing new technology, infrastructure investment, training of workers, industrial parks, research on pollution control etc.

To sum up, the factors which have contributed to rapid growth are:

- Support from Associations, Consortia and Regional Government,

- Sufficient skill base and Innovative Character,
- Strong family orientation,
- Sufficient flexibility and
- Sub-contracting system of production.

## 8.2 Lessons for India

Can India draw lessons from the Italian model?

It is a matter of debate; for most people feel that in spite of some similarities in the two economies, there are many differences. Some of the major differences are:

1. Vast difference in the level of per capita income. India's per capita income is not more than 5 per cent of Italy.
2. The major problem in India is that of poverty and about 30 per cent of the people are still living below the poverty line. They do not have food to eat hence the question of raising self-finance or being skilled does not arise.
3. Some small enterprises in Italy are much bigger than some large units in India. Such enterprises are highly capital intensive and, in the case of one motorbike unit, the investment per unit of employment would work out to Rs. 10 crore, whereas in India the definition of small scale industry means investment of plant and machinery is not exceeding Rs. 35 lakh. It is possible for any unit to use modern machinery and advanced computer system within an investment of 35 lakh? Most of the units in India are basically 'tiny' where investments are below Rs. 2 lakh.
4. India suffers from the problem of over population and a large labour force which is mainly unskilled, whereas with Italy there is now a scarcity of labour.
5. The level of infrastructure development in Italy is very high.

In spite of these differences there are many areas where India can draw some lessons. These are:

Role of Government of India is mainly regulatory and interventionist. A more viable policy with fewer restrictions might induce small units to prosper and multiply and thus the ultimate objective of generation of additional employment opportunity would be achieved. It should be based on a formula of public/private co-operation.

In India even now there are places which are famous for specialised products such as carpets, sericulture, coir, leather etc. This idea can be given a shape and Government should provide specialised infrastructure to suit the product line.

Fragmentation of production within the small units will help the units to multiply and generate more employment but the greatest advantage is that it will help the units to use modern technology even by operating within the prescribed ceiling of investment. Instead of only one unit doing all jobs within Rs. 35 lakh, if 100 units distribute the work among themselves they can have total investment of Rs. 3500 lakh, which is definitely substantial.

Government should promote reinvestment by existing small units and reduce the tax rates etc. to help the units to generate adequate internal capital.

Emphasis on viability can be achieved by modernising traditional industries so that the unemployment is reduced. Hence, a meaningful programme of economic development should not aim merely at the generation of additional employment opportunities but also increasing the level of income. For a wage earner, his wages should be high enough to raise him above the poverty line. Similarly, in the case of self-employed persons, his income must be adequate to meet the day to day needs of the family and also enable him to reinvest.

Organisations like CNA and confedustria could be developed. The existing Associations in India could be allowed to play more active roles.

The experience in tackling rural unemployment through wage employment as National Rural Employment Programme (NREP), Rural Labour Employment Guarantee Programme (RLEGP) or now merged under Jawahar Rozgar Yojana the asset creating Programme of Integrated Rural Development (IRDP) has not been encouraging. In spite of these programmes about 30 per cent of people are still below the poverty line. The programmes themselves suffer from several problems.

It is necessary that rural industries and traditional industries like sericulture, coir, handlooms and handicrafts are modernised in such a way that their production, productivity and marketability increases and consequently the wages of the workers and profit margin of entrepreneurs increase.

The Italian experience has revealed that it is possible to modernise the traditional industries provided they are assisted and promoted on the basis of:

- Industrial districts;
- Fragmentation and sub-contracting of production;
- Adequate emphasis to design and quality;
- Cheap loans available for technological improvements;
- Consortia and co-operatives formed to take care of administrative, accounting, marketing, training and other needs.

Italian model may not be the best, but it is more appropriate to be followed in Indian condition because of large number of similarities in the two economies. There are distinct advantages in paying attention to those centres which have potential rather than spreading the resources thinly. Clusters must form the future strategy of SSI development in India.

## 8.3 Strategy for Cluster Development Initiative in India

Cluster development as a strategy of economic development is a new concept in India. Abid Hussain Committee Report on Small and Medium Enterprises in India (1997) was the first official document strongly reco-mmending cluster as focus of small enterprise development. The phenomenon of a large number of small scale industrial units manufacturing the same (or similar products) existing or historically developing in close proximity to each other (in "Clusters") has been observed in different periods and diverse industrial environments. Clustering as an engine of growth was noticed internationally in the well-networked Clusters (usually referred to as 'Industrial Districts') in developed countries, especially in Italy. This realisation has led to increased interest and research in clustering as well as attempts to replicate the process through planned interventions in the developing countries including India. Much of the research and interventions have been done by the UNIDO, on the international level and particularly in India with the Ministry of Small Scale Industries as the counterpart agency and partner at the national level.

According to UNIDO, a "Cluster" can be defined as a sectoral and geographical concentration of enterprises, in particular small scale enterprises, faced with common opportunities and threats which can

- give rise to external economies (i.e., specialised suppliers of raw materials, components and machinery, sector specific skills etc.)
- favour the emergence of specialised technical, admini-strative and financial services, and

- create a conducive ground for the development of inter-firm co-operation and specialisation as well co-operation among public and private local institutions to promote local production, innovation and collective learning.

A Cluster is generally identified by the product (or product range) and the place where it is located. A complete industry or a sector (like the leather sector) cannot be referred to as a Cluster.

International experiences show that small firms are unable to face competitive pressures because of their isolation and in-effective linkages with relevant support organisations and commercial service providers. In countries like Italy, USA and Germany, clusters of SMEs bound together in strong and dynamic networks and relying upon strong linkages with relevant local/national support institutions have proved competitive in the global context. Clusters could be in existence based on locational or historical factors or it could be induced i.e., created by deliberate programme as IT sector in Bangalore, Hyderabad, Gurgaon and NOIDA.

Examples of historical clusters in India are: ceramic pottery cluster at Khurja, leather and leather garment cluster at Chennai, hosiery cluster at Kolkata, brass at Moradabad, woollen hosiery at Ludhiana, knitwear at Tirupur, glass at Ferozabad etc.

The first noteworthy attempt to prepare a data base of industrial clusters in India was undertaken by UNIDO in 1998 when it came out with a compendium of 138 clusters. The same has been revised to 388 in December 2003. Another major step was the data revealed by the Third Census of SSI which became available in February 2004. It found existence of over 1200 clusters whereas UNIDO Report places the number of units at 4,90,000. First systematic cluster development programme was undertaken by the State Bank of India in 1989 followed by SIDBI in 1991. Current players include office of DC(SSI), NABARD, some State governments, KVIC, NSIC, Textile Committee etc. However, all these initiatives are piece meal and there is lack of co-ordination, often resulting into duplication. To initiate a holistic plan for cluster development, the first requirement is to undertake a diagnostic study, identify gaps, involve all needed players including the banks and training institutions, provide for common facilities and services including those relating to environment and develop a brand name to market the products. Technology upgradation, skill development and infrastructural developments are pre-requisites. Major initiatives are needed from the State Governments and large industries in the development of ancillaries and voluntary organisations to provide necessary linkages. Appropriate credit plans need to be prepared by the banks.

Clusters have the advantage of economies of scale and are capable of improving the quality and cost to suit global needs. The presently adopted approach for cluster development consists of drawing lessons from the experiences of successful clusters and then replicating them through building up of local capabilities with the active participation of various Cluster Actors such as small scale industrial units, industry associations, business Development service providers, policy makers etc. The process of cluster development usually consists of the following steps:

1. Selection of the cluster
2. Selection of a cluster development agent
3. Diagnostic study
4. Preparation of action plan for intervention
5. Approval of the project and release of funds through

leveraging

6. Implementation of trust building between cluster actors and cluster development agent, and also among cluster actors
7. Monitoring and evaluation
8. Self-management phase.

Before launching any development initiative, it is essential to undertake elaborate planning through detailed study of ground level situations and their systematic analysis. There cannot be a uniform criteria for all the clusters. Each cluster has to be viewed as an independent exercise as the critical gaps would not be the same in all the clusters. Similarly, their break even point, viability, replicability, dissemination potential, the scope for creating synergy between clusters etc. would also vary. Whatever be the difference in approach, one thing is now certain that instead of spending the scarce resources on isolated units located in different parts of the country, it is essential that resources are utilised to develop the clusters where there exists scope for maximum output with minimum investment.

# 9

# Export Potential of Small Enterprises in India

The role model prescribed for the Indian Small Scale Industries is as an engine of growth in the new millennium provided it accepts 'competitiveness' as the 'mantra' for ITS future growth. In the struggle for existence it is always the survival of the fittest. The SE sector has the potential to emerge as an engine to take the economy to the desired destinations of globalisation, employment generation, equi-distribution of income, acquiring competitive edge and high rate of economic growth. India's existing share in world trade of not more than 0.7 per cent is a matter of grave concern as this is not adequate to make the country as a major player in the economic affairs of the world. The situation becomes all the more alarming when we compare it with the position in early 50s when India's share in the world trade stood at 1.5 per cent. Another disturbing feature is that our share at 0.6 to 0.8 per cent has been stagnating at this level for more than two decades now.

Since 1971-72, the small scale industrial sector has grown at an impressive rate and its share in the national exports increased from 9.6 per cent in 1971-72 to 26.5 per cent in 1981-82 and further to 31.5 per cent in 1991-92. At present the SSI's share in national exports is about 35 per cent. Despite SSI sector's valuable contribution, stagnancy of our share in world trade at low level shows that in the absence of substantially positive contribution from the SSI Sector our share might have declined further to a figure of 0.3 per cent or 0.4 per cent of world trade. What affects our

International Competitiveness? Are we ready to improve the quality of our exports to find a place in the world market? This chapter goes deeper into the structure of our exports and the scope of improvement both in terms of quality and competitiveness.

## 9.1 International Competitiveness

The issue of international competitiveness has been analysed beautifully by Kumar, Sen and Vaidya in their article "India's Export Competitiveness and Finance" published in India Development Report 1999-2000 which is reproduced as under:

"International competitiveness generally refers to be ability of a country to expand its share in world markets. At a fundamental level, competitiveness of a country in a particular commodity depends on the price at which it delivers the commodity in a foreign market in comparison with the price offered by competing countries for that commodity in the same market. The evolution of overall competitiveness of a country over time is influenced by both macro-economic and micro-economic factors. The most important macroeconomic variable influencing export competitiveness is the real exchange rate. A 'wrong' exchange rate impedes the country from competing successfully in international markets and can lead to balance of payment problems. Moreover, there is evidence to suggest that countries that have been more successful in achieving high export led growth owe much of their success to having been able to maintain the real exchange rate at an 'appropriate' level.

... At micro level, the factor generally considered the most important in influencing competitiveness in different industries/commodities is the evolution of total factor productivity in comparison with trading partners and competing countries. Maintaining a growth rate in productivity that can match, if not out-perform, productivity growth in competing countries is essential in order to retain/increase one's share in world markets."

Export promotion has been one of the principal goals of the on-going economic reforms in the country. Several policy oriented changes have been made in the EXIM policy for meeting the diverse and changing requirements of our exporters. It has been revealed that owing to some specific changes in the demand of products at the global level and structural rigidities at supply level, it has not been possible for us to record a sustained growth in our exports in recent years. India's exports after registering a phenomenal rate of growth during the period from 1993-94 to 1995-96 failed to make any worth-while progress during the next six years. The performance was particularly disappointing in 1998-99 when it recorded a negative rate of growth. The competitiveness of Indian exports has lagged behind due to a variety of reasons. It has made a modest recovery during the last 2 to 3 years.

If India wants to become a dominant economic global player in the current century, it will have to pay special attention to acquiring competitive edges in all the sectors especially in the small scale industrial sector since this sector has vast potential and can emerge as an engine of economic growth in the country. It is crucial that this sector adopts competitiveness as 'mantra', not only for surviving but also to justify the leadership role. It is essential because despite possessing great potential this sector suffers from several handicaps due to its small capital and technological base.

## 9.2 Status of Small-scale Industries in India

The SSI sector has emerged as a dynamic and vibrant sector of the Indian economy in recent years. There are over 35 lakh small scale industrial units in the country. However, the Third Census of SSI has found the number of registered and unregistered small enterprises as high as 105 lakh in 2001-02. In 2003-04, this sector accounted for about 40 per cent of the gross value of the output in the manufacturing sector and about 34 per cent of the total exports of the country. It provided employment to over 250 lakh persons, which is second only to agriculture. A sustained growth in all these areas since mid-seventies is a remarkable feature of the SSI Sector performance during the last two decades. An idea of the overall growth of export from this sector since 1991-92 can be obtained from Table 9.1.

**9.2.1 Export Performance of SSI Sector:** The immense potential of the SSI sector in improving upon the country's share in the world trade and making it a dominant economic player in the next century can be assessed from its past performance as exporting sector of the economy. Exports from the SSI sector have been growing at an annual rate of over 20 per cent per annum at current prices in rupee terms since 1991-92. If one traces the growth of exports from the sector since 1971-72, one realises the great potential of this sector in boosting the over-all exports. The exports growth performance of this sector from 1951-52 is presented in Table 9.2.

In a span of three decades, i.e. 1974-75 to 2002-03, the total exports from the country increased by 100 times, while that from the SSI sector increased by 293 times. During the last 9 years while the total exports increased by 3.6 times, SSI exports increased by 3.4 times.

**Table 9.1: Exports by Small Scale Industries Sector: 1991-92 to 2002-03**

(Rs. crore)

| Year | All India | SSI Sector | Share of SSI in All India (in per cent) |
|---|---|---|---|
| 1991-92 | 44041 | 13883 | 31.5 |
| 1992-93 | 53688 | 17784 | 33.1 |
| 1993-94 | 69751 | 25307 | 36.4 |
| 1994-95 | 82674 | 29068 | 35.2 |
| 1995-96 | 106465 | 36470 | 34.3 |
| 1996-97 | 117524 | 39248 | 33.4 |
| 1997-98 | 126286 | 44442 | 35.2 |
| 1998-99 | 141604 | 48979 | 34.6 |
| 1999-00 | 159161 | 54200 | 34.0 |
| 2000-01 | 202510 | 69797 | 34.4 |
| 2001-02 | 207746 | 71244 | 34.3 |
| 2002-03 | 252790 | 86012 | 34.0 |

Source: Various publications of DCSSI including *Small Scale Industries in India – An Engine of Growth.*

**Table 9.2: Export Performance since 1973-74 to 2002-03**

(Rs. crore)

| Year | All India | SSI Sector | Share of SSI in All India (in per cent) |
|---|---|---|---|
| 1973-74 | 2523 | 393 | 15.58 |
| 1983-84 | 9771 | 2164 | 22.15 |
| 1993-94 | 69751 | 25307 | 36.40 |
| 2002-03 | 252790 | 86012 | 34.00 |

Source: Small Scale Industries in India – An Engine of Growth.

It shows that export growth of SSI sector though higher has not been able to maintain the over impressive growth trend after 1990-91. However, this does not belittle the role of SSIs as dominant export sector of the economy. The information provided in Table 9.2 is with respect to direct exports from the sector only. In fact it also contributes towards indirect exports which are estimated at around 10 per cent of the country's total exports. These take place through merchant exporters, trading houses and export houses. Sometimes these are also in the form of export orders from large units or the production of parts and components for use in finished exportable goods.

The unorganised sector of the Indian economy consisting of small scale industries, handicrafts, handlooms, power-looms, sericulture, coir etc., dominates the export scene of the country and accounts for about 60 per cent of the country's total exports. After small scale industries, handicrafts play very important role and make significant contribution to India's exports particularly through export of gems and jewellery and hand knitted carpets. Table 9.3 presents the export performance of various segments of Village and Small Industries Sector in 2001-02 and 2002-03.

**9.2.2 India's Export Performance:** Despite the significant contributions made by the unorganised sector, particularly the SSI sector, towards the total exports of the country one cannot miss the fact that India's share in world's exports is very low, at about 0.8 per cent. The total exports of the country has been hovering around $33 billion between 1995-98 and rose to $44.5 billion by the end of 2001-02; then it fell to $38 billion in 2002-03 and thereafter showed good improvement in 2003-04, but this could not cross $50 billion limit. This constitutes only an insignificant and small fraction if we compare the same with world's exports which was $3730 billion in 1993-94 and was expected to go up to $5500 billion by the end of 2000 A.D. India is now a member country of the World Trade Organisation (W.T.O.) and it has to undertake a series of measures to increase its exports significantly within the framework of rules of game allowed by it. Efforts will have to be made to double the volume of India's exports in the next five years if India wants to become a significant global player. The task becomes more difficult as the country has been losing grounds in the export of primary products and traditional items and also because of the fact that the large scale industrial sector's inability to enter into global market in a big way.

**Table 9.3: Export Performance of Village and Small Enterprises Sector: 2001-02 to 2002-03**

(Rs. crore)

| | 2001-02 | 2002-03* |
|---|---|---|
| SSI | 71244 | 81930 |
| Powerlooms | 6146 | 6883 |
| Khadi & Village Industries | 22 | 26 |
| Handlooms | 2065 | 2616 |
| Handicrafts | 9205 | 10934 |
| Sericulture | 2235 | 2200 |
| Coir | 320 | 375 |
| **TOTAL** | **91237** | **104964** |

*Projected

Source: *SIDBI's Annual Report, 2002-03.*

Competition is increasing day by day and the task is becoming more daunting because of the increasing manufacturing efficiencies of the developed and newly industrialised countries, greater emphasis on quality, higher investment on export promotion the world over and the emergence of fortified trade blocks. In such a scenario, it is but natural that our attention is drawn towards the SSI sector because of its past impressive performance and vast potential. However, before we analyse and assess the prospects of the SSI sector in this regard, it would be imperative to know the reasons for our failure in recording impressive exports growth rates.

The dismal performance is the result of a combination of factors. The economy faced deceleration in export growth for three years in succession up to 1998-99. Export growth slowed down from 5.6 per cent in US $ terms in 1996-97 to 2.1 per cent in 1997-98 and suffered a decline of 4 per cent in 1998-99.

East Asian crisis, global demand deceleration and decline in Domestic industrial production are some of the reasons for the same. As per the Economy Survey i.e. 1998-99, the following factors have been responsible for this state of affairs:

- A decline in the growth of world trade. Import growth of the advanced economies, which are India's major trading partners has decelerated sharply from 18.2 per cent in 1996 to 3.7 per cent in 1996 and further to 2.5 per cent in 1997.
- A reduction in export prices of major items of manufactured goods. World prices of manufactured goods which constitute three fourth of our total exports have declined cumulatively by 14 per cent in last three years.
- An appreciation of the rupee in real effective exchange rate terms in 1997 against currencies of major trading partners.
- The massive depreciation of the currencies of the East Asian economy. This has affected the price competitiveness of our exports in sectors such as man-made

yarns, finished leather, fabrics and processed minerals. Other items like textiles, automotive parts, chemicals, iron ore, machinery and electronic goods have also been affected.

- Domestic factors such as growing infrastructural constraints, high transaction costs, and restrictions on agricultural exports are some of the other important factors which have adversely affected the supply of exportable surplus.

The scene however, changed in 2000-01. The exports grew by 19.6 per cent in US dollar terms accelerating sharply from 9.5 per cent growth in the previous year. The recovery experienced in recent years has been summed up in the *Economic Survey, 2002-03* which is as under:-

"Export growth, despite some deceleration during August to October 2002, has been robust in 2002-03, growing (in dollar value) by 20.4 per cent in April-December 2002 as against a decline of 2.2 per cent in the corresponding previous period. Although the trend is in line with a world economic recovery, the buoyant performance assumes significance given the slower than expected recovery in global economy and trade. An anticipated rise in international commodity prices in 2002 and the recovery of the domestic manufacturing sector is likely to aid this upturn in exports in the current year".

## 9.3 WTO and India's Compulsions

India is a founder member of both GATT (1947) and the successor organisation, the W.T.O., which came into being on 1.1.1995. By virtue of membership of W.T.O., India automatically gets entitled to Most Favoured Nation Treatment from all W.T.O. members for its exports and for its participation in this increasingly rule based systems aimed towards ensuring more stability and predictability in the governance of international trade. At the same time this has put India within the framework of certain stiff conditionalities as indicated below:

- As a member of W.T.O. India has bound about 67 per cent of its tariff lines whereas prior to Uruguay round of GATT only 6 per cent of the tariff lines were bound. For non-agriculture goods, ceiling bindings of 40 per cent ad-valorem on finished goods and 25 per cent on intermediate goods have been undertaken. The phased reduction to this bound level is to be completed by March 2001.
- Quantitative Restrictions on imports for 1429 tariff lines had to be phased out due to improvement in BOP situation at the time when India lost its case with USA in 1998, an agreement has been reached with many countries (except USA) to phase out QRs over a period of 6 years beginning 1997. The EXIM Policy announced in March 2001 completed the process of removal of Ors on BOP ground by dismantling the remaining 715 items out of the 1429 tariff items. The WTO condition has put in place necessary mechanisms to provide a level playing field to domestic players vis-à-vis imports. These mechanisms include shifting of imports of certain products under the state trading category making imports subject to various domestic regulations on health and hygiene and environment and need for bio-security and sanitary and phyto-sanitary permit for imports of primary products of plant and animal origin. The policy has also established a monitoring mechanism to monitor imports of 300 sensitive items on a regular basis. The list includes 67 SSI sensitive items.
- Agreement on Trade Related Intellectual Property Rights

(TRIPS) establishes certain minimum standards relating to the availability, scope, use and enforcement of IPRS and extends the basic principles of non-discrimination and transparency to these spheres.

- Under Trade Related Investment Measures (TRIMS) India has already notified TRIMS maintained.

## 9.4 General Implications of WTO

It is a tribute to the human civilisation that sovereign nations have agreed to subordinate their freedom (to act) and have agreed to work within the framework of rules to promote global trade. The Uruguay Round of negotiations resulted into formation of WTO, a rule based system which is expected to lead to smooth and orderly international trade. In nutshell, the implications - both threats and opportunities, has been summarised in FISME and SIDBI Handbook (1998):

- The WTO and its Agreements are going to affect every economic activity may it be agriculture, trading, service or manufacturing.
- World markets are opening up due to lowering of tariffs and dismantling of other restrictions in developed and developing countries.
- Enlightened and awakened entrepreneurs have greater opportunities to benefit from the comparative advantages possessed by them.
- Domestic markets will be subject to increased threats because of lowering of tariffs leading to freer entity of foreign goods and because of foreign companies establishing manufacturing bases locally.
- Whereas the developing countries will have greater opportunities in the sectors in which they have cost based comparative advantages e.g. Textiles, Agriculture

etc., while the Developed countries will benefit by opening of service sector and tightening of Intellectual Property Regime.

- Exports Market will become tougher because of competition among developing countries with similar comparative advantages.
- There is a wave of standardisation blowing across the globe; products from developing countries are to face tougher quality standards in developed markets particularly in the areas where they have comparative cost advantage.
- Every company - whether serving domestic or international market, will have to undertake internal exercise to identify factors affecting its international competitiveness in terms of cost as well as quality. It will need to examine if it can stay competitive in the market if the product becomes freely importable and or tariffs are further lowered.
- The WTO regime will bring greater advantages for those countries which show wits and skills in the ongoing dialogue. The Governments that are in constant touch with their industries and affected groups will be able to determine with clarity how and what should be negotiated at multilateral negotiations to the best of their advantage.
- The International Trade is increasingly becoming knowledge based. The entrepreneurial abilities and qualities will come to fore in the new emerging environment.
- The concepts of liberalisation of international trade, deregulation and privatisation of internal economy, have now been strengthened and legalised under WTO. The choice of a direction other than that dictated by the new developments is fraught with dangerous consequences.

The countries that have understood this have moved swiftly forwards fine-tuning their domestic and international trade policies creating a winning environment for their businesses. Those who are still debating the issue or are in the stage of bewilderment will help neither themselves nor their businesses.

- It is essential for the SSI entrepreneurs to understand the rules and regulations of WTO since even a minor violation may adversely affect the export performance.

**9.5 Item-wise SSI Export Performance**

Today the Small Scale Sector produces a wide range of items, numbering over 7,500. The items which play dominant role in terms of exports are readymade garments, leather products, processed food and marine products, engineering goods, electrical and electronic goods, plastic goods, basic chemicals and pharmaceuticals etc. Broad itemwise export performance and the share of SSI in total exports is given in Table 9.4.

The share of SSI sector in export of certain items, is as high as 100 per cent. In 2002-03, the Sector accounted for 100 per cent of the country's exports of sports goods, Cashew Kernel and lac, 95 per cent of wool and woollen products, 90 per cent of readymade garments, 70 per cent of processed food and leather and leather products. The share of marine products, basic chemicals, pharmaceuticals and cosmetics has also increased in recent years. In the case of engineering goods its share was 32.81 per cent in 2002-03. An analysis of the performance of SSI exports reveals some disturbing features which must be given due consideration while formulating any policy for the growth in future. Some of the disturbing features of the performance are listed below:

**Table 9.4: Export Performance/Share of SSI in Country's Total Exports during 2002-2003 (Rs. crore)**

| Product Group | Total exports | Share of SSI sector | % share of SSI sector |
|---|---|---|---|
| **Non-traditional items** | | | |
| 1. Engineering Goods including electrical and electronics | 38093 | 12500 | 32.81 |
| 2. Basic Chemicals, pharmaceuticals, cosmetics | 21701 | 9659 | 44.51 |
| 3. Chemicals and Allied products | 10027 | 3355 | 33.46 |
| 4. Plastic Products | 4470 | 1863 | 41.67 |
| 5. Finished Leather and Leather products | 8780 | 6108 | 69.57 |
| 6. Marine Products | 6881 | 3251 | 47.25 |
| 7. Processed Foods | 13828 | 9680 | 70.00 |
| 8. Woollen Garments and Knitwear | 1289 | 1225 | 95.00 |
| 9. Sports Goods | 317 | 317 | 100.00 |
| 10. Readymade Garments | 26005 | 23404 | 90.00 |
| 11. Rayon and Synthetic Products | 7811 | 1484 | 19.00 |
| 12. Processed Tobacco, Snuff and Bidi | 1066 | 675 | 63.33 |
| 13. Electronics and computers | 52100 | 9860 | 18.93 |
| Total (A) | 192369 | 83382 | 43.34 |
| **Traditional items** | | | |
| 14. Cashew Kernal and cashew nut shell liquid | 2015 | 2015 | 100.00 |
| 15. Lac | 101 | 101 | 100.00 |
| 16. Spices | 1790 | 515 | 28.77 |
| Total (B) | 3905 | 2630 | 67.35 |
| Total (A + B) | 1,96,275 | 86,013 | 43.82 |

Source: DCSSI

1. Within the sector itself, five items alone accounted for 80 per cent of total exports. These items are readymade garments (27.21 per cent), engineering goods (14.53 per cent), processed food (11.25 per cent), basic chemicals (11.23 per cent), electronics and computers (11.46 per cent), leather products (7.10 per cent). Barring electronics and computers which is a new entry, all others are traditional items. This shows lack of diversification and consequent instability to go to new areas.
2. The share of SSI in some of the emerging areas such as electronics, engineering goods and chemicals and allied products, and marine products is very low despite large potential in the manufacturing sector. There are many other items which still remain to be tapped, particularly, glass and ceramics, toys, marble and tiles, paper, wood products and consumer electricals.
3. Even within those items where the present contribution of the sector is significant, their share in total global export is almost negligible. Leather products which have great potential currently account for only 2-3 per cent of the global exports.
4. Similarly, India's share in the total exports of fruits and vegetables and processed food is abysmally low despite vast potential existing in the area. This could be gauged from the fact that about 30 per cent of the fruits and vegetables produced in India are going waste and less than one per cent of the total production of these items is being processed.
5. Most of our exports are going to the recognised markets of developed countries, where not only the competition is tough but there also exists trade blocks. There is a need for exploring the potentiality/viability of the new

markets of Asia and Africa.

6. Of the total value of production within the SSI sector, the share of export is not significant. The total value of production in the sector in March 2003 at current prices was Rs. 7,63,013 crore whereas the value of exports stood at Rs. 86,012 crore which is about 11.3 per cent of the total production. This contribution cannot be considered high enough to improve India's share in world exports. Further, going by the achievement so far, additional efforts are needed to achieve the target.

**9.6 Export and Expand: New Strategy**

In fact the exports from the Indian Small Scale Industrial Sector present a paradox of high share in national exports and low share in sector's production. While the share of SSIs in national exports is as high as 35 per cent, the share of SSI exports in its total production is as low as 11.3 per cent. This means that about ninety per cent of SSI production is meant for the domestic market only. About 98 per cent of SSI units belong to tiny/micro enterprises category where investment in plant and machinery is less than Rs. 25 lakh. Due to low capital base of this segment, the level of technology used by them is low and of traditional type. This affects the productivity as well as quality of products and hence their competitiveness.

In such a situation one may be interested in knowing about the factors which have helped the SSI sector to grow so far. One of the factors which has facilitated the growth of SSI sector so far as the existence of a 'niche' market at lower/middle income levels where there exists demand for low price and low quality products. Only in a very small segment of SSI units the level of capital investment is high and the level of technology used by them is comparatively high. As a result in this segment productivity is high, quality of products is reasonably good and they are in a position to compete on their own in domestic as well as in export markets. As a matter of fact, the number of SSI units which are engaged in production of exportable goods may not be more than forty to fifty thousand out of a total of over 34 lakh SSI units in the country.

With the opening up of the Indian economy as a result of economic reforms and also on account of India's membership of WTO, the survival of the captive market at lower middle income level is at stake. Due to placement of large number of items under OGL, lowering down of tariff rates and host of other measures in the wake of economic reforms, the degree of protection enjoyed by the SSI sector has considerably narrowed down. With domestic markets becoming more and more competitive and the export markets difficult to capture, the SSI sector cannot survive in the changed scenario unless it adopts competitiveness as the 'mantra', exhibits aggressive selling techniques, concentrates on the quality aspects of its products and assumes export orientation. Productivity growth and technological up gradation require investment in technology and human capital and availability of the capital from various sources to finance these investment. The SSI units must feel free to operate and expand.

## 9.7 Potential-item Specific Analysis

With a change in strategy from growth led export to export led growth, it has become essential to provide for better integration of small industries with large industries and to attend the basic problems adversely affecting the functioning of SSI units relating to credit, infrastructure, technology, marketing and information. An analysis of the items which are being exported from the sector and which can conveniently be thus exported would clearly establish the vast scope of export potential existing in the sector.

**9.7.1 Leather Industry:** Leather industry is highly labour intensive and provides employment to about 1.5 million persons in the unorganised sector. A vast segment of manufacture of leather products is reserved exclusively for small scale units. Large units can produce these items with 50 per cent export obligations. The growth of Indian Leather Industry has been sustained by the country's large livestock population. India claims to have the highest livestock holdings in the world, having 57 per cent of buffalo population, 16 per cent of the cattle, 30 per cent of goat and 4 per cent of sheep population. Thus, the basic raw material for the leather industry i.e. hides obtained from cows and buffaloes and skins obtained from goat and sheep is found in abundance within the country.

However, in view of the fact that the livestock population is increasingly only at the rate of 1.2 per cent per annum, the availability of indigenous hides and skins has almost become stagnant. This easy availability of raw material whilst on one hand has sustained the sector over all these years, it has, on the other, now started falling short of demand and as a result the country is forced to import raw leather. The external markets are mainly dominated by Italy, China and South Korea. The major consumers of leather goods are USA, Germany, U.K., France, Netherlands, etc. and the major competing countries are China, Italy, South Korea, Taiwan, Indonesia, Malaysia, Brazil etc. Of late, Columbia and some African countries like Tunisia are also making their presence felt in the world leather trade.

India has been losing its export market in leather and leather manufactures including leather footwear, leather travel goods and leather garments since it declined from $ 1731 million in 1995-96 to $ 1590 million in 1999-2000. A marginal increase has been noticed in 2000-01, when the exports moved up to $ 1951 million, but showed some decline in 2001-02.

A major setback has been suffered in the export of finished leather which stood at $383 million in 1994-95 and this came down to $265 million in 1998-99. While the exports of finished leather witnessed a declining trend, the exports of leather goods exhibited a positive growth of 10.76 per cent in dollar terms in 1998-99. The exports of Indian leather goods to countries like USA, UK, Germany, Italy, France, the Netherlands, Spain and Portugal are showing encouraging trends in the recent times. But the overall export scenario of the industry is not satisfactory and the levels of present exports volumes are much less than the potential existing in this segment. This is due to the following reasons:

- The current depression in the international markets due to unfavourable economic conditions in the European markets.
- Mass closure of tanneries in the State of Tamil Nadu under the directive of Supreme Court on the environmental considerations and
- Liquidity crunch faced by the leather exporters.

A close examination of the performance of this industry reveals that the exports of Indian leather goods to countries like USA, UK, Germany, Italy, France, the Netherlands, Spain and Portugal are showing a rising trend and the share of Indian products in the major leather and leather goods importing countries is also increasing. The main items exported from the country under the category include finished leather, leather footwear, footwear components, leather garments, leather goods and saddlery and harness. While leather goods exports has shown tremendous growth, other items showing positive growth in dollar terms are leather footwear (2.95%); footwear components (3.36%); and saddlery and harness (28.57%). However, finished leather and leather garments showed a downward trend in dollar terms compared to the previous year.

Footwear was declared as an extreme focus sector in 1992. As a policy decision, this liberated the sector from several constraints coming in its way for growth. The UNDP and the Government of India launched in 1992, an integrated programme for the development of leather sector titled "National leather Development Programme" which aims at development of HRD, R&D support service, pollution control and export promotion. NLDP is regarded as a successful technical assistance programme. The Government of India took another important step to help the sector in the form of launching of Leather Technology Mission in 1995. It is funded by the Government of India through the CSIR and implemented by the Central Leather Research Institute.

The Mission aims at improving enhancing and harnessing the proper potential of this sector to augment socio-economic benefits, catalyse the revival of the share of India leather products in global trade to 10 per cent, evolve the most suitable organisational structure to integrate the development of rural, semi-urban and urban sub-sectors, provide extension services to the industry in the adoption of cleaner technologies and upgraded techniques, evolve a development grid for the leather sector to achieve a balanced development of all segments i.e. flaying, processing of raw hides and skins, processing of wet blue leather and manufacture of leather products from finished leather, carry awareness exercises and national campaigns for quality standardisation in leather sector and enhance the traditional and new skills through innovative training programmes.

Several policy initiatives were taken by the Government during 1998-99 to improve India's exports from the leather sector. The National Leather Development Programme with UNDP assistance for integrated development of the leather industry aims at removing the critical gaps which need to be removed for sustained growth of the industry and to enable it to face the challenges in the international market with confidence.

Input value restriction under the Quantity-based Advance Licensing (QBAL) Scheme has been removed. Advance licences with actual user condition have been allowed and the requirement of minimum value-addition has been dispensed with. Relocation of tanneries from Calcutta city to the Calcutta Leather Complex is getting completed and effluent treatment plants are being constructed with funds provided by the Ministry of Environment and Forest. Further, as part of brand promotion under the Market Development Assistance (MDA) Programme of the Ministry of Commerce, it was decided to extend soft loans from MDA for the purpose of brand promotion of Indian leather products.

In the revised Exim Policy (1997-2002) announced on 31st March, 1999, many favourable measures were announced. These included increase in pre-export credit entitlement under the Duty Entitlement Pass Book (DEPB) Scheme from 5 per cent to 10 per cent, allowing import of items under Special Import Licence (SIL) on surrender of SIL equivalent of 3 times the CIF value of imports, relaxation in the admissible limits for import and export samples, reduction of value-addition norms for exports to Russia from 100 per cent to 33 per cent etc. In the EXIM

Policy for 2002-07 announced on 31st March 2002, duty free imports of trimmings and embellishments up to 3 per cent of FOB value hitherto confined to leather garments has been extended to all leather products.

The Government of India have launched the Tannery Modernisation Scheme in January 2000 for encouraging modernisation of the existing tannery units by providing financial assistance in the form of capital subsidy against purchase of eligible machinery for bringing about a positive environmental impact, making them globally competitive, achieve better capacity utilisation and reduce wastage. The main incentive under the scheme is the availability of capital subsidy from Government of India for eligible machinery items to the extent of 30 per cent and 20 per cent of the cost of such plant and machinery for SSI and non-SSI units respectively subject to a ceiling of Rs. 28 lakh and Rs. 35 lakh respectively. SIDBI has been designated as the nodal agency under this scheme.

A section of the persons concerned with the development of the sector hold the view that reservation of this industry for the SSI sector had adversely affected quality and export promotion potential. This is not correct because the policy pronouncements provide for export of the 50 per cent of output if manufactured by the larger units. This sector was dereserved in 2002-03. The industry has immense potential for expansion and has wide scope for value addition and needs to be supported and encouraged as one of important employment providers and export earners industry in the small scale sector.

**9.7.2 Readymade Garments:** Readymade garment industry comprising of woven and knitted garments occupies a prominent place in the unorganised sector of the country in terms of production, exports and employment generation.

The production in this industry was estimated at Rs. 80,000 crore in 2000; of which Rs. 29,585 crore approximately constituted the value of garment exports. The demand for readymade garments in India until the 1970's was fairly low and the mass production of apparel was almost non-existent. The formation of Apparel Exports Promotion Council in 1978 was a major step towards boosting the exports from the sector. The real growth of apparel exports started in the early 1980's.

After recording a high rate of growth in the eighties and first half of nineties, there has been some decline in growth rate after 1995. The growth rate suffered a set back due to factors like recession in major Western and East Asian markets, low productivity, narrow product mix and fabric base and increased competition. The exports have again picked up since 1995-96. It stood at Rs. 26,005 crore in 2002-03.

According to AEPC 37.43 per cent of our exports in 1998-99 was directed to USA, Canada, Brazil, Mexico, 36.22 per cent to Germany, France, UK, Italy and Spain and only 1.90 per cent to African countries and not more than 3 per cent to East Asian countries.

Major quota countries of exports are USA, EU, Norway, and Canada. These countries are imposing quota restrictions on Indian garments based on bilateral agreements. Australia, Japan, Switzerland, CIS, Hungary, UAE etc. constitute non-quota countries. India exports large variety of garments for gents, ladies and children. Major items of exports to these countries are ladies blouses, knitted shirts, gents shirts, ladies skirts, coats, jackets, children wear etc.

Though Indian garments are being exported to over 125 destinations, three quarters of them are sold in 18 markets of North America and Europe. These 18 markets are in USA,

Canada and EC nations. Each of these markets restricts Indian exports by means of quotas administered under the MFA system. Delhi and Mumbai accounted for two thirds of the value exported and the rest is shared between seven other regional centres at Tirupur, Chennai, Bangalore, Ludhiana, Jaipur, Calcutta and Cochin. The trade is divided equally between the manufacturer exporters and merchant exporters. The brand names which have emerged are able to influence the sales more in the domestic urban market than the export market.

The major problem being faced by the industry is low productivity levels on account of poor technological base. According to an ICRIER Study, in 1993 Indian manufacturer exporters averaged 10.18, 9.12, 6.25, 9.62 and 6.84 pieces/shift in ladies blouses, gents shirts, ladies dresses, ladies skirts and trousers respectively against the Hong Kong benchmarks of 20.56, 20.87, 20.17, 19.25 and 19.25 pieces/shift. In spite of sizeable increase in quantity, the value realisation from the export of ready made garments has not been adequate, because of the Indian readymade garment sector producing largely low value added items and operating in low income markets. The major problem encountered by this industry is lack of modernisation and technology up gradation which in the face of phenomenal modernisation by the competing neighbouring countries makes our product uncompetitive and unattractive both in terms of price and the quality.

Most of the machines installed are indigenously manufactured and away from the state of art technology. As a result, the productivity of garments units and quality of garments manufactured are comparatively poor. Recently some steps have been taken by a segment of manufacturing industry to upgrade technology. The pace is however, not fast and is confined to upper segment of the SSI sector. Some ancillary supporting units like dyeing and finishing houses have also updated themselves with latest version of machinery and equipment. It may be mentioned that when foreign buyers place orders for fabric or garment, they include quality specifications in their purchase order such as shrinkage after washing, colour fastness to washing and rubbing, fabric weight per unit area, shade matching, stitching quality etc. Every exporter of garment and hosiery need to take care of above characteristics in order to maintain the consistency in quality of the products. The existing technology needs to be upgraded to take care of not only productivity aspects but also efficiency aspects as listed above. Moreover, removal of trade restrictions as per WTO agreement will also compel the industry to modernise to survive rather than face the threat of extinction where already India's realisation in terms of value realisation is not much.

In order to fully realise the potential possessed by this industry not only in terms of export earnings but also in generating mass scale employment, Government of India has launched recently (1999) the Scheme of Technology Upgradation Fund for Textile Sector. The Fund would provide interest subsidy up to 5 per cent to textile sector for technology up gradation and modernisation. The issues of design, fashion and quality also need to be addressed on priority basis so as to enable this sector to play its important role in boosting the over-all exports from the country.

**9.7.3 Electronics and Software:** The electronics industry has registered a phenomenal growth in the last decade. The industry had a compound growth rate of 35 per cent during the period 1981-90. There has also been an increase in exports of electronics from Rs. 55 crore in 1981 to Rs. 1044 crore in 1993-94 and further to Rs. 12,800 crore in 1998-99 out of which Rs. 11,000 crore was in the form of software exports. Total exports from electronics and computers group was Rs. 52,100 crore in 2002-03, of which the share of small enterprises was Rs. 9,860 crore which is less than 20 per cent. The SSI sector accounts for about 40 per cent of the total output in the industry and 30 per cent of the total exports (both hardware and software) from the sector.

While SSI sector has been mainly exporting items like transistor radios, P.A. systems since early 1950s, it has now penetrated the global markets and is exporting a wide range of hi-tech products in consumer electronics, computers, electronic instruments, telecommunication products and electronic computers. But in spite of these encouraging developments India's share of electronics exports in the global market is less than 1 per cent which is very low and about 80 per cent of exports are from Export Processing Zones. However, a heartening feature of this industry is that it has been drawing qualified engineers within the SSI fold and some of them have really distinguished themselves within a short span of period. We have quite a large number of technically qualified persons in the country who are willing to take to self-employment ventures in the industry provided support in terms of developed industrial sheds/parks and credit is made available to them. There are tremendous opportunities for exports in electronics, software and contract manufacturing.

With proper guidance and inputs, the SSI sector can emerge as a global player in this field. While electronics sector (music system) by and large is facing tough competition, telecommunication sector is poised to grow at a very fast rate in near future and computer (software) sector has already created a revolution in the field of information technology during last five years.

Computer as a productivity tool made an emergence on the Indian industrial scene in the early 70's. But it was in mid-80s that the analysts and policy planners began to understand the potential of Indian talent in computer software industry. This realisation led to the formulation of the computer software policy in 1986. In the middle of eighties the total worth of the industry was placed at a mere Rs. 300 million ($10 million) but currently the Indian software industry is worth Rs. 42 billion. If the value of the in-house software development that takes place in a large number of commercial corporate end-users is added, the total value of software industry is close to Rs. 50 billion or 1.4 billion US dollars. The compound annual growth rate of the industry in last 5 years (1993-98) has been 54 per cent. The industry provided employment to nearly 1,60,000 software professionals in 1997. Present total employment in electronics and software industry is about 20 lakh.

Electronics and Information Technology is fast becoming a viable tool for increasing productivity in the factories, offices and homes. Keeping in view its role in export, employment and productivity, the Working Group on Electronics Industry had strongly recommended that the electronics and information technology industry should be classified as a basic growth 'infrastructure' industry and thereby special status be accorded to this sector. India's share in software production in the total global production is meagre 1 per cent and keeping in view the vast potential the sector offers, sky can be the only limit.

The government is paying utmost attention to the development of this fast growing industry through development of R & D, facilities for EPZ, EOU, EHTP enhancing product range, increasing productivity, quality, communication and satellite services, development of strategic components, high resolution technologies, air-navigation system, radar technologies, micro-electronics, surface mount devices, colour display devices etc. SIDBI launched a Venture Capital Fund dedicated to providing requisite assistance to SSI units in IT/Software related sectors in 1998-99 with participation from Central/State Governments.

**9.7.4 Food Processing Industry:** India produces a very wide variety of fruits and vegetables and is ranked the second largest producer in fruits and vegetables in the world. But the irony is that less than one per cent of this total production is commercially processed. India's share in the world trade of processed fruits and vegetables is also less than one per cent. This figure of very low processing of fruits and vegetables in India is in sharp contrast to the healthy figures of 30 per cent for Philippines and 83 per cent for Malaysia.

Judging by the resource potential of this industry, it offers unlimited opportunities of commercial exploitation. The food items involving processing are grain processing including rice, wheat and dal, consumer food industries covering items like bakery, cocoa products, soft drinks, beer and alcoholic drinks, fruits and vegetables products, meat and poultry processing, and fish processing. A vast segment of these activities are carried out in unorganised sector particularly small scale industrial sector. The number of rice mills as on 1.1.1999 was 1,38,898 of which 34,688 were in modernised sector and the balance belonged to unorganised sector.

There is an urgent need for rapid development of food processing facilities so as to harness the full commercial potential of the Industry and towards this end the

Government has embarked upon a bold programme inter-alia consisting of:

- Scheme for development of infrastructural facilities such as post-harvest infrastructure and cold chain facilities, establishment of food processing industrial estates/food parks facilities for preservation and processing of fish.
- Scheme for setting up/expansion/modernisation of food processing industries including dissemination of low cost preservation technology.
- Schemes for development and modernisation of meat processing, poultry and egg processing.
- Item specific research and development projects, development of processing technology for production of intermediate and finished food products including design and building of prototype equipments/pilot plans.
- Fortification of cereals products.
- Upgradation of packing and storage technology.
- Development of new cost effective packaging for different types of food products.
- Scheme for strengthening of traditional fish processing technology and marketing and utilisation of low value fish to value added products.
- Scheme for setting up innovative dairy projects.
- Scheme for development of marketing, quality control, storage and transportation of meat and meat products.
- Promotional support through exhibitions, seminars, workshops, programmes of entrepreneurial development, etc.

The list can only be illustrative and not an exhaustive list of exportable items, but it definitely shows the potential of SSI sector which can be tapped to the full extent if issues like simplification of procedures, easier access to bank credit and improvement in infrastructure are settled expeditiously and to the full satisfaction of all concerned. The process of liberalisation has provided opportunities to attract the infusion of these things into small scale sector. In the liberalised economic environment of today, it would not be difficult for the small scale industries to rise to the occasion and help the country to achieve a target of at least 1.5 per cent of share in the world export of fruits and vegetables processing in the next 15 years. However, this requires crossing of several hurdles in its way. Some of them are domestic and some are the products of emerging global economic environment. These have posed many threats and challenges. In 2002-03, out of a total export of processed food which was Rs. 13,828 crore, the share of small enterprises was 70 per cent.

### 9.8 Future Scenario

Is the Indian SSI sector geared enough to face the challenges? What are those challenges and what are the options before the SSI sector? Let us examine those issues. These are relevant for the SSI sector as whole and not only specific industries.

**9.8.1 Hurdles and Way Out:** The writing on the wall is clear that a time for change in strategy for development of the Indian small scale sector has come. The 'niche' (lower/middle income) market is waning. With the removal of quantitative restrictions on imports in March 2001, the issue of ensuring competitiveness of the SSI sector has assumed urgent propositions. Some of our neighbouring countries are having an edge in the production of some of these items which are important in our export basket. In addition, China enjoys commanding position in production of toys and many East Asian countries and China dominate in production of consumer electricals and electronic items.

East Asian crisis is showing symptoms of getting over but the recovery in these countries may not be export led hence Indian exports will face stiff competition in terms of price, quality and timely delivery in these markets.

The current economic reforms have ushered in some challenges before this sector. While some of the challenges are on account of its small size, others are on account of the type of technology used and their location in rural and backward areas and some arise on account of their difficulty in obtaining adequate and timely credit and due to lack of infrastructural facilities. These challenges briefly put are as follows:

- Increased competition particularly in the consumer goods sector.
- Inadequate access to institutional credit, delayed delivery and higher cost of credit.
- Vulnerability in terms of access to technology information and advanced management practices.
- Inadequate standardisation of products, components, parts, sub-assemblies etc. which discourage linkage between small and large units.
- Predominance of large number of rules and regulations, procedural hassles and their inability to cope up with all of them.

However, one need not jump to the conclusion that this sector suffers from weaknesses only and has no strong points or inherent strengths to face these challenges. Small enterprises, unlike the big enterprises with the layers of control and separation of ownership, are inherently flexible to react to market signals and changing tastes. This makes the small firms more innovative and open to new ideas. They also interact more closely with their customers to be in touch with changing preferences. In addition, SSI units have better access to cheap labour and have lower overheads which help them to reduce the cost of production.

**9.8.2 EXIM Policy 2002-2007:** The Export-Import Policy 2002-07 is a bold and pragmatic policy available to support Indian exports. Several exclusive measures have been announced to promote SSI sector in this policy. With a view to encouraging the development of clusters working in the SSI sector, several measures have been announced. This includes clusters like Tirpur for hosiery, Panipat for blankets, Ludhiana for woollen knitwear etc. The measures for clusters consist of:

- Common service providers in these areas shall be entitled for facility of EPCG schemes.
- The recognised associations of units in these areas will be able to access the funds under the Market Access Initiative Scheme for creating focussed technological services and marketing abroad.
- Such areas will receive priority for assistance for identified critical infrastructure gaps from the scheme on Central Assistance to States.
- Entitlement for Export House status at Rs. 5 crore instead of Rs. 15 crore for others.

Small firms generally specialise in a few products, in which their strength lies and where small scale production is technologically viable. After choosing and sometimes developing the product through R & D, the fixed costs are minimised by buying second-hand machineries and renovating them to adapt to small scale operations. Large firms suffer from technological rigidities under capital intensive technologies. Small firms are in a better position to adopt new technologies and/or go for their diffusion.

While economic reforms have brought the small scale face to face with competition, they have at the same time presented certain opportunities in the form of impetus to quality, efficiency and better technology, increased availability of raw materials and components and opportunity to restructure and diversify with the dismantling of the control regime. The natural advantages of quick response, flexibility and innovativeness possessed by this sector, will help to convert the challenges into opportunities.

However, to what extent it will be able to take advantage of the opportunities, depends upon the solution to some of the major bottlenecks that this sector faces, e.g. inadequacy of finance, lack of infrastructure, high cost of production and poor quality and lack of information particularly on market conditions in India and abroad. In addition, there are problems arising out of cumbersome export formalities and procedures, which the units being mostly one-man show, find difficult to cope up with.

**9.8.3 Credit Facilities:** The timely availability of adequate credit is the prime requirement of any export oriented SSI unit or for that matter any economic unit. SSI units have to depend on State Financial Corporations and Commercial Banks for their long term and short term credit needs.

According to the Nayak Committee (constituted by the Reserve Bank of India in 1991 to examine the adequacy of credit to SSI Sector), the supply of credit was extremely inadequate from institutional sources. Commercial banks which meet the working capital requirements of these units provide only 8.1 per cent of their total output by way of working capital. Against the minimum norm of 20 per cent prescribed by the Nayak Committee, the actual availability of credit was very low. In the case of tiny units, the supply of credit from the banks was not more than 2.7 per cent of their output. Availability of credit plays a very important role in the successful working of any unit. Credit should be affordable, adequate and timely. The problems of credit become more serious because SSI units do not have access to other sources of finance such as capital market.

A recent study conducted by the Office of the Development Commissioner (Small Scale Industry) has revealed that not more than 15-20 per cent of SSI units avail bank finance. The RBI has issued guidelines to banks to meet 20 per cent output as working capital and the limit of loan has been raised through union budget 1999-2000 up to 5 crore. Composite through single window was also been raised from Rs. 25 lakh to Rs. 50 lakh in 2003-2004. It is essential to have a comprehensive credit scheme targeted at SSI exporters and this requirement. Special line of credit for SSI units needs to be introduced and procedural bottlenecks need to be removed.

One of the major problems faced by the SSI units in the domestic market is the problem of delayed payment. This reduces the availability of capital and also hampers export compliance. This problem could be solved to a great extent by the discounting of small firms' receivables from the large units by the banks and financial institutions under what is popularly known as factoring services, but it should be without recourse. To encourage financing of risk prone ventures, there is need for popularising Venture Capital Fund. The SIDBI has made a beginning in this direction.

**9.8.4 Infrastructure:** Lack of adequate infrastructure, particularly in the field of power supply, communication network and telecommunication facilities affect production, its cost and delivery. Frequent disruption in power supply adversely affects productivity particularly in precision and high technology outputs. Demand for reliable power supply reflects the increasing awareness of small enterprises in maintaining their quality and competitive edge.

Similarly, lack of adequate telecommunication facilities is proving disadvantageous to SSI units in the highly dynamic and hi-tech international market. The demand for better and improved telecommunication facilities reflects the growing appreciation by small units of its relevance. The use of hi-tech application for establishing and nursing market contacts will also lead to cuts in the cost of going global. This area requires adequate and constant attention. The Integrated Infrastructure Development Scheme launched by the Small Industries Development Organisation and the newly created Infrastructure Development Scheme of the Ministry of Commerce and Industry (2003-04) are likely to take care of the problem to some extent. There are many other things as well which with the support of other Ministries and Departments would be required to be undertaken for developing infrastructure. NGO role in managing industrial estates by realising user charges may also be good idea for worth implementing.

**9.8.5 Technology Upgradation:** The SSI sector in India uses wide spectrum of technology ranging from traditional to state-of-the-art. Since over 98 per cent of SSI units are tiny or micro enterprises, they use traditional or local technology called backward or inappropriate and this affects the productivity, quality and competitiveness of the products. Export promotion and technology up gradation are synonymous since it is the door to improving quality and reducing the costs of production. As small units mainly concentrate on serving local markets they prefer to rely less on sophisticated technologies and more on simpler processing techniques. This inertia needs to be broken at the earliest. Some units find it difficult to go for better technology as these are costly and the present investment ceilings of SSI sector do not permit the same.

The Government has been seized of the necessity for technology up gradation and has set up several Tool Rooms, product-cum-process development centres, Regional Testing Centres and Workshops, but they need to be suitably strengthened and multiplied, particularly at the regional level through Mini-Tool Rooms and Common Technology Centres for clusters. Linked with technology up gradation and exploration of market is the issue of availability of timely information, the arrangements for which are extremely inadequate at present. The issue has assumed greater significance as a result of the recent telecommunication revolution which is being used for hi-tech application for market research and looking for business opportunities as a more cost effective substitute for exploratory personal visits abroad. Business queries between trading partners can be easily exchanged over the electronic networks and specifications, drawing and designs can easily be transmitted now. The SSI units, however, have been depending heavily on conventional methods of market exploration through trial and error and private contacts, which is neither adequate nor meets the demands of the changing times.

**9.8.6 Packaging and Development of Popular Brands:** Packaging plays a very crucial role in the present day marketing, especially the export marketing. That is why it has been called a silent salesman. Packaging technology has undergone vast changes in recent years which is based on the recognition that each item needs special attention on account of its nature, volume content, purpose and the packaging must be cost and environment friendly. Packaging is both a science and art and requires special training and awareness.

India faces a formidable hurdle in meeting and matching the packaging requirements of its exportable products in the world market. The international market with deep rooted forces of competition does not respect the inadequacies of the exporting countries. According to a UNO study, 30 per cent of total exports earning from the developing world are lost due to poor packaging. Though the dark side of India's exports may not be as alarming as for other developing countries, yet the possibilities of India loosing about 10 per cent of its export earnings due to poor packaging is not ruled out.

It is also estimated that for many of our products, about 30 to 35 per cent increase in export earnings can be achieved by resorting to exports in acceptable consumer packs. A change in marketing strategy at product level is needed. What sells at present is not a product but a brand name. It is not possible with limited resources to develop their brands. This task will have to be undertaken by consortia in co-operation with organisations like the National Small Industries Corporation and SSIDC.

### 9.9 SSI Sector in the 21st Century

Competitiveness is the name of the hottest game now-a-days. More competitive countries tend to grow faster. As India has already entered the new millennium where the order of the day is increasing economic liberalisation across-the-borders and growing globalisation of world economy under WTO regime, hence the small scale sector is going to face major challenges in the form of intensified competition, both domestic and external. For its existence it has to be competitive otherwise with present levels of technology in use and infrastructural and environmental constraints, it may find itself in a fierce battle for survival. Both the products and producers need international exposure.

The sector has vast potential of being developed into a major economic player but there is need for change in strategy adopted so far for its survival and growth. This change in strategy calls for a shift from individual industry to cluster approach, linkages between large and small units, use of state-of-art technology, efficient system of delivery of input and output with full support and active involvement of financial institutions, associations and the government. It is also very necessary to adopt electronic commence which has brought a revolution in the field of marketing strategy.

The strategy required has to be multi-dimensional. To quote Kirit S. Parikh (India Development Report 1999-2000, page 27), "Globalisation is now a fact, not an option. The communication revolution has turned the world into a global 'village'. Where everyone knows what is going on and what is available.... The emergence of multinational firms and a global market has also led to a deeper integration of production. Parts and components are sourced from different countries and intra-firm trade has become a large part of global trade. A modern car or a computer would generally have components coming from scores of countries. ... The diseconomies of scale have been pushed back as IT has made it possible to manage larger firms efficiently."

The present mode of micro level production is becoming irrelevant in the present global context. The future of international trade will be primarily be based on global product and trading chain. For being a part of global village, the industrial units will have to be part of the globalisation. There are at present two types of international production network, (i) Producer driven commodity chain (PDCC) and (ii) Buyer driven commodity Chain (BPCC). According to Shri K. Parikh PDCCs are found in those industries in which large, usually transnational corporations (TNC) play the central role in co-ordinating production network, including their backward and forward linkages. This is characteristic of capital and technology intensive industries such as automobiles, aircraft, computers, semi-conductors, and heavy machinery. BDCCs are found in those industries where large retailers, branded marketers and trading companies play the key role in setting up decentralised production networks in developing countries. This is common in labour-intensive consumer goods such as garments, footwear, toys and consumer electronics.

The East Asian Newly Industrialised Economies (NIEs) became successful exporters in 1960s and 1970s primarily by mustering the dynamics of BDCCs. Apparel was leading export sector for each of the four East Asian newly Industrialised Economies namely Hong Kong, Singapore, South Korea and Taiwan. Similarly, all the countries except Singapore exported toys and South Area and Taiwan also exported footwear. East Asian firms became full range package suppliers for foreign buyers. Today China is the foremost volume exporter of low tech consumer goods.

K. V. Ramaswamy in his article "Exporting in a Globalised Economy" - published in India Development Report 1999-2000 suggests that the linkages with the global economy can be viewed as connected through four export roles:

- Export processing assembly operations
- Component supply sub-contracting
- Original Equipment Manufacturing (OEM) and
- Original Brand-name Manufacturing (OBM)

The NIEs of both East Asia and Latin America have been engaged in this kind of labour intensive production. Countries like Mexico, which has the world's largest export processing sector has extended the benefits of export processing zones to all export oriented firms, without requiring them to be located in the special zones. China has set up special economic zones within which all economic activities manufacturers, banking, export and import, and foreign investment take place in a more liberal environment. East Asian experience in electronics industry where firm gained entry by OEM, and secured a market channel and acquired technology is another example worth consideration.

India has greater opportunities to assume and develop the export role of assembly, component supplier and OEM exporter. The main avenue to enter international network according to Ramaswamy is through FDI. Cross country studies of FDI indicate that infrastructure quality, labour cost and domestic market size are predominant factors that influence international investors vis-à-vis short-term incentives like corporate tax rebates.

India has the advantage of a large domestic market but critical problem areas are in infrastructure and labour productivity. Labour costs are rising in South Korea, Taiwan, Indonesia and Singapore; foreign investors from developed countries could be looking for cheap labour cost locations with macro-economic stability. If India could improve its infrastructure and provide for a relatively liberal economic environment similar to that in the special Economic Zones of China, it would be possible to attract large scale FDI in India.

A study of India's garments exports by K.V. Ramaswamy reveals the absence of structural change and policy reforms. Buyers in world markets are expecting more services in terms of minimum performance standards. Delivery and service emerged as the main weaknesses of Indian exports as perceived by importers in the EU, Japan and the US. Access to imported inputs, shipping facilities and proximity to fabric sources have become more important determinants of outsourcing by foreign firms than mere manufacturing capability. In this context the policy of product reservation of garments also needs to be looked into afresh.

New slogan for development of SSI should be 'Export and Expand' to help India become a global economic player in the Twenty First Century. With the production and marketing strategy to change from 'I will sell what I make' to 'I will make what you need'.

# 10

# Employment Potential of Small Enterprises in India

Employment generation has always been one of the main objectives of the policies aimed at economic development and growth of the nation. A rise in economic growth has always led to increased employment opportunities and similarly enhanced employment generation has always contributed significantly towards economic growth. However, identifying and creating employment opportunities has always been a challenging task in our country, the reasons for which are plenty and well known. More disturbing in this context is the realisation that there has not been commensurate growth in employment vis-à-vis economic growth as demonstrated by the GDP indicators over the past decade. The general impression that the acceleration in growth experienced during mid 1990s would create sufficient employment capable of absorbing increased labour force and reduce the backlog of employment has not proved fully correct.

From the NSS survey results in 2000 it emerges that during the six year period between 1993-94 and 1999-2000, the rate of growth of employment was just above 1%; this is less than half of what could have occurred had the earlier targeted elasticity of employment of 0.4 would have fructified. The NSS data indicated a significant lowering of labour force participation rates mainly among younger age groups and rural women. During the Tenth Five Year Plan, the SSI sector has been assigned a target of creating 4.4 million additional jobs. During the Ninth Plan, the sector achieved the target. However, during the Tenth Plan some disturbing factors have been noticed. These are decline in labour intensity of small enterprises and decline in flow of credit as percentage of net bank credit from 17.5 per cent in 1998 to 11 per cent in 2003. Under these circumstances, will this sector be able to achieve the target of employment? Should we be happy with just employment creation or should we not pay attention on improving the quality of employment. Improvement in quality of job is dependent on skill and entrepreneurial development. The focus in this chapter is on examining the ability of small enterprises in realizing the targeted growth in employment on the one hand and scope of improvement on the quality of job on the other.

There were over 36 lakh small enterprises all over the country, at the end of 2003-04 of which about 1 lakh are in the organised sector (factory sector). It may be mentioned that these figures and analysis subsequently are based on data on SSI sector which were available before the result of the Third Census became available in February 2004. The unorganised sector comprises of SSI units engaged in manufacturing apart from those in the handlooms, handicrafts, coir and KVIs sectors. The organised sector includes powerlooms other than the manufacturing SSIs.

There is also a large sub-sector within the SSI sector known as Tiny Industries which consist of micro units which are comparable to rural and cottage/ household industries. The Small Scale Sector currently provides employment to over 20.0 million persons, dispersed in every corner of the country and has been contributing significantly to its socio-economic development. With the initiation of wide-ranging economic and structural reforms in the early 90's Public Sector employment has experienced a decline and the expected growth in the private sector employment has not been encouraging either. The reasons for this can be traced to rapid automation, adoption of new technology to operate in the competitive markets and in the process laying off excess labour force. There has been very slow growth in employment in the organised private sector during the past decade which has been experiencing jobless growth. Also, the growth rate of employment in the Agriculture sector has been experiencing a negative trend. This has led to shift in the focus of employment generation to the largely unorganised sector including Small Scale Sector and growing service sector. In fact, a large segment of the service sector exists as small enterprises covering vast spectrum of industry related services including IT, Bio-technology, food processing and preservation technology sectors. According to the Report of Task Force on Employment Opportunities (2001), popularly known as Ahluwalia Committee, the service sector will be the major source for employment generation in future providing about 70% of the new job opportunities in this economy. Adequate attention has not been given to the many sectoral policy constraints, which hold back employment in services.

SSI units are set up in the private sector. The decision to set up the SSI units is governed by the desire to become their own masters through self-employment and it is essentially the function of availability of credit, which includes self-finance and institutional finance. Availability of adequate and timely credit is the primary requirement for the growth of sound and sustainable SSI sector. The decisions are also, to a great extent, governed by factors like availability of adequate infrastructure and a market for their products. The role of Central and State Governments is primarily to act as facilitators to promote entrepreneurship, technology, marketing, to remove hurdles in the way of its growth, provide a level playing field and enhance SSIs' competitiveness.

Small and Medium Enterprises have emerged the main contributor to employment all over the world. To quote from the Report of the Special Group on Targeting Ten Million employment opportunities per year (S.P. Gupta Committee Report) May 2002, in U.S all firms under the Small Business Act contributes nearly 50 per cent of the private workforce along with more than half of the GDP. Similarly, in Japan, of the total 54.16 million people engaged nation (excluding those in primary industries), 42.07 million i.e. 78 per cent employment is in small and medium enterprises and the total value in manufacturing from SME is 51 per cent, in whole sale 64 per cent and in retail 78 per cent. In Germany also, 64 per cent of all employed have their job in small and medium firms, which (produces) contributed at least 48 per cent to the Gross National Domestic Product and 27 per cent to exports for the year 1990. Lastly, in Korea, there are nearly 96000 small and medium manufacturing enterprises, which employ 1 to 300 persons each. They represent 99.1 per cent of all manufacturing enterprises and account for 69.2 per cent of total employment in this sector".

Assistance to Small and Medium Enterprises is also not something unique in India. It exists in one form or other in other countries also. In Korea, USA, Japan, China, there are Credit Guarantee Schemes as introduced in India in 2000, which helps small enterprises to have access to bank loans without collaterals. Technological supports are provided to SMEs in Korea, Japan, China etc. Equity support, which is available under National Equity Fund Programme in India where soft loan is available at 5 per cent interest, is also available in Germany where under 'Equity Support Programme' special support is given to young entrepreneurs and new starters. This programme includes among many two year free of interest, a comparatively low interest rate, 10 year grace period and 20 year repayment period.

### 10.1 Policy Support to SSI Sector

The policy environment enabling this sector to grow includes:

1. SSI sector comes under the Priority Sector Lending programme of Banks.
2. Fiscal support to SSI units in the form of Excise Exemption, some direct tax benefits by the Central Government, sales tax/loan deferment by the State Governments.
3. Protection through product reservation (currently 675 items out of about 8000 items manufactured in the SSI sector are reserved).
4. Price Preference (up to 15 per cent) and Purchase Preference in respect of 358 items purchased by Government Departments.
5. Support for technology upgradation through Small Industries Service Institutes (SISIs), Product Cum Process Development Centres (PPDCs), Regional Testing Centres (RTCs), Tool Rooms, financial incentives for acquiring ISO 9000 certification, adoption of bar coding etc.
6. Entrepreneurship development programmes conducted by various National level Institutes and support to State level Industries.
7. Encouraging Ancillaries, Vendor development, sub-contracting exchanges etc.
8. Development of Infrastructure.

### 10.2 Performance of SSI Sector since 1990

Table 10.1 shows the status of the SSI sector in terms of

number of units, growth of output and employment since 1990.

**Table 10.1 Performance of Small Scale Sector**

| Years | No. of units (lakh ) | Production (Rs. crore) (at current prices) | Employment (lakh ) |
|---|---|---|---|
| 1990-91 | 19.48 (6.86) | 1,55,340 | 125.30 (4.77) |
| 1991-92 | 20.82 (6.88) | 1,78,699 | 129.80 (3.59) |
| 1992-93 | 22.46 (7.88) | 2,09,300 | 134.06 (3.28) |
| 1993-94 | 23.88 (6.32) | 2,41,648 | 139.38 (3.97) |
| 1994-95 | 25.71 (7.66) | 2,98,865 | 146.56 (5.15) |
| 1995-96 | 26.58 (3.38) | 3,62,656 | 152.61 (4.13) |
| 1996-97 | 28.03 (5.45) | 4,11,858 | 160.00 (4.84) |
| 1997-98 | 29.44 (5.03) | 4,62,641 | 167.20 (4.50) |
| 1998-99 | 30.80 (4.60) | 5,20,650 | 171.58 (2.62) |
| 1999-00 | 32.12 (4.30) | 5,72,887 | 178.50 (4.03) |
| 2000-01 | 33.11 (3.08) | 6,39,024 | 185.64 (4.00) |
| 2001-02 | 34.64 (3.08) | 6,90,316 | 192.23 (3.55) |
| 2002-03 | 35.15 | 7,63,013 | 199.65 (3.55) |

Figures in brackets give the percentage increase over the previous year.

Small Scale Industries (the modern segment of small enterprises) in India contribute about 40 per cent of industrial production, 35 per cent of national exports and contributes 6.75 per cent of GDP.

The average rate of growth of production in SSI sector is estimated at 7.7% and the average growth in employment was about 3.7% per annum during the Ninth Plan respectively. During first two years of the Tenth Plan, the average growth remained almost the same lent over 2 per cent higher than growth in overall industrial sector. This gives an employment elasticity of about 0.5 for the SSI sector. The target of employment generation in the SSI sector by the terminal year of the Ninth Five Year Plan was 185 lakh persons in 2001-02, giving an additionality of 25 lakh persons from the base year i.e. 1996-97. The estimates of additional employment generated in the SSI sector during Ninth Plan was that of about 32 lakh persons. This is much higher than the target of additional employment fixed for the Ninth Five Year Plan.

## 10.3 Types of Employment in SSI Sector

Employment in the SSI sector is mainly generated in two forms:

**10.3.1 Autonomous (Growth Related):** wherein every new SSI unit set up provides employment to entrepreneurs, skilled, semi- skilled and unskilled workers; and

**10.3.2 Induced (Programme Related):** through specialised employment generation programmes like the Prime Minister's Rozgar Yojana (PMRY), Rural Employment Guarantee Programme (REGP), etc. The focus of this chapter is however, to explore and examine the possibility of generating 11 million jobs in the SSI sector by 2012 i.e. the end of Eleventh Plan as a result of natural growth in the SSI sector.

The SSI sector provides whole-time and sustainable and durable employment. According to 2nd All India Census of Registered SSI units the average employment per SSI unit was 6.3 persons in 1987-88. As a result of modernisation and technology upgradation of SSI sector and emergence of capital intensive products, the average employment per unit during Ninth Five Year Plan has been estimated at 5.5 persons per unit there are indications of significant decline in the average per unit employment in recent years. The Third Census has revealed decline in per unit employment to 4.5 persons. At the same time there are also indications of increase in productivity per unit of capital employed in the SSI sector.

## 10.4 Employment in SSI Sector: Autonomous

The number of SSI units increased at a rate of nearly 4.8% during the Ninth Plan Period, where as the employment grew at the rate of 3.7 per cent per annum during the same period. This is depicted in Table 10.2.

**Table 10.2: Growth of Autonomous Employment in SSI Sector**

| Years | No. of Units (lakh) | Employment (lakh) | Additional Employment (lakh) |
|---|---|---|---|
| 1996-97 | 28.03 | 160.00 | - |
| 1997-98 | 29.44 (5.03) | 167.20 (4.50) | 7.20 |
| 1998-99 | 30.80 (4.62) | 171.58 (2.62) | 4.38 |
| 1999-00 | 32.12 (4.29) | 178.50 (4.03) | 6.92 |
| 2000-01 | 33.11 (3.08) | 185.64 (4.00) | 7.14 |
| 2001-02 | 34.64 (4.62) | 192.23 (3.55) | 6.59 |
| 1997-02 | | | 32.23 |

Note: Figures in brackets are the percentage growth over previous year.

**10.4.1 Tenth Five Year Plan (2002-07):** The Report of the Special Group of the Planning Commission, under Dr. S.P. Gupta, Member Planning Commission, on targeting 10 million additional jobs per year during the 10$^{th}$ Five Year Plan, has placed major emphasis on the growth of unorganised sector including on Small and Medium Enterprises in meeting the target of additional employment opportunities in the Tenth Plan. This places enhanced expectation on the Small Scale Sector in generating additional employment opportunities so as to achieve this target. The targeted rate of growth for SSI sector has been kept at 12% on the ground that economy is expected to grow at 8 % (GDP) in the Tenth Plan.

With liberalisation of the economy and its assimilation into the globalised world order, latest and state-of-the-art technology needs to be adopted by new units coming up in the Small Scale Sector, while the existing units need to carry out technological upgradation from time to time to enhance their competitive strengths. This also entails commensurate improvement in the quality of employment and labour. Emphasis would have to be given to quality of labour rather than to quantity of labour to bear the onslaught of globalisation and survive in the changing economic scenario with increasing competitiveness. The Small Scale Sector is poised to be the engine of employment generation/growth in next 10 years as is clear from the projections made by the Sub Group–I of the Working Group on Small Scale Industries for the 10$^{th}$ Five Year Plan. The growth in employment is dependent on the growth in the number of units, growth rate of the SSI sector and nature of growth i.e. the type of industries i.e. capital intensive or labour intensive. Taking all these factors into account, the Sub-Group has made a projection of growth in the number of units, production and employment with year-wise break up as given in Table 10.3.

Taking into account the increased capital intensity in the SSI sector, the current employment per unit is estimated around 5 persons. Taking the 2001-02 figure of number of SSI units as the base and applying a growth rate of 4.6 % per annum over it we get the number of SSI units coming into existence each year. This annual number of new units is multiplied by 5.0 i.e. the average estimated current employment per unit as found in the new units. A relatively lower per unit employment has been visualised for the Tenth and Eleventh Five Year Plan periods because of the increased emphasis on technology upgradation and modernisation of the SSI sector, which is considered essential in order to enhance the competitiveness necessitated by the ongoing process of liberalisation globalisation and adherence to the WTO agreements.

**Table 10.3: Projection of SSI Output and Employment in Tenth Plan**

| Years | No. of Units (lakh ) | Production (Rs. crore) | | Employment (lakh.)* |
|---|---|---|---|---|
| | | At current prices | At constant prices (1993-94) | |
| 2002-03 | 36.71 (4.5) | 824363 (12.5) | 527837 (8.5) | 200.79 ( 4.0) |
| 2003-04 | 38.36 (4.5) | 932354 ( 13.1) | 575871 (9.1) | 209.03 (4.1) |
| 2004-05 | 40.09 (4.5) | 1060087 (13.7) | 631730 (9.7) | 217.80 (4.2) |
| 2005-06 | 41.89 ( 4.5) | 1213800 ( 14.5) | 698062 ( 10.5) | 227.17 ( 4.3) |
| 2006-07 | 43.78 ( 4.5) | 1401939 ( 15.5) | 778339 ( 11.5) | 237.17 ( 4.4) |
| Av. Growth (10th Plan) | | 13.9 | 9.9 | 4.2 |
| Total growth in 5 years (base yr 2001-02) | | 91.3 | 60.0 | 22.8 |
| Average | | 18.3 | 12.0 | 4.6 |

Note: Figures in brackets indicate the percentage growth over the previous year.

There are also indications that in times to come, SSI sector will be moving to product lines having higher capital intensity. There is likely to be impetus for setting up more and more self-employment ventures because of introduction of Voluntary Retirement Scheme in the Public Sector Undertakings. Similarly, there are also indications that the major part of the service sector will grow as small enterprises. All these factors will help to generate additional employment of 44.10 lakh persons as against 32 lakh persons in the Ninth Five Year Plan. Considering the potential, a larger increase in employment is also not ruled out. Similarly during the Eleventh Plan the per unit employment has been taken at 4.5 persons mainly because of structural shift in products towards bio-technology, Information Technology, and higher capital intensity due to intensification of move towards technology upgradation.

It is worth noting in Table 10.4 that in the terminal year of the Tenth Five Year Plan period, i.e., 2006-07, it has been projected that an additional 1.0 million jobs would be created in the Small Scale Sector alone. This may be an ambitious target but not unachievable, given the strengths of the SSI sector. It has grown over the past 10 years due to its capacity to adjust, implying flexibility and innovativeness.

**Table 10.4: Projection of Employment in The Tenth Five Year Plan**

| Years | No.of units (lakh) | Net addition per year | Estimated current employment per unit (persons) | Total employment generated (lakh persons) | Cumu-lative Employ-ment |
|---|---|---|---|---|---|
| 2002-03 | 36.71 | 1.58 | 5.0 | 7.72 | 7.72 |
| 2003-04 | 38.36 | 1.65 | 5.0 | 8.24 | 15.96 |
| 2004-05 | 40.09 | 1.73 | 5.0 | 8.77 | 24.73 |
| 2005-06 | 41.89 | 1.80 | 5.0 | 9.37 | 34.10 |
| 2006-07 | 43.78 | 1.89 | 5.0 | 10.00 | 44.10 |

While making projections for the Eleventh Plan i.e. 2007-2012 two assumptions have been made. The rate of growth in the number of units has been assumed at 5 per cent per annum as against 4.5 per cent in the Tenth Plan. Secondly, per unit employment has been assumed to decline further to 4.5 persons per unit by 2012 as a result of intensification of technology upgradation. This is evident from Table 10.5.

With 44.10 lakh jobs in the 10th Plan and 56.90 lakh jobs in the 11th Plan, additional 110 lakh or 11 million jobs would be created by end of 2012 in the small scale sector in India. Since the Third Census has revealed an employment of 25.0 million persons at the end of 2001-02, by the end of Eleventh Plan the sector will provide employment to over 35 million persons.

**Table 10.5: Projection of Employment in the Eleventh Plan**

| Year | No. of units (lakh) | Net addition per year (lakh) | Employ-ment Per unit | Total employ-ment (lakh) | Cumulative employment (lakh) |
|---|---|---|---|---|---|
| 2007-08 | 45.97 | 2.17 | 4.9 | 10.70 | 10.70 |
| 2008-09 | 48.27 | 2.30 | 4.8 | 11.00 | 21.70 |
| 2009-10 | 50.68 | 2.41 | 4.7 | 11.50 | 33.20 |
| 2010-11 | 53.21 | 2.53 | 4.6 | 11.70 | 44.90 |
| 2011-12 | 55.81 | 2.66 | 4.5 | 12.00 | 56.90 |

## 10.5 Factors Affecting Employment

The Special Group on Targeting Ten Million Opportunities per year has highlighted in the Report some of the major problems and constraints experienced by the SSI sector in India. The constraints exist in the form of:

- Lower Productivity
- Increased competition due to globalisation, removal of QRs and cheaper imports from China.
- Increased capital intensity in the SSI sector.
- Of these, the problem of lower productivity is more serious and needs special attention through measures designed to upgrade technology, improvement quality of products and skill development of the workers and

employees.

As per the Special Group Report, the major problems faced by the SSI sector relate to

- Credit
- Infrastructure
- Technology
- Skill Development , and
- Marketing.

The advantage possessed by the SSI sector exists in the form of higher labour elasticity and better efficiency in the use of capital. In spite of industrial slow down during 2001-03, the SSI sector had grown 3 to 4 per cent higher than overall industrial sector. The sector contributes 35% to national export which proves its ability to compete globally.

The indicators of autonomous growth in recent times have been stifled due to the impact of WTO agreements affecting India, like removal of Quantitative Restrictions (QRs), dumping of certain goods/items, power related problems and credit related drawbacks, etc. The employment generated through induced measures can serve as a supplement to the efforts not fulfilled by the autonomous measures. Direct employment should not be viewed in isolation. It has forward and backward linkages and generates large scale employment in the service sector. In addition the role of fast emerging information, bio technology sectors should not be ignored. In many ways they are catalysts to employment generation. India possess distinct advantages in this sector. India's success can be attributed to a combination of factors such as resource endowment, availability of cheap skilled labour, favourable government policies. Further there are a few industries like food processing and leather where India has vast resource endowment and not more than 25% of potentials have been tapped so far.

## 10.6 Strategy for Quality Employment Generation

The Small Scale Sector has the required potential to create additional employment as it is a low-capital consuming and labour intensive sector, although, adoption of advanced technology to improve efficiency of small units has displaced some labour, skilled and unskilled. In this regard, the Ministry of Small Scale Industries, in pursuance of the Comprehensive Policy Package, 2000, has paved the way for greater opportunities in the Small Scale Sector, removing the existing major roadblocks. The sector however suffers from several handicaps starting from poor capital base to inability to adopt modern marketing techniques. The problems are accentuated to factors like poor/errant power supply and their inability to have their own captive power generating plants, coping with plethora of rules and regulations popularly known as "Inspector Raj" also pose major problem. Ahluwalia Committee has observed that

"Inflexibility in our labour laws affects all units, but it has a more damaging effect upon small scale units because they are generally more labour intensive and, therefore, the share of wage cost in total cost is high. The high 'transaction costs' involved in dealing with the bureaucracy and banks, which is another source of complaint, also involves economies of scale which give larger units an advantage".

The Task Force on Employment Opportunities observed that the problems faced by SSIs have to be tackled at the root by implementing reforms in the power sector and addressing labour laws. In addition, the Task Force has suggested that there are a number of SSI specific policy support measures which should be considered to effectively target three key concerns - Credit, Marketing and

Technological upgradation. Special Group has also acknowledged the role of these factors, in addition it has also highlighted the importance of infrastructure and skill formation. The Special Group has also is of the view that the main focus of the strategy should be on decentralized production and centralized marketing, centralized designing and centralized quality control. The employment generating capacity of small enterprises is very high and boosting of growth at 12 per cent in this sector will improve the employment generation per unit of output. The special groups finds the target of generating 50 million additional jobs in the tenth plan achievable provided the policies and programmes are supported by labour intensificative activities and technologies. It is relevant to quote from the Special Group Report on the strategy which needs to be adopted for this purpose:-

"To sum up, the employment strategy for future, to meet the Plan's employment goals is to encourage the use of labour intensive and capital saving technology, in general to rejuvenate the growth of the unorganized sector in particular, which at present 92 per cent to the country's employment and enjoys more than 10 times labour intensity per unit of production, as compared to the organized sector. However, the unorganized sector needs to be made more productive to sustain itself against the domestic and international competition by proper choice of programmes and policies compatible with India's economic reforms and WTO results".

The policy measures included in the Comprehensive Policy Package consist of fiscal and credit support, infrastructural, technological and marketing support along with streamlining of rules/regulations, entrepreneurship development, rehabilitation of sick units, etc. These measures would pave the way for setting up of more Small Scale units which would, in turn, generate employment opportunities for entrepreneurs, skilled, semi-skilled and unskilled labour. On technology front there should be more linkages between laboratories and entrepreneurs in the small scale sector. Technology upgradation should aim at improving productivity. The forward and backward linkages attached to these new units would have a multiplier effect on the employment opportunities also, contributing towards achievement of the targets set.

According to the Special Group the ability of the SSI sector is to survive and generate additional employment opportunities is linked intimately with labour productivity. The labour productivity of the unorganized manufacturing sector is seven times less than organized sector and nine to ten times less than organized private sector. This indicates the extent of the challenge that this sector has to face to catch up with productivity levels of the organized sector. Since the QR regime has been dismantled and the tariff rates are coming down this sector is facing hard competition from abroad. There however, is a silver lining as the unorganized sector has improved its labour productivity by nearly 4 per cent per annum between 1993-94 and 1999-2000. In fact in the upper range of the SSI sector which is high tech and export oriented segment, the labour productivity is already very high and these sectors have high growth possibilities. Fortunately many of these sub sectors exist in the form of clusters and with a little effort big results can be realized.

The supporting evidence of improvement in labour productivity comes from the results of Second census of 1987-88 and Sample Survey of 1999-2000 conducted by the office of DC(SSI) which found that per unit employment has declined from 6.3 per cent per unit to 3.6 persons per unit but the average production per unit was Rs. 31.31 lakh in 1999-2000 against Rs. 7.38 lakh in second census. This gives a clear indication of increasing productivity per labour through adoption of improved technology. For making projection for 2012, lower per unit employment at 5 persons has been taken and not 4.5 persons since as per information from the registering authorities at the state government, it has been found that in the newly registered units employment per unit is high; in fact higher than 5 persons. There are also indications of increased capital investment since it has moved from Rs. 0.93 lakh to Rs. 1.62 lakh per unit during the same period. As per the Third Census (2001-02), the per unit investment in registered and unregistered units was as shown in Table 10.6.

**Table 10.6: Capital and Labour Intensity of SSI – Third Census**

| | Registered | Unregistered | Total |
|---|---|---|---|
| No. of Units | 13,74,974 | 91,46,216 | 1,05,21,190 |
| Per unit employment (number) | 4.48 | 2.05 | 2.37 |
| Per unit original value of plant and machinery (Rs. lakh) | 2.21 | 0.27 | 0.52 |
| Per unit fixed Investment (Rs. lakh) | 6.68 | 0.68 | 1.47 |
| Per unit gross output (Rs. lakh) | 14.78 | 0.86 | 2.68 |

Evidently the small producers are improving their productivity and technology and are growing in size. In this context, it would be interesting to have a comparison of capital and labour intensity of registered SSI units between $2^{nd}$ (1987-88) and $3^{rd}$ (2001-02) Census, evident in Table 10.7.

**Table 10.7: Comparative Labour/Capital Intensity of Registered SSI Units – 2nd and 3rd Census**

| | 2nd Census | 3rd Census |
|---|---|---|
| Per working unit fixed investment (Rs. lakh) | 1.60 | 6.68 |
| Per working unit production (Rs, lakh) | 7.38 | 14.78 |
| Per working unit Employment | 29 | 4.48 |

There is also evidence of improved capital efficiency in the unorganized sector. According to Special Group Report which has analysed the RBI data on flow of credit has observed that while the unorganized sector produces nearly 60 per cent of GDP (agriculture, SSI, cottage industries, service sector etc.) the net outstanding credit of scheduled commercial banks to this sector is only 37.1% of total bank credit. More disturbing is the fact this allocation ratio has come down from 53.1 per cent in 1993-94. If we consider SSI sector, alone which contributes 40% of industrial production, its share in total net bank credit is in the range of 14 to 16 per cent only

Another problem faced by the unorganized sector labour is the threat of exploitation which is likely to intensify due to growing unemployment. Hence the emphasis should also be on improving the quality of labour and empowering them.

The experience during the Eighth and Ninth Five Year Plan period, is that the targets set for employment generation have not only been achieved but also exceeded during each of these years. To enable this trend to continue over the $10^{th}$ and $11^{th}$ Five-Year Plan period, it is of utmost importance to realise that a shift in focus from quantity of labour to quality to labour should take place and it would be more profound once the effects of WTO Agreements start showing up.

Economic growth becomes really meaningful when the people participate extensively in the production processes. The real challenge of growth is to provide full employment. The small-scale sector is the symbol of that facet of our economy which reflects production by masses rather than mass production. With decline in agricultural employment and virtual stagnation in the organised manufacturing sector, employment in SSI sector has emerged as the only ray of hope.

The projections for the 10th Five Year Plan period, as submitted in the report of Sub-Group I of the Working Group on Small Scale Industries set up by Planning Commission, would have to fulfil certain pre-conditions to be actually realised. The rate of growth of the SSI sector would have to be pegged at 12% to attain the targets set for additional employment.

Areas of concern like credit, availability of power, delayed payments, etc. would have to be given due attention and within the SSI sector certain fast growing sectors would have to be identified and earmarked for achieving the high growth targets.

Credit is lifeline for any business whether in the organised or unorganised sector. The organised sector because of its bargaining strength is in a better position to raise capital from banks, capital market, foreign investment. SSIs have to depend primarily on bank credit. Adequate and timely credit at reasonable rate of interest without collaterals is the essential requirement of the small scale sector in India. In India some major initiatives have been taken in this direction which consist of creation of Small Industries Development Bank of India as an exclusive refinancing agency, launching of Credit Guarantee Scheme which aims at providing loans up to Rs. 25 lakh without collaterals provided the loans are availed through member lending institutions of Credit Guarantee Fund Trust, general scheme of banks of collateral free loan up to Rs. 5 lakh and even up to Rs. 15 lakh in deserving cases, setting up of specialised bank branches for SSI lending, raising the limit of composite loan up to Rs. 25 lakh and soft loan under National Equity Funds on projects costing up to Rs. 50 lakh. However, some major areas of concern are high cost of credit to SSI and some reluctance towards small loaning due to higher NPAs and more paper work. A time has come to move from traditional system of loaning to innovative finance in the form of venture capital and factoring services. While former encourages risk capital to skilled entrepreneurs in new areas of information technology, bio-technology, food processing, the latter addresses to the problem of delayed payments faced by the SSI units on their supplies to large units including PSUs. This encourages bill culture but it must be without recourse.

Training and technology upgradation are two important tools for increasing productivity in the unorganized sector. Training is required both for the new entrants and the existing workers. Training should aim at bottom end of this sector which is much larger in size than the middle and top levels. The skill development should include expansion of vocational training facilities, improving the effectiveness, efficiency and relevance of existing training programme, post training follow up, specially designed training programmes for educated unemployed youths in the informal sector, entrepreneurship development to address new challenges rising out of globalisation and W.T.O agreements. Labour need at the same time some social protection and a better environment. The intended single legislation for the SSI sector supported by self-certification will help the labour to great extent to come out from the purview of plethora of rules and regulations and routine inspections.

To sum up, the strategy to be adopted would have to lay focus on:

1. Ensuring adequate and timely flow of credit to SSI sector calculated at minimum of 20% of normative requirement of annual turnover of the SSI sector as recommended by the Nayak Committee (1992). Introducing innovative financing like Venture Capital and Factoring Services. The realisation of target of additional employment by 2012 is dependent to a great extent on the availability of credit.
2. Ensuring adequate and regular power supply to the SSI units and especially to the clusters.
3. Encouraging technology upgradation of the existing units and adoption of latest state-of-the-art technologies by the new units to raise their efficiency and competitiveness.
4. A bold and innovative Marketing Development Programme with statutory support of compulsory purchase by Government Departments from SSI sector. US Small Business Act provides for compulsory purchase of 24% of Government purchases from small business. Similar statutory provisions, as also recommended by the S.P. Gupta Study Group Report on Small Scale Enterprises (March 2001) needs to be made.
5. Sunrise industries (such as IT, Bio-Technology) would have to be given adequate attention and encouragement and their growth would have to be ensured through availability of latest technical and financial information, innovations being carried out world-wide which are relevant for Indian conditions.
6. Cluster development has to be accorded priority for

existing ones and potential clusters would have to be identified and action plan for their integrated development in the next 10 years will have to be worked out. The programme needs support in the form of adequate infrastructure to the clusters and active involvement of Industry Associations in maintenance of services.

It would not be out of place to quote again from the report of the Special Group, "All available studies show that the growth and quality of jobs in the unorganized sector has been very much affected by the absence of timely low cost credit, improved technology, good infrastructure, quality consciousness, modern marketing, proper organization and synergy with the large organized industries." The solution lies in addressing to the above problems effectively. The only caution however, needed is that the changes taking place at global and domestic levels are very fast. Small enterprises are also not static. They are also changing at fast pace. Hence to achieve the target of 11 million additional jobs by 2012, our action at all levels has to be very fast.

# 11

# Small Enterprises in India: Vision 2012

Growth is nothing but change in attitude. Small Enterprises (SEs) sector in India have been undergoing this attitudinal change but silently. The SEs that we see today are not the same which existed 50 years ago and will not be the same after another 50 years. The process of change has been catalysed in recent years due to macroeconomic transformation taking place both domestically and globally. In the present era of borderless and market oriented economy, the two big global economic forces which are competing for world attention are (a) the emergence of a 'new economy' underpinned by information and communication technologies and (b) growing instability and uncertainty linked to globalisation. With the emergence of WTO a new trade environment has been emerging. With the removal of Quantitative Restriction (QRs) on import of 715 items w.e.f 1st April, 2001and those done earlier, a large number of items are now under Open General Licence (OGL). There has also been reduction in import duties in recent years.

These have emerged as challenges before the SSI sector since these warrant that the SSI sector must be more competitive and efficient. There are changes in the type of products and services demanded, in the quality of products and services and change in fashion and tastes. There has also been change in the mode of production and technology. To cope up with these changes, the SSI sector will have to undergo many internal and external transformations. Will it be able to do so? Since it has changed in the past, it is assumed that it will change in future as the small enterprises have the advantage of flexibility and innovativeness. The harbingers of this change are the 105 lakh Small Scale Industries and industry related enterprises, (as the number as revealed by the Third All India Census of SSIs 2001-02) entrepreneurs coming from the equal number of units in the country. A large number of them are first generation entrepreneurs and quite a significant number is accounted by technocrats, skilled manpower, scientists, MBAs, Ex-Government, Ex-Army personnel who are ready to change the work culture and work environment in the context of the emerging requirements on account of liberalisation and globalisation. Many of them are IT proficients and have branched to newly found areas such as bio-technology.

The main objective of this concluding chapter is to trace the changes which have taken place in the field of small enterprises in the last ten years and workout a blueprint of the changes which are likely to emerge in the next eight years i.e., by 2012 which will be the terminal year of the Eleventh Five Year Plan.

## 11.1 Changes Witnessed in Recent Years

The Small Enterprises sector is silently making a move from the zone of protection to promotion through active involvement of institutions and the non-governmental organisations. There was a time when any talk of de-reservation was greeted with protest. Now in 2004, a situation has come in which nobody talks about increasing the list of reserved items for exclusive manufacturing in the small scale sector. In fact, the stake holders are themselves advocating and recommending the items which are to be de-reserved or the items in whose case the investment ceiling should be enhanced. It is on their suggestions that during last three to four years, more than 150 items have been de-reserved.

Quite a large number of them are significant in terms of their number, contribution to production, employment and exports, viz. readymade garments, leather goods, leather shoes, toys, rice milling, dal milling, ice creams, packaging material, and auto components. Similarly, it is based on their suggestions that the investment ceiling in plant and machinery for the SSI sector has been raised from Rs.1 crore to Rs. 5 crore in respect of group of items belonging to knitwear, hand tools, stationery items and pharmaceuticals.

T0he history of funding of the small scale enterprises for the last 50 years reveals that the sector has mostly been relying on self finance and debt finance through banking system. The young and technically qualified entrepreneurs are now moving to new areas of financing particularly, lease finance and venture capital financing. The time is not far off when one can find the Indian small enterprises getting linked with the capital market and equity financing emerges as the strong support line in the financing of small enterprises in India. While banks are moving from their traditional and developmental role to commercial operation as per the requirement of market led economy, many new instruments of innovative financing in the form of lease finance, venture capital, equity finance are emerging. At the same time a realisation has dawned that an economy to be able to reap the maximum advantage of globalisation must not and should not ignore the vast mass of the population living below the poverty line or those who are poor. For them in most of the countries 'Micro Credit has emerged as a powerful tool of removal of poverty and women empowerment.

Changes in the structure of small enterprises and in the product lines are also visible. There are evidence that quite a significant section of the small enterprises in India have made a shift from the domain of exclusive manufacturing to that of industry related services. This has no doubt been facilitated also by the inclusion of Small scale Services & Business Enterprises (SSSBE) within the SSI sector provided the fixed investment does not exceed Rs.10 lakh. According to Third All India Census of SSI the service sector which accounted for 3% of registered SSIs in 1987-88 have moved up to 34 per cent in 2001-02. In the case of unregistered small enterprises its share was as high as 64 per cent. The sector which produces about eight thousand items and a product range is as diversified as paper clip on one hand to components of the spacecraft on the other. The Tool Rooms under the Ministry of SSI have assisted in the development of tool design of several components of the spacecrafts. One can clearly see that the sector is silently making a move from traditional line of production to modern line of production. They are ready to upgrade the technology and modernise the production process. In fact, many of the items have got recently included in the SSI basket did not exist 10 years ago.

A significant change that can be witnessed in the field of quality of job creation in the small enterprises. The focus is shifting from 'number of labour force employed' to 'quality of labour force employed' i.e. whether the existing and new labour force joining the small enterprises have contributed to the improvement in productivity. What is the efficiency of labour vis-à-vis the capital? The quality of labour is measured through productivity and this in turn is the function of twin forces of (a) Skill development and (b) Technology upgradation. The Tenth Five Year Plan talks not only in terms of addition of over 10 million jobs through the small enterprises in the country but also at achieving an annual rate of growth of 12 per cent as against annual growth of 8 per cent in GDP. Hence clearly the emphasis is on improving the quality of labour.

One can also see that the training programmes which used to be mostly of general nature earlier have now changed to product specific training in the field of cosmetics, herbal medicines, processing of agro based items, biotech items etc. The training programmes are moving to the realm of specialisation with specific product related training on packaging, IPR and W.T.O conditionalities.

Similarly, the concept of the marketing of the products in the SSI sector is also changing. Till a decade ago one could have clearly seen the existence of 3 or 4 types of markets in the SSI sector which existed in the form of niche/captive/domestic/international markets. The increased awareness of WTO conditionalities and exposure from the electronic media have led to enhanced awareness of international quality and the popular brands with which they have to compete. As a result of this, now the entrepreneurs do not want to have product differentiation. They try to maintain same quality whether this produce for domestic market or international market. They are getting increasingly aware that it is only the quality and cost which are relevant and not the production of inferior goods for one market and superior goods for the other. Very soon one will see that the Indian small enterprises develop their own brands which would be able to compete with the popular brands of external market.

The changes witnessed in the fiscal policy particularly the reduction in the rate of customs and excise duties which reduced the area of protection of the small enterprises drastically and changes in trade policies and removal of qualitative restrictions have also played important role in changing the attitude. The sector has now realised that they have to operate only in a 'market led economy' and they must change if they have to survive in this era of competition. The $10^{th}$ Plan document has also acknowledged this fact. It has been stated in the document that "Taking into consideration the higher potential for growth in the unorganised sector, mainly VSI and food processing sectors, in terms of output, employment and exports, it would be prudent to strengthen these sectors to enable them to remain competitive in the market led economy".

The eagerness of the entrepreneurs to acquire more and more knowledge facilitated by 'Internets' can also easily be seen. The experiences of the overwhelming response to awareness programmes on WTO, Intellectual Property Rights, Anti-dumping etc., organised by the Office of the Development Commissioner (SSI)and other organisations is also indicative of the eagerness on the part of entrepreneurs to be abreast with the latest in the field of knowledge. They are aware that the Twenty First Century belongs to 'Knowledge' and hence for sustainable development it is essential to have as much knowledge as possible.

For quite a long time, the SSI Associations have been approaching the Government. for one or the other protection. They are now active participants in the programme of small enterprises development. One can see their active involvement in shaping the taxation policy sector, credit policy and trade and investment policy. They have been actively airing their grievances and concerns. One classic example is the concern expressed by them at the rise in iron and steel prices since June 2002 and their active intervention which led to reduction in the rates of customs and excise duties in the beginning of 2004. They have been operating Sub-Contracting Exchanges, organising Vendor Development Programmes, taking lead in setting up infrastructural development centres. Quite a large number of these Associations are engaged in arranging global level summits, National and State level Small and Medium Enterprises (SME) Conventions and organising seminars and workshops on issue of topical importance.

The adoption of Cluster development as the strategy of future growth of the SSI sector in India is also indicative of the attitudinal change and is indicate of the awareness that for optimisation of the results it is essential to allocate the limited resources to those areas which have potential. Clusters allows you to reap the economies of scales. It is with this end that the Government has launched five National Programmes of Cluster Development with UNIDO's assistance covering product lines such as toys, stones, hand tools, machine tools, and locks. Out of over 380 important clusters (as per UNIDO) which exists in this field, the Ministry of Small Scale Industries has already completed studies in respect of 25 clusters covering product lines like bulk drug, fruit processing, foundry and forging, pottery, neem and perfumery, herbal and aromatic plants, auto components, diesel pump, brass and bronze metal works, jewellery etc.

The RBI has also asked the banks to formulate credit plans for the 60 clusters which could be integrated with the State Credit Plan. More focus on Cluster development as the strategy of SSI development will definitely help in linking the Indian small enterprises with global market as it would be possible to source their requirements from one place rather than collecting small supplies from various SSI units scattered in different parts of the country. In order to have the maximum advantage from these clusters particularly in employment generation a holistic approach needs to be adopted. The specific areas requesting attention would be revealed by the diagnostic survey of the cluster.

The attitudinal change could also be seen in the initiatives and programmes of the Government both at the Centre and the state level. The role of the Government has gradually been changing from protection to facilitator. Many State Government. have discontinued the Capital Subsidy Scheme for backward areas. Similarly, there has been drastic reduction in the number of schemes aimed at providing direct financial assistance to SSI units from the budgetary sources. To a large extent the financial needs must be met from institutional sources and not from budgetary sources. All autonomous bodies are now required to raise their own revenue whether it is a tool room, regional training centre, a training institute or small workshop attached to Small Industry Service Institutes. The launching of Credit Guarantee Scheme by the Government is just one of the examples of Government's initiative to encourage institutional financing of small enterprises.

## 11.2 Agenda for Vision 2012

The Small Enterprises also been experiencing structural transformation. As seen in the foregoing paragraphs many changes have already taken place in last 10 years. There are indications of the increased use of capital, increased ancillarisation, women empowerment through small enterprises and efficiency in the use of man and material. Most important changes is to become more competitive, more efficient, and to become a part of global player. To speed up the process of change some interventions are needed. The areas of intervention have been outlined in following paragraphs.

**11.2.1 Concept of Small Enterprise**: All over the world, unorganised manufacturing sector is known as Small and Medium Enterprises (SMEs) while in India this is known as SSI defined in terms of investment in plant and machinery. During last 50 years the limit of investment has been changed several times. It changed from Rs. 5 lakh in sixties to Rs. 100 lakh in 1999. Within the SSI sector, further two sub segments have been created one for Tiny Units having investment in plant and machinery up to Rs. 25 lakh and other for Industry Related Service and Business Enterprise (SSSBE) sector defined as investment in fixed assets excluding land and building not exceeding Rs. 10 lakh. The SP Gupta Study Group on Small Enterprises (1999) in its interim report, has recommended that a time has come to move from 'Industry' to 'Enterprise' and also to include Medium Enterprise also within the SSI sector. This is essential in order to bring Indian SSI sector at par with the global SMEs sector. Some of the immediate requirements of the Sector are

1. It must adopt SME concept by defining 'Medium Sector and changing the concept from 'Industry' to Enterprise.
2. It must enhance the investment ceiling prescribed for the SSI sector from existing Rs. 1 crore to Rs. 5 crore. This is essential in order to enhance the competitiveness of the sector and make it at par with the investment ceiling of Rs. 5 crore already applicable to sectors like hand tools, knitwears, pharmaceuticals etc.
3. At the same time it must take measures to safeguard the interest of the smaller among the SMEs by reserving a major portion of facilities available to them in terms of credit, raw materials, fiscal concessions, plots/sheds etc.
4. Attempt need also be made to base the definition on parameters like 'Employment' and 'Turnover' as applicable in most of the countries rather than investment in plant and machinery.

**11.2.2 Government as Facilitator:** Small enterprises assume special importance in India because of its role as creator of large scale employment opportunities apart from contributing significantly to industrial production, exports and regional dispersal. In the next 9-10 years there may not be drastic changes in the structure of SE but there may be some changes in the composition of the SSI sector in India. In the changed atmosphere only an efficient, viable and competitive SSI units will survive. The contribution of this sector, which is currently 40 per cent of industrial production and, 35 per cent of exports, will further improve The SSI sector currently provides employment to 250 lakh persons as revealed by the Third Census.

According to Working Group on 10$^{th}$ Plan on SSI, 44.1 lakh additional employment would be provided by the end of 10$^{th}$ Plan. This has also been accepted by Dr. S.P.Gupta Special Group Report (May 2002) on Targeting 10 Million jobs per year during 10$^{th}$ Five Year Plan. At present our share in the world trade is only 0. 7 per cent, which is very low by any international standards. This will have to be improved to 1.5 per cent in next 10 years. The target by the end of 10$^{th}$ Plan is to be raise in our world trade to 1%.The SSI sector is expected to be contribute significantly to our national exports; may be to the tune of 50%. For which this sector will need certain support so that it is able to over come the handicaps due to inaccessibility to economies of scale and due to the use of somewhat obsolete technology, inadequate and delayed supply of credit, poor infrastructure. Some form of hand holding to this sector because of its very nature cannot be ruled out. Moreover in all parts of world whether it is advanced country like USA or developing countries, small enterprises are provided special support. Though the policy of reservation in the present form may not exist but the sector will need some support which helps it to attain a level playing ground.

The Comprehensive Policy Package announced by the Prime Minister on $30^{th}$ August 2000 and several policy supports announced by the Government thereafter may be able to improve the situation with regard to the availability of credit and infrastructure level of technology in use and marketing of products. The role of the Government will be changing from one of the protector to facilitator. In fact during last ten years i.e. after the introduction of economic reforms, one can already experience a change in the role of the Government. In the developing countries, where the infrastructural facilities for development are inadequate and entrepreneurial activities are limited, the promotional role of the government assumes special significance.

The State will have to assume direct responsibility to build up and strengthen the necessary development infrastructural such as power, transport, guidance on promoting technologies through Tool Room, Process cum Product Development Centres, Testing Centres etc. The role of Government in ensuring a level playing field to SEs will continue and hence fiscal, monetary and other incentives will continue. Such incentives exist even in advanced countries. While support will continue, interventions, will come down. The Government's policy measures have to be clearly divided on the nature of SMEs and their level of development. The programmes would be focused more to address to the requirements of clusters. The sunrise industries and new ventures would require different attention. In a market oriented liberalised economy the role of the Government will to create a situation in which market forces are allowed a free play. In fact the role of handholding also be taken over to a great extent by the mentors.

**11.2.3 Concept of the Market:** As mentioned earlier in this chapter, at present three types of market exist for the SE. These are (i) 'niche' market (ii) domestic /local market and (iii) global /international market. With the introduction of non discriminatory trade laws under WTO and with the removal of QRs and placement of the items under OGL, the small enterprise sector will have to produce only one type of product which is competitive in terms of cost and quality in all the three types of markets. In other words in next 10 years one may not be surprised to find only one market i.e. international market as there may be no distinction between global and domestic market and the watchword for the same would be the quality to be attained by use of the state of the art technology. The small will continue to be beautiful even in changed market because it has the advantage of flexibility, lower inventory and innovativeness. The next ten years will see emergence of large number of market consortia and Indian SSI Associations becoming part of global chain and information network.

**11.2.4 Credit Flow to SSI:** The traditional SSI sector in India has been utilising primarily two types of capital known as fixed capital and working capital. These are arranged either through private sources or by institutional sources such as commercial banks, state finance corporations and other state owned bodies. This involved raising of loans through securities, guarantees, collaterals and margin money. There are many skilled and educated potential entrepreneurs who are unable to raise even the minimum equity support. Hence arrangements were made to assist those entrepreneurs who had skill but had no capital of their own hence through schemes like National Equity Fund. To meet the growing credit requirements of SSI sector, a refinancing bank called SIDBI was created in 1990-91. To facilitate credit without collaterals a new Credit Guarantee Scheme has been launched in August 2000.

In addition RBI's guidelines also exist on providing loans to SSIs by the banks without collaterals up to a limit of Rs. 5 lakh. This limit has been raised to Rs. 25 lakh that in deserving cases. To facilitate credit at reasonable rate of interest i.e. 2 per cent below Prime Lending Rate (PLR), Government also announced a SME fund of Rs. 10,000 crore in January 2004 to be operated through SIDBI. The nature of credit requirements, however, has been changing. Need for separate line of a credit for technology upgradation has also been felt. To address to the requirement of technology upgradation and modernisation, schemes like Technology Development and Modernisation Fund (1995) and Credit Linked Capita Subsidy Scheme for Technology Upgradation (2000) have been launched. New ventures have emerged which are still untried and belong to the category of risky ventures. New product lines are emerging in the field of information technology, electronics, bio technology, geo technology etc.

Knowledge based industries are taking precedence over others. Other sectors where new products are emerging are in the field of communication, entertainment, toy, dimensional stone, auto components etc. The qualified software professionals need venture capital support. During last few years Venture Capital Funds have been created for Information Technology and Bio Technology sectors. In coming years more innovative finance in the form of Venture Capital Funds, Factoring Services and Lease Finance would be becoming popular. It would be essential to set up large number of incubation centres. A beginning has been made by the SIDBI, at IIT Kanpur and several private sector firms. Hence the traditional pattern of credit would to some extent be yielding to innovative finance in next 10 years. A large segment of small enterprises would be availing institutional finances as against only 15 to 20 per cent of them availing at present.

**11.2.5 Technological Requirements:** The 'mantra' of the day is competitiveness, which is the function of productivity of man and machine and the extent to which the sector has the competitive advantage in the production of final good. The competitiveness of any economy depends on how efficiently all the resources in the process of production are utilised and how efficiently these are marketed. Hence the entire chain of production and marketing has to be efficient. Many of the items produced in the small scale sector or which were being produced in the past are becoming redundant because of the change in tastes and preferences and fashions and also due to emergence of new technology.

The entry of foreign brands in the white goods segment has not only given consumers a wide choice of hi-tech and good quality products at competitive prices but has also given them improved after sales services. It is an age of shopping in super departmental stores. Only those SSI units goods can find a place in these stores which can meet both quantity and quality requirement at competitive prices. This means that the process of production has to be cost efficient and meet quality needs of the consumers. This improvement can come through the use of latest technology. Hence the need for change in technology is more relevant for SMEs than large units. It is heartening to note that the new technologies which are emerging are more SME friendly unlike in the past when they favoured only the large enterprises.

Unlike in the case of old technologies which relied on

centralised practices and supported large enterprises, the emerging technologies rely on computer aided design (CAD) and computer aided manufacturing (CAM) and they favour flexible manufacturing systems and thus they favour the SMEs. As a result all over the world large companies have been withdrawing from direct manufacturing activities and concentrating more on marketing, technology creation, diffusion and networking with SMEs in manufacturing related activities. It is the efficiency of small firms which will govern the economics of industrial production. The next ten years will experience a revolutionary change in the use of technology which is relevant, appropriate, forward looking and also state of art.

**11.2.6 Regulatory Environment and Labour Laws:** It is said that the plethora of rules, regulations and laws is killing the small scale sector and making it inefficient. At present a lot of time of the entrepreneurs are wasted in filling up large number of forms some of which are routine in nature. There is a need to club many of these returns into one and to eliminate those returns and remove those regulations, which have become redundant. Government at Centre and states are fully aware of this problem. A new environment in which the rigours are reduced and the laws regulations etc. do not hamper the production process is the need of the hour. Already changes have taken place in some of the states like Andhra Pradesh, Maharashtra, Haryana, Uttarpradesh. It is expected that other states will also follow suit to reduce the rigours of Inspector Raj.

In next ten years definitely an environment would be emerging where the system operates in a friendly and harmonious manner. In the meantime a single legislation on SSI may also be in vogue. A beginning towards lessening of rigours has already been made by the acceptance of the idea of self-certification in the place of regular/routine inspections. Single unified legislation for the small enterprises proposed under Small Enterprise Development Bill is expected to herald a new era of rigors free small enterprise sector.

**11.2.7 Impact of Impending WTO Conditionalities:** Removal of Quantitative Restrictions (QRs) and application of WTO conditionalities from 2005 and their impact on small enterprises is a matter of hot discussion these days. Some of the WTO provisions which could impact on SMEs relate to provisions pertaining to intellectual property and patent rights, investment measures, sanitary and phyto-sanitary measures, non tariff barriers and subsidy provisions and also the issues like continuance of reservation, price and purchase preference, excise exemption, income tax relief etc, to the SMEs. Direct tax benefits and subsidies, which are not WTO compatible, will have to be phased out. SE will definitely be affected due to removal of subsidies /benefits like DEPB scheme, Income tax exemption etc. The general impression is that most of SSI incentives are not against WTO rules and they can continue. Many others need interpretation as the exact position is not yet known and further that most of the incentives exist in advanced as well as developing economies. WTO conditionalities is a mixed basket and some provisions, no doubt, would be adversely affecting the SSI sector in India. At the same time some other provisions will also help the SSI. What is needed to take advantage of the positive provisions and for this the immediate need is to have awareness of the provisions.

There are certain product lines in which large companies may not be able to supply goods. The SSIs can continue to manufacture products for 'niche market' for some time more without incurring huge expenditure in packaging the machinery and products because those product lines are appropriate only for small production. Already one can witness that the MNCs are increasingly outsourcing their components from SE. The SSI sector has good opportunity in products groups like automotive parts, computer components etc.

The TRIPS agreement would cover the entire gamut of goods and services. At present India does not have the product patent laws but only has the process patents. With effect from 2005, the product patents would come into force thereby the Indian IPR legislations would become more stringent. The components of SSI sector which have essentially survived so far due to concept of reverse engineering, infringement of copy right laws would be hit hard. Particularly in industries like auto- components parts, music cassettes, light engineering goods, light machinery, chemicals, drugs and pharmaceuticals etc.

The sanitary and phyto sanitary measures would require paying greater attention on healthy products for consumption and standardards for goods meant for human animal and plant uses. In quite a few countries particularly the developed countries far more strict legislation and high standards exist for making the goods which are exported. In the initial stage our products may find it tough to pass their quality tests and standards. In this context agricultural products, leather products, chemicals, fertilisers, pesticides, food products and marine products are likely to be affected. Under TRIMs, absence of local content by a company may affect automotive component industries sector and ancillaries to the large corporation, which would be permitted to outsource their components from anywhere in the world if the quality of the present supplier is found not up to mark.

**11.2.8 Role of the Entrepreneur:** The basic requirement of an entrepreneur is to bear risk and uncertainty. An entrepreneur is one who has the initiative, skill for innovation, and who looks for high achievements. His role in a country like India in creating wealth, opening up employment opportunities and providing forward and backward linkages is laudable. This will continue. But in the changing environment, he is expected to perform some additional functions. Since he will no longer be operating under protected market, he will have to be competitive both globally and domestically, For this, he will have to be conversant with the modern managerial techniques. He has to emerge as a dynamic entrepreneur capable to compete globally. He will have to understand as to how a change in economic policy of any country is going to affect his own cost of production and demand of his product. He will have to address to the requirement of a new product lines, be it software, bio technology, or traditional items like shirt, shoes or food. He will have to conversant with environmental regulations and WTO conditionalities. This means the existing entrepreneurship institutes have to reorient their training programmes to address to the new requirements of entrepreneurship. SMEs will no longer be one man shows. Next ten years will see the emergence of highly qualified first generation entrepreneurs. In next 10 years, knowledge based industries are likely to acquire greater prominence. SMEs are likely to come up in big way in areas of pharmaceuticals, IT and biotechnology sectors.

**11.2.9 Concern for Ecology and Energy Efficiency:** Last but not least important changes which I visualise the small enterprises in India to experience in next 10 years is with regard to concern for ecology environment and energy efficiency. There are a few high energy consuming activities such as foundaries, furnaces, brick kiln, glass making, cement making textile, bio mass based industries etc. which will undergo serious energy audit and will try to economise not only the consumption but will also adopt a technology which is environment friendly. In this process some alternative means of energy other than the conventional ones will also come into prominence.

A beginning has already been made in wind energy and could be seen at the southern part of Tamil Nadu. More and more institutions like The Energy And Resource Institute (TERI) will undertake energy efficiency studies of various small enterprises related activities under the overall guidance of Institute of Global Environmental Strategies of Japan. The National Strategy Study (NSS) for implementation of Clean Development Mechanism (CDM)in India has been initiated to assess issues and opportunities presented by potential international markets for greenhouse gas reductions through CDM and to evaluate processes and methodologies to facilitate implementation of CDM projects in India. It is relevant to quote from United Nations Framework Convention n Climate change popularly known as Kyoto Protocol 91997) which is as under." Stabilisation of greenhouse gas concentration in the atmosphere at a level that would prevent dangerous anthropogenic interference with the climate system. Such a level should be achieved within a time frame sufficient to allow econsystems to adopt naturally to climate change, to ensure that food production is not threatened, and to enable economic development to proceed in a sustainable manner".

We are already aware of the intervention by Supreme Court on shifting of polluting industries from Ferozabad and Agra region which has been affecting the Taj. (historical monument at Agra) and from Delhi. Before such strict ions are passed in other areas/ clusters it is essential to take measures to reduce pollution levels of these industries. To facilitate change over to safer and cleaner technology SIDBI has launched a new scheme in March 2004. To start with studies on extent of pollution of various industries in various locations be undertaken and thereafter specific remedial measures must be undertaken. Consciousness towards cleaner technology is increasing and hence in next 10 years small enterprises would be adopting more and more cleaner and environment friendly technology.

### 11.3 Concluding Remarks

The Indian small enterprises must embrace change if they have to survive and find a place for themselves in global competitive environment. The most important change is needed in attitude of the stake holders and mindset of the institutions which are engaged in the task of small enterprises development. The effort should be to take fullest advantage of the opportunities made available by WTO and globalisation. The constraints will have to be overcome through adoption of aggressive export and marketing strategy like China. Competitiveness and quality improvement have to be accepted as watchwords. Indian small enterprises have proved their worth in the past and with adoption of necessary changes they can capture future. In the ultimate analysis the survival of the small enterprises and their ability to find a place for themselves in the global market and that too within WTO framework depends on their ability to bring out major change in the quality of output, exports and employment. It is not a question of providing employment but providing gainful and sustainable employment to the masses by 2012.

# Select Bibliography

50 years of Small Scale Industries in India Policies and Programmes by Dr. C. S. Prasad and K. C. Kaushik (January-December 1997).

A Brief Guide to the WTO for Small Business – published by FISME (May 1999).

Annual Reports of the Ministry of SSI & ARI and Ministry of SSI since 2000 to 2003, brought out by Government of India, New Delhi.

Arthik Udarikaran Ek Dasak Evam Laghu Udyog – by Shri Babu Lal Varma Mimeograph (2004).

Attacking poverty with Micro Credit – Edited by Salehuddin Ahmed and M. A. Hakim published by the University Press Limited, Dhaka, Bangladesh (2004).

Attitudinal Changes in the SSI Sector by Dr. C. S. Prasad (April-September 2003).

Bridging the differences – 5 issues of WTO Agenda Edited by L. Alan Winters and Pradeep S. Mehta published by CUTS, Jaipur (2003).

Characteristics and contribution of SMEs by Shri S.K. Tuteja (January-March 2002).

Cluster Development and Sectoral Programmes brought out by Development Commissioner, Small Scale Industries,

Ministry of SSI, Government of India, New Delhi (August 2003).

Comprehensive Policy Package for Small Scale Industries and Tiny Sector announced on 30th August 2000 published by Office of DC (SSI), Ministry of SSI, New Delhi (2000 and 2003).

Creative Marketing – a Strategic Tool for SMEs by Dr. J. S. Juneja (April-September 2002).

Decent Employment through Small Enterprises – ILO's publication Geneva (2003).

Draft Tenth Five Year Plan (2002-07) brought out by Planning Commission New Delhi (2002).

Economic Surveys of various years particularly from 1991 to 2003. Published by Ministry of Finance, Government of India, New Delhi.

Handbook of Statistics on Indian Economy, Reserve Bank of India (2002-03).

How can Indian SSEs meet the challenges of globalisation by Dr. S. K. Jain (April-September 2001).

India 2020 – A Vision for the New Millennium by APJ Abdul Kalam with Y. S. Rajan published by Viking, New Delhi (1998).

India Development Report 1999-2000. Edited by Kirit S. Parikh, Indira Gandhi Institute of Development Research, Mumbai.

Indian Economy and the WTO – New Challenges and Strategies by Vibha Mathur published by New Century Publication, Delhi (2002).

Indian Small Scale Industries in Emerging International Scenario by Dr. C.S. Prasad (October-December 2002).

Innovative Financing for SMEs by Dr. C.S. Prasad (January-March 2003).

Laghu Udyog – Bharat Ki Pragati Ke Adharstambh – Publication of DC (SSI), Ministry of SSI, Government of India, New Delhi (August 2003).

Laghu Udyog Samachar (various issues) a journal of the office of DC (SSI) Ministry of SSI, Government of India, New Delhi with particular reference to following articles.

Ninth Five Year Plan (1997-2002) – Planning Commission, New Delhi

Partnership for SME Development – Ancillarisation/Sub-contracting by Shri S. K. Tuteja (April-September 2001).

Quick Results of the Third All India Census of Small Scale Industries (2001-2002) published by the Office of DC (SSI), Government of India (August 2003)

RBI's Mid Term Review of Monetary and Credit Policy for the year 2003-04 published by RBI (November 2003).

Report of the Expert Committee on Small Enterprises Chairman Dr. Abid Hussain published by NCAER, New Delhi, January 1997).

Report of the Second All India Census of Registered SSIs (1987-88) published by the Office of DC (SSI), Ministry of Industry, Government of India (1991).

Report of the Special Group on Targeting Ten Million Employment Opportunities per year, Chairman Dr. S. P. Gupta, Member, Planning Commission, published by Planning Commission, New Delhi (May 2002).

Report of the Study Group on Development of Small Scale Enterprises Chairman Dr. S. P. Gupta, Member, Planning Commission, published by Planning Commission, New Delhi (March 2001).

Report of the Task Force on Employment Opportunities, Chairman, Shri Montek Singh Ahluwalia, Member, Planning Commission, published by Planning Commission New Delhi (July 2001).

Report of the Working Group on Small Scale Industries for the Tenth Five Year Plan, Ministry of SSI, New Delhi (2002).

Report on Sample Surveys of Registered SSI units (2000-01) published by the office of DC (SSI), Government of India, New Delhi (February 2002).

Reserve Bank of India Report of the High Level Committee on credit to SSI Chairman Shri S. L. Kapur, Former Secretary (SSI) Government of India (1998).

Reserve Bank of India Report on Credit Flow to Small Scale Industries and other related issues, Chairman, Shri R. P. Nayak then Deputy Governor RBI (1992).

SIDBI's Annual Reports 1991 to 2003 published by SIDBI Lucknow every year.

SIDBI's report on Small Scale Industries Sector 1999, 2000 and 2001.

Small and Medium Enterprises and their Role in Employment Generation by Dr. S.P. Gupta (April-September 2002).

Small and Medium Enterprises Emerging Issues by Shri P. B. Nimbalkar (October-December 2002).

Small Enterprises Protection to Promotion by Dr. Abid Hussain (January-September 1998).

Small Industries Development Organization in Global Perspective by Shri Suresh Chandra (October-December 2002).

Small scale Industries in India – An Engine of Growth – published by the office of DC (SSI), Ministry of SSI, Government of India, New Delhi (August 2002).

Small Scale Industry Policy in India – A critical Evaluation by Dr. Rakesh Mohan, NCAER, New Delhi (May–June 2000).

Structure and promotion of Small Scale Industries in India – Lesson for Future Development by National Council of Applied Economic Research (NCAER), New Delhi and Friedrick Naumann Stiftung New Delhi (December 1993).

Targeting 10 Million Employment in SSI Sector – Vision 2012 by Dr. C.S. Prasad (April-September 2002).

Technology for Small Scale Industries – Current Status and Emerging Needs – A Report of SIDBI published by Tata McGraw Hill (October 2001).

Tenth Five Year Plan (2002-07) published by Planning Commission, New Delhi (2002-03).

Third Census of SSI Units, by Dr. C. S. Prasad (April-September 2001).

Uruguay Round – Final Act Marrakesh ($15^{th}$ April 1994).

WTO – A Threat or An Opportunity by Dr. B. R. Sabade Centre for Business and Industry, Pune (January 2001).

# Index

S



T